Global Gender Politics

Accessible and student-friendly, *Global Gender Politics* analyzes the gendered divisions of power, labor, and resources that contribute to the global crises of representation, violence, and sustainability. The author emphasizes how hard-won attention to gender and other related inequalities in world affairs is simultaneously being jeopardized by new and old authoritarianisms and depoliticized through reducing gender to a binary and a problem-solving tool in global governance. The author examines gendered insecurities produced by the pursuit of international security and gendered injustices in the global political economy and sees promise in transnational struggles for global justice.

In this new re-titled edition of a foundational contribution to the field of feminist International Relations, Anne Sisson Runyan continues to examine the challenges of placing inequalities and resisting injustices at the center of global politics scholarship and practice through intersectional and transnational feminist lenses. This more streamlined approach includes more illustrations and discussions have been updated to reflect current issues. To provide more support to instructors and readers, *Global Gender Politics* is accompanied by an e-resource, which includes web resources, suggested topics for discussion, and suggested research activities also found in the book.

Anne Sisson Runyan is a professor in the Department of Political Science at the University of Cincinnati, where she directs a Political Science doctoral concentration in Feminist Comparative and International Politics and holds an affiliation with the Department of Women's, Gender, and Sexuality Studies, which she formerly headed. Her other books include *Gender and Global Restructuring* (two editions) and *Feminist (Im)Mobilities in Fortress(ing) North America*.

"*Global Gender Politics* opens at the centre of today's most pressing political questions, it asks how a growing consensus around the importance of gender can happen alongside the rise of right-wing authoritarianisms and backlash, and it offers sophisticated yet accessible analytical tools to understand both 'gender' and 'global politics'. It is a must-read for students at all levels."

– Sandra Whitworth, Professor of Political Science and Associate Dean, York University Toronto, Canada

"Anne Sisson Runyan is one of the foremost feminist analysts of the workings (often insidious) of gender injustices in today's globalized economies. *Global Gender Politics* is sure to inform, engage and energize our students."

– Cynthia Enloe, author of The Big Push: Exposing and Challenging Persistent Patriarchy

"*Global Gender Politics* is a fantastic resource for students, scholars, practitioners and anyone interested in the global workings of gender. Complex concepts are discussed and illustrated in super accessible ways, but crucially without any dilution of the serious, political, intellectual and epistemological messages. A tour de force combining current issues and wide-ranging theory. Fabulous."

– Marysia Zalewski, Professor of International Relations, Cardiff University, UK

"*Global Gender Politics* is a must-have resource for students and researchers alike looking to understand the wide variety of ways in which gender matters in global politics. It is rich but accessible, complex but fascinating – a great guide!"

– Laura Sjoberg, University of Florida, USA

Global Gender Politics

Fifth Edition

Anne Sisson Runyan

NEW YORK AND LONDON

Fifth edition published 2019
by Routledge
711 Third Avenue, New York, NY 10017

and by Routledge
2 Park Square, Milton Park, Abingdon, Oxon, OX14 4RN

Routledge is an imprint of the Taylor & Francis Group, an informa business

First edition published by Westview 1993
Fourth edition published by Westview 2013

Library of Congress Cataloging-in-Publication Data
Names: Runyan, Anne Sisson, author.
Title: Global gender politics / Anne Sisson Runyan.
Other titles: Global gender issues in the new millennium.
Description: Fifth Edition. | New York: Routledge, 2019. | Revised edition of the author's Global gender issues in the new millennium, [2014] | Fourth edition published by Westview Press, 2013. | Includes bibliographical references and index.
Identifiers: LCCN 2018015588 | ISBN 9781138320215 (hardback) | ISBN 9780813350851 (pbk.) | ISBN 9780429453458 (ebook)
Subjects: LCSH: Women–Political activity. | World politics–21st century.
Classification: LCC HQ1236.P45 2019 | DDC 320.082–dc23
LC record available at https://lccn.loc.gov/2018015588

ISBN: 978-1-138-32021-5 (hbk)
ISBN: 978-0-8133-5085-1 (pbk)
ISBN: 978-0-429-45345-8 (ebk)

Typeset in Times New Roman
by Sunrise Setting Ltd., Brixham, UK

Visit the eResources: www.routledge.com/9780813350851

For my husband, Albert Adrian Kanters, and my sisters everywhere

For my husband, [illegible] Ratna, and my sisters [illegible]

Contents

Illustrations

Charts and Photo

Tables

Boxes

Acknowledgments

New times have brought a new title, a new publisher, and my single-authorship of this book that began life in the early 1990s as *Global Gender Issues*. In the early days of the rise of feminist International Relations (IR) scholarship, V. Spike Peterson and I embarked on the project of mapping what such inquiry entailed and how it challenged conventional thinking in IR and about world politics. Through four editions that spanned the end of the Cold War, when women appeared virtually absent in state-centric world politics and gender analysis was only nascent in the discipline of IR, to the era of neoliberal global governance, in which women's empowerment became a fulcrum for addressing global problems and feminist IR, which also opened spaces for queer and trans IR, had become well established, we tracked such momentous changes. However, we did so critically, finding that, in fact, the more things change, the more they remain the same, and can even worsen.

The presence of women has substantially increased in many national and international structures, the latter of which have also expanded dramatically in terms of both intergovernmental and nongovernmental organizations (IGOs and NGOs), and the advancement of gender equality as key to the advancement of more representative governance, human rights, peacemaking, and sustainable development is a common refrain within IGOs and NGOs. However, as we found through an intersectional feminist lens and this book continues to find through that lens, inequalities have actually widened and deepened among women and among men within and across states, while equality between women and men is far from being achieved. Despite some increased international recognition of the rights of women, workers, ethnic and indigenous peoples, and sexual and gender minorities, some decline in interstate warfare since the twentieth century accompanied by increasing understandings about the relationship between international and gender violence, some amelioration of the most absolute poverty, and some consensus on the costs of climate change, wealth concentration at the top has risen exponentially around the world. This concentration of private wealth has been at the expense of public funding for rights enforcement, social welfare, human security, and environmental protection and, thus, the realization of rhetorical norms forged at the international level by transnational feminist and other social movements seeking greater global justice. The resulting incapacitation of public structures to significantly address widening and deepening inequalities and injustices has paved the way for the rise of what has been called new authoritarianisms, which have joined older ones in both the global North and South.

It is in the moment of the ascendancy of the far-right, particularly in Western democracies, that this book was written. Earlier editions did document the trends leading to this, including signaling that civil society within and across states can always contain regressive elements, made more so and more susceptible to divide-and-conquer narratives in times of economic anxiety. The undermining of not only public systems and services, but also democratic principles by neoliberalism and imperialist wars in the early twenty-first century was also observed. Still, what we did not wholly anticipate was this particularly virulent development of today. The last edition I alone reworked tracked a time of more progressive popular uprisings, such as the Arab Spring in resistance to authoritarianism and the Occupy movement in resistance to neoliberalism. Although the former has since mostly deteriorated, the latter has taken new forms, which are also more visibly feminist and intersectional, such as the 2017 global Women's March, for the rights of women and peoples in all their diversity that are now subject to considerable roll-backs in a range of national contexts but particularly in the US, which, under Trump, seeks roll-backs in international human rights (and particularly women's reproductive and LGBTQ rights), peacebuilding, and climate change amelioration norms, all of which entail gender agendas to realize them.

One could argue that this very open assault will result in even greater resistances and more widespread activism for global justice. That is the hope of this edition, retitled *Global Gender Politics*, to emphasize an intersectional gender analysis-informed global politics for social justice. This more streamlined edition, now published by Routledge, not only updates the repositioning of women and men (including those who identify as one or the other or neither) in global politics in the context of trends in gender and gendered divisions of power, violence, and labor and resources, but also addresses how crises of representation, insecurity, and sustainability arising from these divisions are being exacerbated by the democratic crisis reflected by the rise of the far-right or the new authoritarianism that has been constituted by neoliberalism in combination with the deep and persistent ideological and structural forces of masculinism, heteronormativity, gender normativity, racism, classism, and neocolonialism that neoliberalism has not excised, and, in many ways, has been built upon. The power of gender, shorthand for the dichotomizing and stratifying moves in thought and action that derive from hierarchical oppositional constructions of sex and gender and operate in other hierarchical oppositional categorizations, remains a conceptual fulcrum of the book. More visuals appear in the book and more suggestions for discussion and activities as well as more resources are included in the book and in the e-resource that accompanies this book, a new innovation for this edition.

The reorganization of and greater explicit attention to feminist IR in relation to other critical and conventional IR in this book is a reflection of my own shift back to teaching in a political science department after leading and teaching in women's, gender, and sexuality departments and programs for many years. I was motivated to do this by the opportunity to be a part of a critical mass of feminists that now make up the Department of Political Science at the University of Cincinnati (UC) and to launch and direct a Political Science doctoral concentration in Feminist Comparative and International Politics there, the first of its kind as far as we know and a testament to decades of struggle to change the study of IR. In addition to teaching graduate courses that contribute to this concentration, I also now teach an online Global Gender Politics course. Members of that course in Spring 2017, including students at UC and at the Future University of Egypt in Cairo with which my department is partnered and where I also lecture on occasion, made suggestions as to how to revise this text. Suggested revisions were also offered by several anonymous faculty reviewers who had used past editions. I could not incorporate all suggestions, but I did what I could and am so grateful for all the insights and feedback of student and faculty reviewers alike. I also am grateful for the assistance of editorial staff at Westview Press who asked me to prepare a fifth edition, helped me to finalize my revision plan, and executed my contract. Once Westview was bought by Taylor & Francis while I was completing the manuscript, editorial staff at Routledge, who I also greatly thank, have assisted me in the final production.

Special thanks go to my graduate research assistants, Crystal Whetstone, Murat Yilmaz, and Sayam Moktan, all doctoral students or candidates in Political Science at UC, who worked with me from Spring through Fall 2017, to update empirical material, develop visuals, add new references and resources, and generally support this effort. They have been a joy to work with on this project, and each are engaging in critical and/or feminist comparative and international politics inquiry in their own work. It is also my privilege at present to serve on the doctoral dissertation committees for Crystal and Murat, from whom I have learned so much.

I am also so gratified that several of my graduate students and colleagues at UC in both Political Science and Women's, Gender, and Sexuality Studies participated in the fifth annual conference of the *International Feminist Journal of Politics* (*IFJP*), which I, as an associate editor of that journal, organized and hosted at UC in 2016 on the theme of decolonizing knowledges in feminist world politics. This brought my campus and professional communities together, and I am pleased that the work of some of my students and colleagues appear in the March 2018 special issue of that journal arising from the conference, which I guest-edited and to which I contributed some of my current work on the relationship between gender and nuclear colonialism visited on indigenous peoples. My *IFJP* community, which includes members of the Feminist Theory and Gender Studies section and the LGBTQA and Women's caucuses of the International Studies Association, has been integral not only to the advancement of feminist IR, but also to my work and well-being as a scholar, activist, and person. The scholarship this community has generated and the friendships and collaborators I enjoy within it, too numerous to list here, have made this book, its previous permutations, and all of my other past and ongoing work possible. The sabbatical and UC Taft Research Center fellowship that extended it, which were awarded to me with the support of my department, as well as a Fulbright research chair fellowship I recently held in Canada at York University have also enabled me to complete this book in the midst of other projects.

My deepest thanks, as always, go to Spike Peterson. Our work together on past editions is still reflected within this one, and our friendship and mutual support transcends space and time. Should some future editions of this book be desired, I know she joins me in hoping future generations of feminist IR scholars will carry it on for us.

Finally, and as always, I am most grateful to Albert Kanters, my partner in life for over 43 years, to whom this book is dedicated for his consistent and loving support of my work and life throughout. He lost his dear father and last parent as I prepared this, one of many family members and friends we have lost on our journey together. But through thick and thin, we are always there for each other and hope for a world in which all have the support and care of not only loved ones but also a larger world based on social justice and compassion.

Acronyms

1325	United Nations Security Council Resolution 1325
9/11	attacks on the United States on September 11, 2001
AIDS	acquired immunodeficiency syndrome (*see* HIV/AIDS)
BCE	before common era
BPA	Beijing Platform for Action
CEDAW	United Nations Convention on the Elimination of All Forms of Discrimination Against Women
CEO	Chief Executive Officer
COP	Conference of the Parties
DAV	Disabled American Veterans
DDR	disarmament, demobilization, and reintegration
DOD	Department of Defense (US)
DRC	Democratic Republic of Congo
ECOSOC	United Nations Economic and Social Council
EPZs	export-processing zones
EU	European Union
F(I or G)PE	feminist international or global political economy
FMF	Feminist Majority Foundation
FSS	feminist security studies
GAD	gender and development
GBV	gender-based violence
GDI	Gender-Related Development Index
GDP	gross domestic product
GEM	Gender Empowerment Measure
GFC	Great Financial Crisis
GI	military, non-civilian serviceperson (*formerly* government issue)
GII	Gender Inequality Index
GJM	global justice movement
GPE	global political economy
HIV/AIDS	human immunodeficiency virus/acquired immunodeficiency syndrome
HR Council	Human Resources Council
ICC	International Criminal Court
ICERD	International Convention on the Elimination of All Forms of Racial Discrimination
ICJ	International Court of Justice
ICTR	International Criminal Tribunal for Rwanda

ICTs	information and communications technologies
ICTY	International Criminal Tribunal for the Former Yugoslavia
IDEA	Institute for Democracy and Electoral Assistance
IDPs	internally displaced persons
IDWN	International Domestic Workers Network
IFIs	international financial institutions
IFJP	*International Feminist Journal of Politics*
IGLHRC	International Gay and Lesbian Human Rights Commission (now OutRight International)
IGOs	intergovernmental organizations
ILGA	International Lesbian, Gay, Bisexual, Trans, and Intersex Association
ILO	International Labour Organization
IMF	International Monetary Fund
INSS	The Institute for National Security Studies
IOM	International Organization for Migration
IPU	Inter-Parliamentary Union
IR	International Relations
IRA	Irish Republican Army
ISIS	Islamic State of Iraq and Syria
ITC	International Trade Center
IUF	International Union of Food, Agricultural, Hotel, Restaurant, Catering, Tobacco, and Allied Workers' Associations
IWRAW	International Women's Rights Action Watch
LGBT	lesbian, gay, bisexual, trans
LGBTQ	lesbian, gay, bisexual, trans, queer
LGBTQIA	lesbian, gay, bisexual, trans, queer, intersex, asexual
MDGs	Millennium Development Goals (United Nations)
MPs	members of parliament
MST	military sexual trauma
NATO	North Atlantic Treaty Organization
NCRW	National Council for Research on Women (now part of International Center for Research on Women)
NGOs	nongovernmental organizations
OECD	Organization for Economic Cooperation and Development
OSAGI	Office of the Special Adviser to the Secretary-General on Gender Issues and Advancement of Women (UN)
PMSCs	private military and security companies
PR	proportional representation
PTSD	post-traumatic stress disorder
R&R	rest and recreation
R2P	Responsibility to Protect
RAWA	Revolutionary Association of the Women of Afghanistan
SAPs	structural adjustment programs
SDGs	Sustainable Development Goals
SERNAM	Servicio Nacional de la Mujer (National Office for Women's Affairs)
SIPRI	Stockholm International Peace Research Institute
SOFAs	Status of Forces Agreements
SOGI	Declaration on Human Rights, Sexual Orientation, and Gender Identity

TFNs	transnational feminist networks
TNCs	transnational corporations
TSNs	transnational social networks
UK	United Kingdom
UN	United Nations
UNAIDS	Joint United Nations Programme on HIV/AIDS
UNDAW	United Nations Division for the Advancement of Women
UNDP	United Nations Development Programme
UNDRIP	United Nations Declaration of the Rights of Indigenous Peoples
UNEP	United Nations Environment Program
UNESCO	United Nations Educational, Scientific, and Cultural Organization
UNFCCC	United Nations Framework Convention on Climate Change
UNHCR	United Nations High Commissioner for Refugees
UNICEF	United Nations Children's Fund
UNIFEM	United Nations Development Fund for Women
UN-INSTRAW	United Nations International Research and Training Institute for the Advancement of Women
UNSCR	United Nations Security Council Resolution
UN-SWAP	United Nation System-Wide Action Plan
UN Women	United Nations Entity for Gender Equality and the Empowerment of Women
UNWTO	United Nations World Tourism Organization
US	United States (of America)
USAID	United States Agency for International Development
WCAR	World Conference Against Racism (UN)
WEDO	Women's Environment and Development Organization
WEF	World Economic Forum
WHO	World Health Organization
WID	women in development
WIIS	Women in International Security
WILPF	Women's International League for Peace and Freedom
WPS	Women, Peace, and Security
WSIS	World Summits on the Information Society
WTO	World Trade Organization

1 Introduction: Gender and Global Politics

Why does gender matter in global politics? What difference does it make to view global politics through a gendered lens? What becomes visible when we see "international relations" as interconnected relations of inequality—among genders, races, classes, sexualities, and nationalities—as opposed to simply interactions between and among self-interested states? What are the costs of being inattentive to gendered dynamics in global politics for addressing a myriad of world problems that ultimately affect us all?

In this introductory chapter, an overview is presented of the contemporary relationships between gender and global politics. It begins with a conceptual discussion of gender as a dichotomous power relation and normative ordering power, referred to as the *power of gender*, a *meta-lens* that fosters dichotomization, stratification, and depoliticization in thought and action through the processes of *masculinization* and *feminization*, thereby sustaining global power structures and crises that prevent, militate against, or reverse meaningful advances in social equality and justice. It then addresses why adopting not only a *gender lens*, but more importantly a *gendered lens*, informed by *intersectional* thinking, is important for understanding how the gender interacts with other power relations, such as race, class, sexuality, and nationality (including power relations among nations as well as those based on national origin) to produce both *gender* and *gendered divisions of power*, *violence*, and *labor and resources* in global governance, global security, and global political economy, the principal areas of inquiry in the study of International Relations (IR). These divisions, in turn, keep in place and exacerbate the *crises of representation*, *insecurity*, and *sustainability* in global politics, which are also introduced.

In the remainder of this introductory chapter, how gender politics became more salient in national and international policymaking in recent decades is raised. A host of international institutions have been adopting some understandings produced by gender-centered research in IR that make links between raising the status of women worldwide and addressing global crises, including democratic deficits, armed conflict and other violence, and poverty and environmental degradation. However, as also raised, the deepening of such crises has also led to a backlash not only against international institutions, but also with respect to nascent attention to women's rights with the recent rise of ethnic, economic, and belligerent nationalisms in several parts of the world. This rise of such new authoritarianisms associated with "strong man" politics, as also pointed out, is also a feature of contemporary global gender politics. Thus, a gendered lens is required to better understand these conflicting responses to global crises and the insufficiencies and problematics of both to address them.

With these foundations, the chapter then moves to the central conundrum or dilemma focused on in this text: despite some elevation of gender issues on national and international policymaking agendas that have led to some gains by some women, there have also been significant setbacks not only to achieving greater social equity and justice for most women and many men, but also with respect to stemming global crises that, in part, result from the gendered nature of global politics and are, in part, producing more virulent gendered global politics. The central argument throughout this text is that this conundrum arises from the superficial ways in which gender has been taken up in national and international policymaking—namely, simply "adding women" for the most part while leaving global crises in place—thus paving the way for more authoritarian responses to these crises, which, among other things, attempt to reassert so-called traditional social hierarchies. This text further contends that this superficial *repositioning of some women and men* in global politics that leaves global crises unabated, which, in turn, breed desires for re-establishing rigid social hierarchies, is rooted in the power of gender. The power of gender is not fundamentally disturbed by mere repositionings of some women and men within gendered divisions of power, violence, and labor and resources present in global governance institutions, global security apparatuses, and global political economy formations. Moreover, inattention to the intersecting nature of these inequalities has resulted in problematic gender equality policymaking. Such policymaking tends to target only women and fails to take into account inequalities among women and among men. It further deflects attention from such interlocking forces as democratic deficits, militarization, and globalization, which, on the one hand, have, minimized equality and social justice efforts at the international and many national levels, and, on the other hand, have led to authoritarian anti-equality responses to global crises that such forces foment.

The chapter ends with a mapping of the text, briefly outlining the subsequent chapters. While throughout the text, it is emphasized that global crises remain unabated in no small measure as a result of the underlying and as yet undisturbed power of gender to order thought and action in dichotomous and hierarchical ways, the text concludes with the ways diverse women and men are resisting the power of gender, gendered divisions, and the global crises that flow from them at local, national, and transnational levels.

Gender as a Power Relation, the Power of Gender, and a Gender Lens

Gender "is not a synonym for women" (Carver 1996). Rather, it generally refers to the socially learned behaviors, repeated performances, and idealized expectations that are associated with and distinguish between the proscribed gender roles of masculinity and femininity. As such, it is not the same as and may be wholly unrelated to sex, which is typically defined as the biological and anatomical characteristics that distinguish between women's and men's bodies. Contemporary gender studies, informed by feminist, queer, and trans(gender) thought, find that sex, too, is socially constructed because it is only through the meanings given to and the marshaling of particular biological and anatomical characteristics that sex difference, as an unequivocal binary, is naturalized and enforced, including surgically when children born with ambiguous sexual organs are made into either "girls" or "boys" to sustain the idea that there are only two sexes (Fausto-Sterling 1992, 2000). As a result, gender analysts challenge not only the biologically determinist idea that dualistic gender identities and roles arise from natural sex difference, but also the notion that sex difference itself is natural and dualistic, calling into question even our assumptions about a world made up of only "females" and "males," "girls" and "boys," "men" and "women."

Trans movements and scholars (see, for example, Stryker and Whittle 2006) have particularly countered such assumptions, expressing and arguing for the fluidity and diversity of sex and gender forms and identifications and putting into question "cisgender" norms based on the lining up of sexed bodies with gender identifications and roles. They have also complicated reference to any singular categories of "women" and "men" in recognition of trans as well as ciswomen and cismen, the former of which experience particular and particularly harsh forms of gender discrimination and violence (Spade 2015). Queer or LGBTQ (lesbian, gay, bisexual, trans, queer) or sexual minority movements and scholars (see, for example, Peterson 2014; Picq and Thiel 2015; Weber 2016) challenge both gender normativity and heteronormativity, which assume an "essentialized" (natural, universal) binary of sex difference (male and female only), privilege exclusively heterosexual desire (for the "opposite" sex), and maintain that the only natural and hence appropriate or respectable expressions of desire, intimacy, sexual identity, marriage, and family formation are heterosexual. The rigid gender dichotomy presumed in both ideologies fosters the demonization and even criminalization of non-gender normative identities and non-heterosexual relations Thus, the study of gender is as much about the socially constructed and normative categories of "men" and masculinity as it is about the socially constructed and normative categories of "women" and femininity and the heteronormativity that attends such gender normativity.[1]

But gender is also not confined to a "set of ideas" that divide humans up into socially constructed, binary, and gender- and hetero-normative categories of male and female, masculine and feminine, heterosexual and non-heterosexual, but is "more broadly, a way of categorizing, ordering, and symbolizing power" (Cohn 2013: 3). As such, it is a "structural power relation" which "organizes access to resources, rights, responsibilities, authority and life options" (Cohn 2013: 5). Indeed, without attending to the *structural power relation of gender*, we "gravely underestimate both the amount and the kinds of power it has taken to create and to perpetuate the international political system we are living in today" (Enloe 2014: 9). The rise of feminist perspectives in IR (which are addressed in the next chapter) brought about the investigation of gender as a significant power relation in global politics by documenting the institutionalization of gender difference as a major underpinning of structural inequalities in much of the world. Through a complex interaction of identification processes, symbolic and material systems, and social institutions (explored more in-depth in subsequent chapters), gender differences are produced—typically in the form of a *dichotomy* that not only opposes masculinity to femininity but also translates these oppositional differences into *gender hierarchy*, the privileging of traits and activities defined as masculine over those defined as feminine. A *gender lens* (explored more in the next chapter) reveals the political nature of gender as a system of difference construction, hierarchical dichotomy production, and norms enforcement that constitutes virtually all contemporary societies. Gender is about power, and power is gendered. How power operates in this way starts to become visible in an examination of the relationship between masculinity and femininity.

Although the specific traits that mark gender-appropriate behavior vary cross-culturally, they constitute systems of politically significant structural power in the following interacting ways. First, males are expected to conform to models of masculinity (that are privileged) and females to models of femininity (which are subordinated). There are multiple models of masculinity within cultures, but one typically has hegemonic status as the most valued and esteemed model, and it is associated with elite (class, race, and culturally privileged) males. Within particular cultures, these expectations are taken very seriously because they are considered fundamental to who we are, how we are perceived by others, and what actions are appropriate. In this sense, gender ordering is inextricable from social ordering of power, authority, work, leisure, and pleasure.

Second, because masculine activities are more highly valued or privileged than are feminine activities in most of the world most of the time, the identities and activities associated with men and women are typically unequal. Thus, the social construction of gender is actually a system of power that not only divides the world into "men" and "women" and masculine and feminine, but also typically places some men and masculinity above most women and femininity. Consider, for example, how consistently institutions and practices that are male-dominated and/or representative of hegemonically masculine traits and style (politics, making money) are valued more highly and considered more important than institutions and practices associated with femininity (families, caring labor). This elevation of what are perceived as masculine traits and activities over those perceived as feminine is a central feature of the ideology or system of belief of *masculinism*.

Third, because the dichotomy of masculine and feminine constructs them as polarized and mutually exclusive, when we favor or privilege what is associated with masculinity, we do so at the expense of what is associated with femininity. Politics, as conventionally defined, is about differential access to power—about who gets what and how. Therefore, the privileging of masculinity is political insofar as relations of inequality, manifested in this case as gender inequality, represent men's and women's unequal access to power, authority, and resources.

Like other social hierarchies, gender inequality is maintained by various means, ranging from psychological mechanisms (engaging in sexist humor, blaming the victim, internalizing oppressive stereotypes), sociocultural practices (objectifying women, creating "chilly climates" for women's advancement, harassing women sexually, trivializing women's concerns), structural discrimination (denial of equal rights, job segregation, marginalization of reproductive health issues), to direct violence (domestic battering, rape, femicide, or the systematic murder of women). Also, like many social hierarchies, gender inequality is "justified" by focusing on physical differences and exaggerating their significance as determinants of what are in fact socially constructed, learned behaviors. Thus, Arthur Brittan has argued that by denying the social construction of gender, masculinism serves to justify and "naturalize" (depoliticize) male domination because

> it takes for granted that there is a fundamental difference between men and women, it assumes that heterosexuality is normal, it accepts without question the sexual division of labor, and it sanctions the political and dominant role of men in the public and private spheres.
>
> (Brittan 1989: 4)

Like the abstract concepts of family, race, and nation, gender "in the real" sense is always inflected by such dimensions as race/ethnicity and class, which vary depending on culture and context. What does not appear to vary is the *power of gender* to conceptually and structurally organize not only gender identities and sexual practices, but also virtually all aspects of social life in all cultures. Indeed, a gender lens reveals that masculine and feminine "natures" are not simply inscribed on what are assumed to be distinct male and female bodies, but also are applied to other objects, including things, non-human beings, groups, institutions, and even nations and states. Consider references to a ship or car as "she," invocations of "mother nature," characterizations of opposing sports teams as "wimpy" while one's own is "mighty," notions of "motherlands" and "fatherlands," and categorizations of "strong" and "weak" states. Everyday parlance is rife with gender appellations and metaphors, *masculinizing* and *feminizing* subjects, objects, and even concepts. This constant gendering of natural, artificial, and social worlds through language and, thus, thought, is no trivial matter. It directs us to how the power of gender operates to set up and reinforce dualistic, dichotomous, or either–or thinking *and* to foster hierarchical thinking in which those people and objects assigned masculine qualities are valued or given power over those assigned feminine qualities.

Thus, this approach foregrounds not only how a gender lens reveals the nature and extent of gender and other related inequalities (explored more in this chapter) that structure and are structured by global politics, but also, and most insidiously, how the power of gender operates as a *meta-lens* that orders and constrains thinking and thus social reality and action, thereby serving as a major impediment to addressing inequalities and the global crises (also begun to be explored in this chapter) that stem from, sustain, and even worsen inequalities. On one level, the power of gender upholds masculinist ideology, which refers to individuals, perspectives, practices, and institutions that embody, naturalize, and privilege the traits of masculinity at the expense of feminized and other alternatives and are thus engaged in producing and sustaining relations of gender inequality. On another level, the power of gender works to pervade our everyday naming, speaking, clothing, working, entertainment, and sports, but most importantly, as this text argues, dominant approaches to knowledge production, governance, security, and economic relations. At its deepest level, the power of gender as a meta-lens continually normalizes—and hence depoliticizes—essentialized stereotypes, dichotomized categories, and hierarchical arrangements. In these multiple and overlapping ways, the power of gender is political: it operates pervasively to produce and sustain unequal power relations. Thus, lenses that ignore or obscure how gender operates systemically and structurally are conceptually inadequate for understanding how power works in global politics and politically inadequate for challenging interrelated social injustices and global crises.

Intersectional Gender Analysis

Contemporary gender studies that partake of intersectional analysis, which holds that gender cannot be understood in isolation from other identity categories and relations of inequality, recognize that there are multiple genders, as well as sexes, in part because race/ethnicity, class, sexuality, and other cultural variations shape gender identities and performances. The concept of intersectional analysis emerged from the work of black US feminist theorists in the 1980s and beyond (Crenshaw 1991; Collins 1991) who recognized that the lives and experiences of women of color were underrepresented in dominant Western feminist theories about women's subordination that were based on the experiences of largely white, Western, middle-class, and/or working-class women.

Because the particular characteristics associated with femininity and masculinity vary significantly across cultures, races, classes, and age groups, there are no generic women and men, cis or trans. Our gender identities, loyalties, interests, and opportunities are intersected and crosscut by countless dimensions of "difference," especially those associated with ethnicity/race, class, national, and sexual identities. "Acting like a man" (or a "woman") means different things to different groups of people (e.g., trans people, heterosexual Catholics, Native Americans, British colonials, agriculturists versus corporate managers, athletes versus orchestra conductors, combat soldiers versus military strategists) and to the same group of people at different points in time (e.g., nineteenth- versus twentieth-century Europeans, colonized versus postcolonial Africans, pre-puberty versus elderly age sets, women during war versus women after war). Men may be characterized as feminine (e.g., Mahatma Gandhi, "flamboyant" gay men) and women as "masculine" (e.g., Margaret Thatcher, "butch" lesbians). Gender is shaped by race (models of masculinity and femininity vary among Africans, Indians, Asians, Europeans), and race is gendered (gender stereotypes shape racial stereotypes of Africans, Indians, Asians, whites). Moreover, because masculinities and femininities vary (by class, race/ethnicity, sexuality, age), some expressions of gender (Hispanic in the US, Muslim in India, Turkana in Kenya) are subordinated to *dominant* constructions of gender (Anglo, Hindu, Kikuyu). There are thus multiple masculinities that not only vary across cultures but also confer different levels of power. What is referred to as "hegemonic masculinity" (Connell 1987, 1995) is the ideal form of masculinity performed by men with the most power attributes, who not incidentally populate most global power positions. These are typically white, Western, upper-class, straight cismen who have conferred on them the complete range of gender, race, class, national, and sexuality privileges. "Subordinated masculinities" (Connell 1987, 1995) are embodied by those who lack one, some, or all these privileges and are consequently rendered *feminized and thus devalorized* (a process explored more in this chapter) on these scores. Although all femininities are subordinated to all masculinities, it is also the case that some femininities are subordinated more than or differently from others. The idealized image of Western femininity remains associated with Victorian notions of womanhood that celebrated the gentility, passivity, decorativeness, and asexuality imposed on white, middle- to upper-class women, who were the only ones who could enact such standards. Working-class women, women of color, and/or lesbians or trans women are either denied the (dubious) status of feminine because they cannot meet these standards or are feminized in other ways through processes of *racialization* and/or *sexualization*. For example, since the times of slavery and colonization, women of color have been labeled as naturally oversexual, thereby not only being unworthy of (white) male protection but also particularly open to (white) male sexual exploitation.

But beyond such an example, it is important to stress that racialization and sexualization can carry two meanings that are often in tension. They refer in one sense to processes of identifying an individual or group as one or another sexuality (straight, gay, queer) or race (white, black, Asian) by attributing to them particular and often stereotypical ideas and practices associated with that label. In a second sense, the attributing process often emerges from a position of normative privilege and presumed superiority, which effectively stigmatizes (or "others") the objects of attribution, especially by constructing them unidimensionally—as "only" their race, class, or sexuality. It is in this sense that privilege permits whites to be less aware of "having a race" themselves and more often to "racialize" others, even as the social construction of "race" permits some who are excluded from "whiteness" through economic or religious discrimination at one juncture to be "whitened up" by altered alignments at another (southern Europeans, Jews, Irish). Thus, the moniker of "white," particularly when used in this text, can also refer to those who gain the status of "whiteness," regardless of actual skin color, as a result of class and other privileges.

Finally, the specific meanings and values conferred on masculinity and femininity have also changed over time as well as across cultures. For example, Western ideals of "manliness" have undergone historical shifts: from the early Greeks through the feudal period, the emphasis of idealized masculinity was on military heroism and political prowess through male bonding and risk-taking; whereas more modern meanings of masculinity have stressed "competitive individualism, reason, self-control or self-denial, combining respectability as breadwinner and head of household with calculative rationality in public life" (Hooper 1998: 33). This does not mean, however, that older meanings have gone away, as unbridled military toughness and financial risk-taking can come once again to the fore in times of war and economic restructuring. Moreover, not all cultures have associated such conceptions of masculinity with leadership qualities: "queen mothers" in Ghana and "clan mothers" in many Native American societies have been accorded power and leadership roles in these matrilineal contexts on the basis of the feminine quality of regeneration of the people and the land (Okojo 1994: 286; Guerrero 1997: 215). Furthermore, there is some play in gender roles even within patrilineal or patriarchal cultures, given that men are not exclusively leaders and warriors and women are not exclusively in charge of maintaining the home and caring for children. Cultures also vary in the play allowed to the display of non-conforming gender behavior, such as that not associated with a person's assigned sex; sometimes even "third genders" are revered. Polities also vary in terms of acceptance of and resources available to people who choose to change their assigned sex. Due to the variation in meanings attached to femininity and masculinity, we know that expressions of gender are not "fixed" or predetermined; the particulars of gender are always shaped by context.

Because models of appropriate gender behavior are diverse, we know that femininity and masculinity are not timeless or separable from the contexts in which they are embodied, acted out, and observed. This illustrates how gender rests not on biological sex differences but on *interpretations* or constructions of behavior that are culturally specific, that shift as contexts change, and that typically have little to do with biological differences, which themselves are not fixed as some bodies are born neither "male" nor "female" and gender and sex assignments can be altered. In short, there are multiple genders and gender orderings, but gender is always raced, classed, sexualized, and nationalized, just as race, class, sexuality, and nationality are always gendered. Hence, gender analysis must avoid stereotyping (or reducing people to unfounded caricatures), essentializing (or assuming "natural" and unchanging characteristics), and singling out any one identity as descriptive of a whole person. Instead, gender analysis must adopt intersectional analyses to make sense of our multiple, crosscutting, and differentially valorized identities. However, these variations still rest on concepts of gender differences and do not necessarily disrupt the power of gender as an oppositional dichotomy and as a relation of inequality.

Gendered Power Relations Through a Gendered Lens

Here, intersectional analysis is expanded on to go beyond a gender to a *gendered lens*. First, as has already been argued, women and men, cis and trans, have multiple identities simultaneously, describing themselves or being described not only by gender but also by race, class, sexual, and national markers, such as a black, American, working-class, gay male. Second, these identity markers, however, are not just additive, merely descriptive, or politically or socially neutral. Some parts of our identities carry privilege, and others do not. For example, male privilege, which an individual may be able to exercise in the home over women and children, is offset in other, more public arenas if the individual is a racial minority in the larger demographic and thus subject to racism; a sexual minority within the person's own race or a wider demographic and thus subject to homophobia; and/or not a member of the owning or managerial class and thus subject to classism. Being an American may confer some privileges, such as citizenship rights, including voting rights, that are denied to non-naturalized immigrants (of color or not), but we also know that racism (and classism) can trump those formal citizenship rights, as in the case of black Americans who were routinely kept from voting through Jim Crow laws, poll taxes, and literacy tests long after they won the formal right to vote.

Third, different parts of our identities become politically salient at different times. This casts us into pigeonholes that deny the complexity of our identities, and when some aspects of our identities are given rights, but others are not, it can create a kind of schizophrenia within the individual and divisive mentalities within and between seemingly cohesive social groups. Consider the case of suffrage for African American women. The common notion is that African Americans were given the vote before women in the US, but in fact only African American men were enfranchised first; African American women had to await the enfranchisement of women generally. Thus, their gender separated them from the category of "African American," which was coded as meaning only black men. At the same time, although many white women suffragists had been abolitionists, their anger over the enfranchisement first of only black men prompted racist arguments as to why white women were better entrusted with the vote to uphold white civilizational values. This effectively discounted black women, who had to organize separately. Thus, because of their race, African American women were also separated from the category of "women," which was coded as meaning only white women (Giddings 1984). A more contemporary example is the idea that a black man cannot also be gay because dominant constructions of black men's sexuality, foisted by whites and internalized by blacks from slavery on, are so tied to images of aggressive heterosexuality.

This leads to a fourth meaning of intersectional analysis—namely, the kind of masculinity or femininity one is assumed to have rests on the meanings given to one's race, class, sexuality, and nationality. For example, Africans brought as slaves to the Americas were defined by their captors as subhuman with largely animal instincts, which included the assumption that animals mate indiscriminately. The idea that slaves, whether men or women, were "oversexed" was a convenient mythology for male slaveholders who could thereby justify their sexual assaults on female slaves while upholding slavery and, later, lynchings in the name of protecting white women from "naturally" sexually predatory black men. As noted earlier, the contemporary terms for this kind of thinking are the gendered racialization and sexualization of groups to render them as "other" or different and less than the groups doing the labeling. As also raised earlier, hegemonic masculinity—currently identified with and exercised by those individuals, groups, cultures, organizations, and states coded with the full privileges of Western-ness, whiteness, wealth, and cismaleness born out of long histories of conquest and colonization—carries the highest representational (or labeling) power to render others "other." If we focus only on a narrow definition of gender or singular notions of masculinity and femininity, we miss the complexity of unjust social orders and fail to see how they are upheld often by pitting subordinated groups against each other, especially when such groups are coded as homogeneous without both crosscutting and conflicting interests within them that hold potential for coalitions and more comprehensive resistance to unjust social (and world political) orders.

Contemporary feminist scholars engage in intersectional analysis to avoid the practice of "essentialism," or the assumption that, for example, all women or all men or all those within a given race or class share the same experiences and interests. Only by recognizing how, for example, some women have benefited by the racial, class, sexual, and national origin oppression of other women, whereas many men subordinated by these very characteristics still exercise gender oppression, can we advance a more comprehensive notion of gender equality that sees it as indivisible from racial, class, and sexual equality and equality among nations. Thus, a sole focus on gender equality can fail to address other sources of inequality (such as race and class discrimination) that disadvantage certain groups of women. At the same time, when such efforts blame only men, and mostly non-elite men, for gender inequality and fail to address forms of discrimination that subordinated men experience (based on class, race, and/or sexuality), then subordinated men may withhold support for gender equality. A narrow focus on gender equality also maintains the power of gender, even as the socioeconomic positionings of some women and men may be somewhat altered, as is addressed more in this chapter.

Another reason to avoid essentialism is also to avoid "universalism," or universal prescriptions for how to achieve comprehensive gender equality. Not only do women not share the same experiences or interests as a result of their multiple identities derived from their differing social locations in the world, but also the sociopolitical, cultural, and historical contexts in which women live vary significantly, requiring varying strategies for social change. These complex realities have made many feminists skeptical of resorting to "global" solutions just as they have recognized that "global" problems take many and differing "local" forms to which agents of social change must be attentive to create context-specific and context-sensitive solutions that do not backfire (Grewal and Kaplan 1994).

Thus, it is important to attend to the ways in which race, class, sexual, and national power relations intersect with gender power relations to produce multiple and differing subordinated femininities and masculinities, significantly complicating how to address and redress what are, in fact, interrelated inequalities. However, it is also important to recognize how masculinism operates to justify not only gender hierarchies, but also hierarchies of ethnicity/race, class, nation, and sexuality through the process of *feminization* as the central mechanism of the power of gender. Underpinning this claim is the observation that, although structural hierarchies vary by reference to the "differences" emphasized and the disparate modalities of power involved, they typically share a common feature: their denigration of feminized qualities attributed to those who are subordinated (lacking reason, control, etc.). Because the "natural" inferiority of the feminine is so taken for granted, invoking it plays a powerful—though not exhaustive—role in "legitimating" these hierarchies. In a second sense, not only subjects (women and marginalized men) but also concepts, desires, tastes, styles, ways of knowing, cultural expressions (art, music), roles, practices, work, and nature can be feminized. This effectively reduces their legitimacy, status, and value, and fuels stereotypical characterizations that can be deployed to depoliticize unequal valorizations. In both senses, *devalorization through feminization* powerfully normalizes—with the effect of legitimating—the subordination, exploitation of, and various forms of violence against feminized concepts, skills, activities, and persons.

In short, a central argument of this text is that the more an individual or a social category is feminized, the more likely (although not invariably) its categorical difference and devaluation are assumed or presumed to be "explained." This insight contributes to intersectional analysis by enabling us to see how diverse hierarchies are linked and ideologically naturalized by the feminizing of individuals and subordinated social categories. To be clear, however, feminization is only one among a number of normalizing ideologies, nor is gender hierarchy the primary oppression or the most salient or powerful hierarchy in any particular context. As Nira Yuval-Davis notes, "In specific historical situations and in relation to specific people . . . some social divisions . . . are more important than others" (2006: 203). At the same time, some social divisions (e.g., age, gender, ethnicity/race, class) "tend to shape people's lives in most social locations," whereas other divisions (e.g., castes, status as indigenous or refugee persons) profoundly affect those subject to them but "tend to affect fewer people globally" (Yuval-Davis 2006: 203). The objective is not to prioritize the subordination of women or deny the different organizing logics or modalities of power operating in racism, classism, nationalism, and so on. It is, rather, to note that even as social divisions have different bases, they are not historically independent of each other and gender is an important linkage among them, especially with reference to the political project of normalizing, hence depoliticizing, hierarchical (de)valorizations. What distinguishes feminization is the unique extent to which it invokes the deeply embedded, internalized, and naturalized binary of sex difference and gender dichotomy. Despite significant lived experience and intellectual challenges to sex and gender as binaries, most people most of the time take "sex difference" completely for granted—as biologically "given," reproductively necessary, and psychosocially "obvious." As argued earlier, however, sex difference is a mistakenly essentialized binary that falsely "grounds" gender as a system of difference construction and hierarchical dichotomy production. The naturalization of sex difference naturalizes dichotomized gender differentiations (pervading all social life) and thinking in hierarchical, categorical oppositions more generally. Insofar as these naturalizations and masculinist (not necessarily male) privilege constitute common sense, their ideological power is then "available" (through, for example, cultural assignments of reason, agency, and governing to masculinity and irrationality, dependence, and being governed to femininity) for legitimating other forms of domination (for example, colonialism, racism, classism, and homophobia).

The power of gender produces a common sense of privileging the masculine and devaluing the feminine that is culturally and collectively internalized to such an extent that we are all variously complicit in its reproduction. It is also implicitly and explicitly manipulated to reproduce inequalities as if they were natural and inevitable, thus undercutting critique and resistance. In these ways, devalorizing through feminizing produces even as it obscures vast inequalities of power, authority, and resource distribution.

Examples of how the power of gender, as an ordering system that valorizes or privileges what is deemed masculine and devalorizes or subordinates what is deemed feminine in order to naturalize inequalities and power relations, extends beyond hierarchically dividing women and men to hierarchically dividing peoples, places, cultures, practices, institutions, and even ideas and concepts in the global system can be seen in Table 1.1. The processes of *masculinization as valorization* and *feminization as devalorization* powerfully organize our thinking as to what is valued and thus prioritized and what is not valued and thus denigrated in the study (explored more in Chapter 2) and practice (explored more in Chapters 3, 4, and 5) of global politics. To better see how gender as a power relation combines in complex ways with other structural power relations, such as colonialism, imperialism, militarism, racism, and economic and environmental exploitation, to normalize social, political, and economic divisions, inequalities, and injustices, a *gendered lens* is necessary. The term "gendered" is used in this text, unless otherwise specified, as a shorthand to signal the application of an intersectional analysis to examine interlocking relations of inequality in global politics. The next section provides an overview of how hierarchical gender divisions that foreground the normative masculine–feminine dynamic are intertwined with gender*ed* hierarchical divisions that foreground how gender is never separate from and powerfully informs hierarchical

Table 1.1 Gender and Gendered Divisions of Power, Violence, and Labor, and Resources

Masculinized	*Feminized*
Men	Women
Normative genders	Non-normative genders
Heteronormative majority	Sexual minorities
White(ned)	Racialized
(Neo)colonizing	(Neo)colonized
Western	Non-Western
Global North	Global South
War	Peace
International	Domestic
States	Families/communities/social movements
Market economy	Care economy

divisions based on race, ethnicity, class, sexuality, nationality, age, ability, and so on. Adopting a gendered lens also more fully reveals how these divisions are productive of and reproduced by global crises, also introduced in the following section.

Gender(ed) Divisions of Power, Violence, Labor, and Resources and Global Crises

This section introduces the core matrices covered in more depth in later chapters through which gender and gendered, or intersectional, power relations operate in the conventional study of IR and in the conduct of *global politics-as-usual*. These matrices—*gender(ed) divisions of power, violence, labor, and resources*—not only constitute and sustain power relations between and among diverse women and men across the globe, but also are productive and reproductive of the interactive global *crises of representation, insecurity, and sustainability* that reinforce gendered divisions and power relations and are upheld by the power of gender.

Gender(ed) Divisions of Power and the Crisis of Representation

Masculinism pervades politics. Wendy Brown writes,

> More than any other kind of human activity, politics has historically borne an explicitly masculine identity. It has been more exclusively limited to men than any other realm of endeavor and has been more intensely, self-consciously masculine than most other social practices.
>
> (Brown 1988: 4)

In IR, as in political science generally, power is usually defined as "power over," specifically, the ability to get someone to do what you want. It is usually measured by control of resources, especially those supporting physical coercion. The appropriate analogy might be power understood as tools: if you have them, you can use them to get certain things done if and when you choose, and some have more of these tools than others. This definition assumes measurable capacities, privileges instrumental rationality, and emphasizes separation and competition: those who have power use it (or its threat) to keep others from securing enough to threaten them. The emphasis on material resources and coercive ability deflects attention from the fact that power reckoning is embedded in dominant conceptual orders, value systems, disciplinary practices, and institutional dynamics.

In IR, the concept of "political actor"—the legitimate wielder of society's power—is derived from classical political theory. Common to constructions of "political man"—from Plato and Aristotle to Hobbes, Locke, and Rousseau—is the privileging of "man's" capacity for reason. Rationality ostensibly distinguishes man from other animals and explains his pursuit of freedom—from nature and "necessity" as well as from tyranny. Feminist scholarship has exposed how models of human nature presupposed in constructions of political man are not in fact gender-neutral but are *androcentric*, based on exclusively male (especially elite male) experience and perspective. With reference to gender divisions of power, "woman" is excluded conceptually from political power by denying her the rationality that marks "man" as the highest animal. Substantively, women have historically been excluded from political power by states' limiting citizenship to those who perform military duty and/or are property owners. Under these conditions, most women are structurally excluded from formal politics, even though individual women in exceptional circumstances have wielded considerable political power. Women worldwide have largely won the battle for the vote, though definitions of citizenship continue to limit women's access to public power and women's political power is circumscribed by a variety of indirect means (discussed more in Chapter 3). Most obvious are the continued effects of the dichotomy of public–private that privileges men's productive and "political" activities over women's reproductive and "personal/familial" activities. For example, sovereign man and sovereign states are defined not by connection or relationships but by (masculinist) autonomy in decision-making and putative freedom from interdependence and collective responsibilities. Although Aristotle acknowledged that the public sphere depends upon the (re)production of life's necessities in the private sphere, he denied the interdependence that this implies in articulating political theory.

With reference to gender*ed* divisions of power, "political man" also presupposed "civilizational" status: early Greek texts excluded "barbarians" and Persians; premodern European texts excluded "primitives" and racialized "others" within Europe and outside it as colonization proceeded. Indeed, racialization is historically inextricable from the expansionary and colonizing practices of European elites who deployed Enlightenment ideas ("reason," "science") and new technologies (gunpowder, steam engine) to enhance their power over foreign populations, thus enabling the extraction of resources and labor to fuel European "modernization" and geopolitical dominance. "Eurocentrism" is an ideology of European superiority that arose from this conquest and is often used interchangeably with "Westerncentrism" in more recent times. "Orientalism" (Said 1979) is one effect of Eurocentrism (or "Occidentalism"), consigning the "non-West" to the status of cultural, political, economic, and technological backwardness. Such backwardness is assumed, in Eurocentric and Orientalist thinking, to need stimulation from the West to "develop" or "modernize" or "progress." Thus, men and women of various colonized, racialized, and classed groups have been excluded over time from political power by various means: barred on the basis of property claims, denied leadership in their own lands by colonial domination, displaced to other lands and denied power through slavery and debt bondage, and more generally excluded from citizenship rights based on criteria related to birth location, "appropriate" documentation, or "economic" status. Although after World War II resistance to direct colonial rule was largely successful, more indirect "neocolonial" or "neoimperial" rule (sometimes referred to as "recolonization"), in which former colonial or newer superpowers control or seek to control the polities and economies of formerly colonized nations, has continued. Such labels as "developed" versus "developing" countries or the terms "First" and "Third" Worlds attest to the maintenance colonial logics that construct the West (or the North more broadly) as more advanced politically and economically than the rest. Colonial logics also continue through sexualized as well as racialized divisions of power, justifying the invasion or control of "others" by coding the West as uniquely moral and "respectable," as well as racially superior.

Today, most people have a "right" to political participation, but the most powerful decision-makers in global politics are those occupying positions of power in national and international governmental institutions and transnational corporations. Occupants of these positions now include elites from both the global North and the global South, terms used in this text to avoid such problematic and inaccurate references as developed vs. developing countries or First vs. Third Worlds. Such elites, regardless of their geographic origin, continue to reflect privileged statuses, especially of national and economic power, which are derived from being members of the dominant ethnicity/race, class, gender, and sexuality.

Gender divisions of power, which equate being political, acting in the public realm of reason, and exercising power-over with normative masculinity and being apolitical, powerless, and sequestered in the private realm of emotion and necessity with femininity, in combination with gendered divisions of power, which feminize or devalorize colonized, racialized, classed, and sexualized peoples in today's global politics, are reflective of and instrumental in producing a *crisis of representation*. This entails still gross inequalities in political representation, not only in formal power structures such as states and intergovernmental organizations (IGOs), but also in nongovernmental organizations (NGOs) and social movements. While problematic in terms of constraining the political agency and voice of large swaths of people, even in "democracies," without a range of perspectives from varying social locations, solutions proposed by the few (and most privileged) more often benefit them while causing harm to those un- or under-represented. "Democracy" is strategically promoted while its radical promise is undermined by fraudulent elections, political machinations, imperial impositions, and gendered rule. As addressed in greater detail in Chapter 3, "global governance" sounds good and is presumably desirable in some form, but its current form obscures the predominantly nondemocratic and unaccountable forms of international rule.

In these senses, analyzing gendered divisions of power requires greater attention to political, economic, and sociocultural forces below and above the level of the state, thereby revealing the greater complexity of global politics, which cannot be reduced to the actions of state elites and their international organizations or the top-down "problem-solving" orientation they advocate. Such a lens reveals inequalities as a source of conflict in global politics and illuminates divisions within groups—as well as linkages among groups—not only along national lines but also along gender, race, class, sexuality, and culture lines. The corollary of this, addressed in the final chapter, is that many people are resisting global-politics-as-usual by finding common cause with each other across national boundaries and "identity politics" and thus creating a different kind of international relations from that of elite policymakers.

As discussed in Chapter 2, elite power-wielders in global politics (and many who study them) have an interest in stability and, thus, act to maintain current divisions of power and their corollary forms of (nondemocratic) political representation. Non-elites around the world (and most who study them) focus on divisions of power that are created in the name of stability but undermine democracy and accountability and compromise the security of the global majority. People around the world struggling against the tyrannies of sexism, homophobia, racism, classism, militarism, and/or imperialism seek justice, which requires upsetting the status quo. The danger is that even when people struggle for social change, the power of gender typically prevents them from seeing beyond particular interests and oppositional politics to the collective interests of all planetary inhabitants and the complex politics of social justice. It thus (re)produces a crisis of representation by (re)producing global gender and gendered divisions of power.

Gender(ed) Divisions of Violence and the Crisis of Insecurity

Essentializing claims about men's superior strength are favored justifications for gender hierarchy. But such claims are misleading. On the one hand, men's strength varies cross-culturally and within cultures, and a considerable number of women are, in fact, stronger than men. On the other hand, why do we consider men's upper-body muscular strength more significant than women's burden-carrying strength and greater endurance? Decades ago Ashley Montagu undertook a comprehensive review of scientific literature and concluded that "the female is *constitutionally* stronger than the male": she has greater stamina, lives longer, fights disease better, and endures "all sorts of devitalizing conditions better than men: starvation, exposure, fatigue, shock, illness and the like" (Montagu 1974: 61–62).

Historically, the upper-body strength of (some) males was presumably an important factor when the success of hunting large game or the outcome of conflicts depended on this particular strength. Modern technologies, however, have dramatically altered the relationship of muscular strength to success in battle or in the workplace. Yet a cultural preoccupation with power and strength defined in masculine terms endures. With reference to gender divisions of violence, stereotypes of superior male strength are inextricable from hegemonic constructions of masculinity that cultivate male arrogance and overweening power. Most models of masculinity, historically and presently, include elements of courage, competition, assertiveness, and ambition that are difficult to disassociate from physical aggression and even violence, especially when males are systematically placed in situations where proving their manhood involves aggressive behavior. Willingness to engage in violence is then easily mobilized, whether against feminized intimates (lovers, wives) or feminized "others" (opponents, enemies). As one effect, across national contexts, many more men (especially of particular ages) engage in violent behaviors more frequently and with more systemically destructive effect than do most women.

Moreover, gender divisions of violence assure that security is understood not in terms of producing and sustaining life but of acquiring sufficient power to protect "one's own" and keep "others" at bay. The Hobbesian notion that human nature is universally competitive and hostile that undergirds conventional IR thinking is revealed as problematic when we ask how helpless infants ever become adults. Through a lens on child-rearing practices—necessary for life everywhere—it makes more sense to argue that humans are naturally cooperative, for without the cooperation required to nurture children, there would be no men or women.

With reference to gender*ed* divisions of violence, Europeans manipulated ideologies of superior (masculinist) "strength" to justify colonial wars and obscure their racist, economic, and heteronormative dynamics.[2] What surfaces repeatedly are characterizations of the colonized as feminine: weak, passive, irrational, disorderly, unpredictable, and lacking self-control. This afforded European power-wielders (not only men or all men) a justification for military interventions by casting themselves in favorable masculinist terms: as uniquely rational, sexually and morally respectable, and more advanced economically and politically. In colonial wars and geopolitical "othering," civilization became a code word for European heteronormative masculine superiority. Through this lens, imperial violence was perhaps a regrettable but nonetheless necessary component of "enlightening" and "civilizing" primitive, unruly, feminine "others." As Zillah Eisenstein observes, although Europeans extolled the virtues of reason as a progressive force, they positioned rationality "against savagery (natives), emotionality (women), and sexuality (racialized others)" (Eisenstein 2004: 75).

At the same time—and complicating simplistic models of gender—the development of European nationalisms and normalization of bourgeois respectability produced an idealized model of (bourgeois) femininity: passive, pure, dutiful, maternal. This superficial valorization of femininity did less to empower women than it did to render them perpetual dependents, as feminine virtue and morality were best assured by confining these qualities and "good women" to a private sphere of domesticity and assigning men the public-sphere responsibility of defending and protecting feminized dependents. The patronizing and protectionist logic of bourgeois norms provided imperial governments a moral—as well as rational—justification for militarized colonization: the barbarity of "other" men was proven by their (allegedly) oppressive treatment of women, and this *called for* the rescue of victimized females by honorable, civilized men. In short, the defense of idealized femininity—to paraphrase Gayatri Spivak's (1988) apt analysis—justified wars by white men to "save" brown women from brown men.[3] This protectionist and crusading rhetoric obscured exploitative agendas and appeared to legitimate militarized violence. As discussed in Chapter 4, it resurfaces, with particular vengeance and new complexities, in contemporary global security practices, including increased militarism, particularly on the part of new (and older) authoritarians, and militarization—the extension of military thinking and practices into civilian life—and imperialist projects, such as the ongoing "war on terror."

Today's *crisis of insecurity* relates not only to the *direct violence* of international conflict, but also to the *structural violence* of political, economic, and social priorities and inequalities that leave much of the world's people subject to unemployment and underemployment, poverty, disease, and malnutrition as well as other forms of direct violence—namely domestic and sexual violence. The link between direct and structural violence is revealed particularly when we consider how military spending and war-making undermines access to basic human needs. As a result of debts racked up by runaway "defense" spending for the "war on terror" that reduce social welfare spending, massive displacements of peoples within and beyond state borders as the result of war-fighting, and the destruction of land and resources entailed by war and preparations for it that undermine people's lives and livelihoods, more and more people are becoming insecured. Structural violence disproportionately affects women and groups subordinated culturally and economically, and when we ignore this, we ignore the insecurity of the planet's majority and the planet itself.

Gendered and gender divisions of violence are deeply implicated in these multiple aspects of the crisis of security. The masculinized and feminized poles of self vs. other and us vs. them constructs a world shaped by fear of difference and justifies war or other forms of violence against "othered" nations or groups placed on the devalued feminized pole. At the same time, gender divisions of violence that associate masculinity with aggression and soldiering, and femininity with passivity and victimhood, construct a world in which war can be further justified in the name of protecting those feminized (and deemed worthy of protection) from such "others." In this self-perpetuating cycle, threats (real or fictive) increase preparations for defense and/or retaliation that are inextricable from conditions of structural violence, perpetuating inequalities. This cycle further disallows thinking and acting nonviolently as that is also feminized—seen as soft and ineffectual—under the gendered division of violence. Moreover, while gender and gendered inequalities provide motives for conflict and fuel militarization, wars also provide profit-making opportunities for some that delay the resolution of conflicts and deepen the crisis of insecurity for all.

Gender(ed) Divisions of Labor and Resources and the Crisis of Sustainability

Divisions of labor within households and the global workforce and divisions of the planet's resources are shaped by masculinist and capitalist ideologies, both of which entail relations of inequality and exploitative dynamics. Gender divisions of labor rest on how "work" is defined and "counted," what kinds of work are most valued, who does what work, and how much—if anything—they are paid. Hierarchical gender dichotomies of public–private, productive–reproductive, mental–manual, skilled–unskilled, formal labor–informal labor, and provider–dependent generate quite rigid labor patterns not only between men and women, but also between the rich and poor and North and South under gendered divisions of labor. Just as the public is seen as (politically) more important than the private (ostensibly less skilled), reproductive, manual, and informal (low-end, self-employed) labor is monetarily devalued, accorded less status, and rendered less visible, even though such labor underpins and makes possible what "more important" workers—especially elite men—do. And just as women are deemed feminine by their dependence within the family, "less developed" nations and their people are "unmanned" by their position of dependence in the global economy.

As examined in greater detail in Chapter 5, for the past several decades geopolitical elites have promoted neoliberal, or market-based, policies that effectively restructured production and financial arrangements worldwide. Many conventional IR scholars, who draw on neo-classical economic theory to study the global political economy, have endorsed neoliberalism as the optimal strategy not only for pursuing economic growth and prosperity but also for promoting "democracy" worldwide. Neoliberal commitments to deregulation and economic liberalization, most associated with the process of globalization, were assumed to be the most efficient and, therefore, most desirable approach to national and international economic relations. Deregulation has favored private capital at the expense of public provisioning and shifted risks and responsibilities from the collective to the individual. Increasing "flexibilization" and feminization of work arrangements has dramatically reduced not only many women's but also more men's access to paid, safe, and secure ("formal," long-term, with benefits) forms of employment. With reference to gender*ed* divisions of labor, male workers in general face increasing un- and underemployment (work "below" their skill level), and the poorest workers in the global North and South face declining prospects for any "meaningful" work or income sufficient to escape poverty. Greater numbers of men and women are on the move globally in search of work, and these racialized flows alter identity politics and heighten conflicts over immigration. Women virtually everywhere are increasingly entering the workforce, but for the vast majority, they find work only in low-status and poorly paid jobs.

Although women often seek paid work because males in the household are un- or under-employed, the gender division of labor in the household is rarely transformed when women work outside the home. Rather, studies worldwide confirm that women who work for pay rarely do less unpaid work at home because even when men are unemployed, they resist doing "women's work" in the home. One effect is a global trend of women doing more work than ever: still carrying the primary responsibility for child care, the emotional and physical well-being of family members, and everyday household maintenance, but now also earning income for the family and often being called upon to nurture community survival networks in the face of worsening socioeconomic conditions. This is consistent with masculinist branding of "women's work" as that which serves others—both at home and in the workplace. Women are seen to work "for love" or as secondary income earners to sustain families, rather than primarily for income or status as most cultures expect men to do.

The larger problem, however, is not simply a failure of men to "do their share" but the effects that neoliberal capitalism has had on the viability of social reproduction, or the capacity to meet basic human needs that enable people to live and work. In the context of deteriorating economic conditions and reduced public support, there are ultimately limits to how far and how long women can "stretch" their energy and labor to meet survival needs and ensure the daily reproduction of social life. Isabella Bakker and Stephen Gill refer to "a global contradiction between the extended power of capital (and its protection by the state) and not only sustainable but also progressive forms of social reproduction for the majority of the world's population" (Bakker and Gill 2003: 4). The increasing breakdown of social reproduction in daily life is also the result of environmental degradation arising from gender and gendered divisions of resources.

Gender divisions of resources are problematically revealed when we consider how women are assigned primary responsibility for social reproduction, which requires basic resources, but they have little control over how local and global resources are used, distributed, and controlled. Worldwide, but particularly in the global South and among the poor, females are more dramatically affected by environmental degradation than are males. As food providers, women find their workload increases when water, food, and fuel resources deteriorate; as last and least fed, they suffer most from starvation and malnutrition; and as caretakers, they have to work harder when economic, health, and environmental conditions deteriorate and when families and communities are victims of toxic pollution and environmental disasters brought on of late by climate change. As a result, women's bodies are rendered more disposable, too.

Gender*ed* divisions are institutionalized with the growth of science and industrial technologies in service to capitalist and colonial projects. At the core, the modernist, Eurocentric ideology of limitless growth presupposes a belief in (white, Western) "man's" dominion over nature (promoted, for example, in Christian and capitalist belief systems) and the desirability of (white, Western) "man's" exploiting nature to further his own ends. Conquering nature, digging out "her" treasure and secrets, proving (white, Western) man's superiority through control over and manipulation of nature—these are familiar and currently deadly refrains. The feminization of nature is not an accident but a historical development that is visible in justifications by elites for territorial and intellectual expansion. Exploitation is most readily legitimated by objectifying who or what is exploited. Understanding people or nature as "objects" denies them agency, purpose, feelings, intelligence, a right to exist and/or to warrant respect. Through the ideology of (white, Western) man's dominion, it is taken for granted that natural resources are there for humans to exploit and control: no questions asked; such resources are "there for the taking." In various ways throughout history, aboriginal peoples, women, colonies, and the earth's bounty have all been treated as such natural resources (Mies, Bennholdt-Thomsen, and von Werlhof 1988). Such gendered divisions of resources as subject–object, culture–nature, and users–exploitable and disposable resources feminize the natural environment and are all associated with it at great cost to human and ecological sustainability.

Thus, the contemporary global *crisis of sustainability* is two-fold. It is a crisis of both social reproduction, borne of gender(ed) divisions of labor, and of resource depletion, borne of gender(ed) divisions of resources. The (over)valorization of skills, work, and "production" associated with hegemonically masculine identities and activities presuppose (white) man's dominion over feminized people and nature, as well as capitalist commitments to neoliberal restructuring. But as also suggested in this section, the crises of representation, insecurity, and sustainability are all interrelated. The power of gender to naturalize and normalize hierarchical dichotomies through processes of masculinization and feminization sets up the ideological and material gender(ed) divisions of power, violence, and labor and resources. These disempower much of the world's people to have meaningful and more equitable says in what constitutes security and how to better sustain livelihoods and human and non-human life; disable alternatives to armed conflict and other forms of violence that destroy lives, livelihoods, and ecosystems and militates against equitable decision-making and economic redistribution from "guns to butter"; and undermine not only the capacities of people to make decent livings and provide care for each other, which are prerequisites for active political participation and senses of security, but also the carrying capacity of the planet on which all depend. Thus, the crises of representation, insecurity, and sustainability have to be addressed together and through an understanding that the power of gender significantly underpins them all.

Global Crises, Gender Agendas in International Policymaking, and the Repositioning of Women and Men

As many have observed, the language of crisis has beset the world in recent times. Invocations of crises, ranging from the Great Financial Crisis (GFC) and North Korean nuclear crises to the global refugee crisis and the climate change crisis, are calling forth a sense of "emergency" on many fronts (Sjoberg, Hudson, and Weber 2015: 530). Too often such crises are not seen as connected, some crises deflect attention from others, and what may be actually more serious crises do not rise to the level of being seen as crises on the world stage. The invocation of crisis can also lead to top-down emergency responses that worsen some crises while trying to "fix" others and/or reproduce the sources of the crisis trying to be addressed. In this section, a preliminary discussion is provided on why gender has begun to be taken seriously in crisis-ridden global politics, but also why gender agendas in international policymaking are insufficient and problematic, leading only to some *repositioning of women and men* in global politics without disrupting the deeper problem of the power of gender and gender(ed) divisions and global crises it breeds. This core argument of the text is expanded upon in subsequent chapters, which are mapped at the end of this introductory chapter.

Decades of feminist IR scholarship (addressed in detail in Chapter 2) and the centuries of international feminist thought and activism most catalyzed during and since the United Nations (UN) Decade for Women (1975–1985) are most responsible for putting gender inequality on the map of global politics. But it was only with the inauguration of the UN Decade for Women that gender inequality begun to be taken seriously in international policymaking. High-level attention to gender can be traced to tracking the positionings of women in world affairs that became possible when governments around the world—since the first UN conference on women, held in 1975—committed to provide data regularly to the UN that disaggregated the roles men and women play in state governance, militaries, diplomatic machineries, and economies. By the end of the last millennium, the data regarding how men and women are situated differently around the world revealed, starkly, the extent of gender inequality. The United Nations Development Programme (UNDP) unequivocally concluded that "no society treats its women as well as its men" (UNDP 1997: 39). Such a conclusion was based on reports to the UN Committee on the Status of Women that, although women composed one-half of the world's population, they performed the majority of the world's work hours when unpaid labor was counted, yet in aggregate were poorer in resources and poorly represented in elite positions of decision-making power (Tickner 1993: 75).

Such findings precipitated a host of gender equality measures dedicated largely to *repositioning women*, which were championed by the UN and adopted, albeit very unevenly, incompletely, and selectively, by national governments. Examples of such measures (detailed more in subsequent chapters) include, first, the UN Convention on the Elimination of All Forms of Discrimination Against Women (CEDAW),[4] initially adopted in 1979 following the UN Decade for Women and going into force in 1981, which recognized that women have human rights and that women's human rights expand definitions of human rights. By 2000, only 25 countries (including, most glaringly, the US, as well as a smattering of Muslim and the poorest countries) had failed to ratify CEDAW, making it the second most widely ratified human rights convention (UN 2000: 151). As of 2017, only the US, Iran, Sudan, Somalia, Palau, and Tonga remain as outliers (see Chart 1.1). Through CEDAW and subsequent UN conferences on human rights, particularly throughout the 1990s, women's movements and NGOs made the case that "women's rights are human rights," achieving international recognition that reproductive and, to some degree, sexual rights are just as important as and connected to political and economic rights. As long as women are denied choices about if, when, and under what conditions they bear children or terminate pregnancies, are subject to sexual and domestic abuse, and are limited in their sexual expressions and orientations, they will not be able to exercise their political and economic rights. Although women's and other human rights continue to be violated on a massive scale, the widespread ratification of CEDAW has

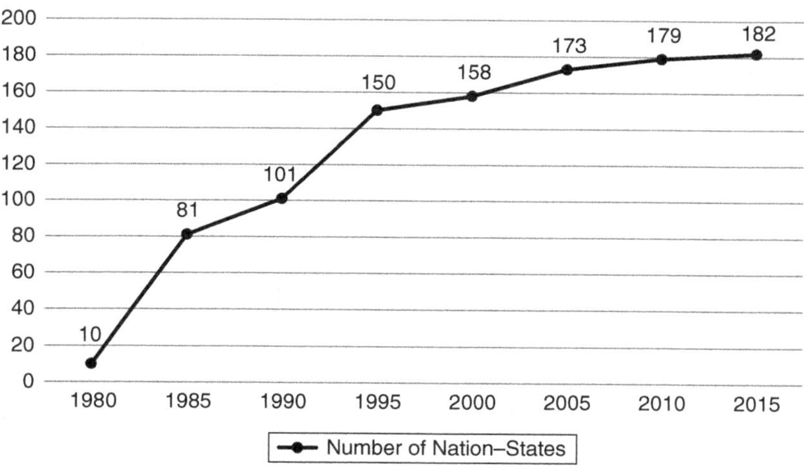

Chart 1.1 CEDAW Adoptions over Time

Source: Drawn from United Nations Treaty Collection at https://treaties.un.org/Pages/View Details.aspx?src=TREATY&mtdsg_no=IV-8&chapter=4&lang=en#8 (accessed December 12, 2017).

given women's movements throughout much of the world a major tool through which to hold their governments accountable for continued abuses.

Since 1990 when the UN Economic and Social Council (ECOSOC) supported the goal lobbied for by women's movements to have 30 percent of world decision-making positions held by women by 1995, the adoption of gender quotas have become a "global trend" (Dahlerup 2006b: 6). As of 2017, 48 countries had reached or exceeded the 30 percent target in their national legislatures (IPU 2017b), with postgenocide Rwanda still topping the list at 56 percent (and in 2008 becoming the first country with more female than male legislators). Almost all these have legal or party gender quota systems in combination with proportional representation systems (defined and discussed in Chapter 3). Although quota systems vary in form and efficacy, they were specifically promoted in the Platform for Action arising from the UN Fourth World Conference on Women, held in Beijing in 1995, which was unanimously supported by the world's governments, as the "fast-track" way to increase women's political representation.[5] There are many reasons for this recent "contagion" of gender quotas, but among them is a growing international consensus or norm, advocated by women's movements worldwide and supported by feminist scholarship, that gender equality in the form of women's greater political representation, ideally to the point of parity with men, is necessary for polities claiming or aspiring to be modern and democratic. The wide use of gender quotas has not yet had a significant effect on the numbers of women heads of government given that, as of 2017, there are only 16 such women, most of whom rose to power in the 1990s. However, greater pools of women aspiring to such office are enabled by quotas, even though they are not sufficient alone to change the gender landscape at the highest levels.

Gender mainstreaming also gained momentum and increasing acceptance during the same period that gender quotas were advancing. Although definitions vary somewhat, gender mainstreaming refers generally to integrating the principle of gender equality into any (inter) governmental policy (not just those associated with so-called women's issues, such as family and violence against women) to ensure that in practice it does not, wittingly or unwittingly, increase or sustain inequalities between women and men (Squires 2007: 39–40). Gender mainstreaming was first advocated in the context of economic development policies once feminist research revealed that approaches taken by funding bodies like the World Bank, such as the promotion of capital-intensive agriculture for export, tended to privilege men, who had or were given more access to capital, agricultural inputs and machinery, and land ownership. Women, although heavily involved in subsistence agriculture, which was the main source of family food consumption, were not seen as farmers or landowners and, thus, did not benefit from this kind of funding. This disparity not only increased men's power over women in agricultural work and families, but also contributed to producing more hunger and malnutrition when women's work of subsistence farming was increasingly so devalued and unsupported. The World Bank and a number of other supranational institutions, ranging from the UN and the Organization for Economic Cooperation and Development (OECD) to the European Union (EU), as well as many development agencies within states in the North, have been convinced by such findings to adopt gender mainstreaming, also called for in the Beijing Platform for Action (BPA), to try to avoid such outcomes (Squires 2007: 42). There have been numerous downsides to this approach (which are addressed in Chapter 3), but its institutionalization represents a sea change in its recognition that gender is infused in all (world) political issues and legitimizes the need for "gender experts" in global politics.

No less than the UN Security Council, arguably the most male-dominated and masculinist body in the world (that is, steeped in the most hegemonic masculine values associated with power politics), has also acquiesced to giving some attention to gender. For example, Security Council Resolution 1325, passed in 2000 and followed by several more such resolutions that affirm it, calls for women to be present at peace negotiating tables, a goal long advocated by women's peace movements that have claimed women have greater interests and different stakes in ending war, and zero tolerance for wartime sexual violence. As explored in Chapter 4, it is not that women are inherently more peaceful, but rather that their predominantly civilian status means that they often bear the high structural costs of wars over time. In wars, some past and some present, in which there has been little separation between the battlefront and the home front and in which civilians are purposely targeted, civilians constitute the highest proportion of those left homeless, diseased, and hungry; turned into refugees; and made victims of sexual and domestic assault (by enemy and "friendly" combatants) as indirect consequences of warfare. Although for the past few centuries combatants have died from the direct violence of war-fighting in about the same numbers as civilians caught up in armed conflicts, civilian deaths in "total wars," such as the world wars, and in wars in which they are targeted for direct violence, such as massacres, have been higher, and the toll of civilian suffering and death from indirect warfare violence is staggering (Goldstein 2011: 258–260). Although women are increasingly combatants and civilian men suffer a range of similar violences arising from war as civilian women, women tend to be more subject to sexual and domestic violence (in times of war and "peace") and more vulnerable to deprivations as they have less resources and mobility even prior to conflict, and are made more responsible for the mending of postconflict societies through their roles in re-creating households and communities, albeit with few resources. Thus, UN Security Council resolutions, as part of the larger UN Women, Peace, and Security Agenda instigated by former UN Secretary-General Kofi Annan as a result of the advocacy and lobbying of international women's peace movement NGOs and activists, constitute not only some recognition of the relationship between gender inequality and war, but also policies and programs to address it.

Predating this Security Council resolution was a significant codification and prosecution of rape as a war crime following the highly visible use of systematic rape in the early 1990s in the wars in the former Yugoslavia and in Rwanda. Systematic wartime rape not only neutralizes women as threats, but also seeks to weaken men's resolve to fight by "soiling their women" while also trying to wipe out an enemy culture or ethnicity by impregnating women with "alien" seed or keeping them from reproducing altogether. The assumption that rape was merely a natural "spoil of war" (for men) had kept it from being fully recognized as an international war crime until feminist activists and events in Bosnia and Rwanda made it clear that rape was a direct violation of women's human rights, rising to the level of torture as an instrument of warfare. However, this has not stopped rape in wartime, nor does it address it in so-called peacetime, which are among the problems with this addressed in Chapter 3.

Although feminist activists and scholars who have advocated for and performed research to legitimate and implement such international instruments for global gender equality did so for the purposes of uprooting gender and other social injustice, international gender policy agendas have been increasingly directed to empowering women as a solution to a crisis-ridden world. By 2010, a host of IGOs, NGOs, and corporate actors and economists reached a consensus: "Progress is achieved through women" (Kristof and WuDunn 2009: xx). Even national and international security experts had begun paying attention to gender on the basis of a perceived relationship between the marginalization of women in politics and society and the growth of "terrorism," particularly in Islamic countries.

> As the Pentagon gained a deeper understanding of counterterrorism, it became increasingly interested in grassroots projects such as girls' education. Empowering girls, some in the military argued, would disempower terrorists. When the Joint Chiefs of Staff hold discussion of girls' education in Pakistan and Afghanistan, you know that gender is a serious topic on the international affairs agenda.
>
> (Kristof and WuDunn 2009: xxi)

Even though this newfound interest at the highest levels of global political institutions in gender, but more accurately in women, can be read as a feminist success story, the instrumentalist way that gender has become so salient by being reduced to women's empowerment is problematic. For example, it was only when women entered into the formal labor force in huge numbers out of their own economic necessity and as a result of being seen and used as a preferred source of "cheap" and "obedient" labor to fuel the world's factories, that women suddenly were noticed by economic elites as a previously "untapped resource" and an "engine of growth" that could be better harnessed to serve national and transnational corporations and capitalism. "The basic formula was to ease repression, educate girls as well as boys, give girls the freedom to move to cities and take factory jobs, and then benefit from the demographic dividend as they delayed marriage and reduced childbearing" (Kristof and WuDunn 2009: xix). A further dividend of breaking down patriarchal authority in homes and communities and the violence against women and girls that is justified by patriarchal authority is assumed to be a reduction in women's and their children's poverty, as women and children make up the vast majority of the world's poor. As raised earlier and probed later in Chapters 4 and 5, this has instead led to women working even harder for still very little and even increased violence, while still denied comprehensive reproductive rights in many parts of the world. Similarly, women became visible to security elites only when it appeared that raising the status of girls and women could constitute a counterterrorism tool, not only denying that women, too, engage in political violence as discussed in Chapter 4, but also ignoring the range of interconnected global hierarchies, especially arising from the legacies of colonialism and effects of present-day neocolonialisms, that breed both non-state and state terrorism. Thus, the empowerment of women has become only a means to an end, not an end in itself—just the latest mechanism to "manage" serial crises as opposed to representing an actual commitment to gender equality and social justice required to get to the roots of the larger global crises identified in this text. That inequalities might be leavened through repositioning (some) women is secondary to shoring up global politics-as-usual priorities of capitalist economic growth and state and interstate security through simplistic, problematic, and always under-resourced approaches to empowering women. These priorities keep the lurching from crisis to crisis in place, for which empowering women becomes largely a panacea because gender inequality and social injustice are not themselves defined as global crises that would animate far more attention, resources, and serious structural change.

The expansion of serial crises and the deeper crises of representation, insecurity, and sustainability have also produced political backlashes, most visible in the last few years, destabilizing in some quarters the emergent international focus on the value of empowering women to solve global problems. A symptom of this can be seen in the rise of elected ultra-conservative, or "new authoritarian," leaders, some quite recently elected or re-elected and most on the right, in both the global North (such as in the US, the UK, Austria, Hungary, Russia, and Italy) and the global South (such as in the Philippines, Turkey, Venezuela, and Egypt). Although in other recent elections ultra-right-wing challengers failed to capture leadership in places like The Netherlands, France, and Germany, their parties gained in strength in, for example, the national legislature of Germany. Although research continues on how to account for such shifts to (or sustenance of) more illiberal democracies, particularly in the West, widening income inequalities, unemployment, and underemployment attributed to globalization appear to have a hand in the rise of ethnonationalist anti-immigrant and anti-internationalist fervor to which illiberal candidates and parties appeal and which they stoke. Wealth concentration is unprecedented today as there

> has been a 60 percent increase in the wealth of the top 1 percent globally in the past 20 years; at the top of that 1 percent the richest 100 billionaires added 240 billion to their wealth in 2012-enough to end world poverty four times over.
>
> (Sassen 2014: 13)

At the same time "2 billion people" are living in "extreme poverty" while "hunger is now growing in rich countries" (Sassen 2014: 147). As noted earlier, neoliberal economic restructuring has not only deleteriously affected women by superexploiting their productive and reproductive labor, but also has been implicated in many men "falling down" (or staying down on) the economic ladder. This *repositioning of (some) men* may be translating into the phenomenon of what countless media reports call "angry white males," particularly in the US but also in other parts of the West, who blame immigrants, people of color, women, LGBTQ people, and internationalizing forces like globalization that make borders more porous for the loss or diminution of jobs that white, working-class men used to more exclusively hold. "Strong man" political discourses, used also by some ultra-conservative female politicians, appeal to this kind of blaming by promising to expel immigrants, build border walls, crack down on crime which is (inaccurately) attributed to immigrants and racialized minorities, roll back women's and LGBTQ rights to restore patriarchal authority and the heteronormative family, and exit from international institutions and agreements that entail subscribing to international cooperation (for such things as reducing violence, poverty, and climate change) and emergent, albeit still cramped, equality norms.

Thus, just as some women are being repositioned upwards through international policy agendas and some national adherence to them, the repositioning of some men downwards, particularly in the global political economy, is producing extreme anti-equality (and related anti-democratic, anti-environmental, and anti-international) agendas in some states. That this is occurring in some very powerful Western states, which have largely been the architects of international institutions and the international order as well as the main beneficiaries of that (unequal) order, suggests that the "management" of serial crises under global politics-as-usual has done little to stem the deeper global crises of representation, insecurity, and sustainability. As this text argues throughout, these crises are a result of the gendered nature of global politics and are, in part, producing more virulent gendered global politics. The tinkering around the edges that adding and empowering women represents in international gender policy agendas neither significantly challenge nor uproot deeply ensconced gender and gendered power relations. These power relations, expressed in this text as gender(ed) divisions of power, violence, and labor and resources, are also not fundamentally disturbed by the repositioning of some women and some men in existing power structures. As building blocks of the crises of representation, insecurity, and sustainability, their perpetuation leaves these crises largely unabated. Moreover, because gender(ed) divisions are outcomes of the power of gender to naturalize and normalize dichotomous and hierarchical social relations and encourage dichotomous (either–or) and hierarchical (us–them) thinking and action, responses to them and the crises they breed have resulted in both the depoliticizing of inequalities as an instrumentalist and technical matter in international policymaking and political (illiberal, authoritarian) backlashes that attempt to (re)assert (often violently) what are claimed to be natural and essential social hierarchies. Without seeing intersecting inequalities and social injustice as global crises and the sources of many others, interlocking forces of democratic deficits, militarization, and globalization operant in global governance institutions, global security apparatuses, and global political economy formations under global politics-as-usual will continue to not only reproduce inequalities and social injustice, but also produce virulent anti-equality and anti-social justice responses that will only further deepen global crises.

Mapping the Book

To better understand what scholarship informs the analysis and empirical findings in this text and how it differs from conventional IR approaches, Chapter 2 on "Gender(ed) Lenses on Global Politics" provides somewhat of a primer on the development and current state of what is variously called gender and IR or feminist IR or feminist world politics. This is a subfield of IR, but also an interdisciplinary field of study. Feminist IR now appears alongside longer-legitimated conventional perspectives in IR, such as (neo)realism, idealism, or (neo)liberalism, and often in combination with more critical ones, such as older (neo-)Marxist and more recent perspectives, including constructivist, poststructural, postcolonial (including decolonial and anti-racist), and queer and trans perspectives, which also can combine in various ways. These critical perspectives, all of which emphasize social reality as constructed rather than given, and most of which are concerned with producing knowledge that brings about social change and justice, enable the positing of the power of gender and the intersecting power relations that flow from it as a significant, but too often unseen, normative ordering power in global politics.

The gender(ed), or intersectional feminist, lenses that arise from feminist in combination with other critical perspectives on global politics are applied to the traditional categories of global politics inquiry: global governance (Chapter 3), global security (Chapter 4), and global political economy (Chapter 5). It is within these chapters that historical and contemporary gender(ed) divisions of power, violence, and labor and resources and the global crises of representation, insecurity, and sustainability they spawn are fleshed out empirically and analytically. The employment of multiple feminist perspectives and the empirical research they are generating foregrounds the substantial body of work that now exists in feminist IR,[6] which is contributing to, as well as based on, data now being produced by IGOs and NGOs on the gender(ed) effects of global political priorities, processes, and institutions and attempts to ameliorate them. The diversity of feminist IR thought and research also affords more complex and sometimes conflicting gender or gendered analyses of global politics. The benefits of this diversity are that it militates against resorts to "quick fixes" that can do more harm than good and ensures no single or hegemonic analysis that forecloses debate and further investigation within feminist inquiry. At the same time, weaknesses in feminist inquiry and appropriations of gender analysis in policymaking are raised when they fail to address the gendered power relations among women and among men that forestall more comprehensive critiques and resistances to processes that widen and deepen global and local inequalities.

The final Chapter 6, "Engendering Global Justice," examines some resistances, both activist and conceptual, that seek to counter the inequalities between and among women and men and/or transform perspectives on and practices in global politics. Although varied, incomplete, and sometimes conflictual, such resistance strategies attempt to confront the crises of representation, insecurity, and sustainability through enabling more participatory and non-hegemonic governance, nonviolent forms of security, and more just and environmentally sustainable economies to develop less crisis-ridden and more just forms of global politics.

Users of this text are also encouraged to employ the questions for discussion and suggested research activities that appear at the end of each chapter to assist in developing a deeper understanding of the material in the text. These aids are also provided in the e-resource that accompanies this text (www.routledge.com/9780813350851). At the end of this text and in the e-resource are a host of links to additional resources.

Notes

1 Although this text often refers only to "women" and "men" or "males" and "females" or, on occasion, notions such as "both genders," it also at times differentiates between cis and trans women and men or refers to diverse genders in recognition that there are multiple sexes and genders and that "women" and "men" are themselves socially constructed and nonhomogeneous categories. Also frequently referred to are the ideologies of "heteronormativity" and "heterosexism," which assume an essentialized (natural, universal) binary of sex difference (male and female only), privilege exclusively heterosexual desire (for the "opposite" sex), and maintain that the only natural and, hence, appropriate or respectable expressions of desire, intimacy, sexual identity, marriage, and family formation are heterosexual. The rigid gender dichotomy presumed in both ideologies promotes masculinism, devalues what is feminized, and fosters the demonization and even criminalization of non-heterosexual relations. References to "sexual minorities" and "gender minorities" signify individuals and groups who contest or do not conform to heteronormativity and normative gender identifications. Although "queer" and "LGBTQ" can capture an array of sexual and non-normative gender identifications (lesbian, gay, bisexual, trans, and queer identities), it is important to note that engaging in particular sexual practices need not constitute assuming a particular sexual identity, that these Western-originating terms are less widely circulated elsewhere, and that those who engage in same-sex or other minority sexual practices or non-normative gender expression do not necessarily identify as LGBTQ (particularly outside the global North) or fit into these categories (such as intersex people who are

born with ambiguous sex organs). A few other terms used in this text also bear explication here for reference. "Homonormativity" refers to the assumption that all sexual minorities do or should conform to Western conceptions of lesbian, gay, and bisexual identity and to Western forms of LGBTQ politics, which when imposed on other cultures and political contexts is often referred to as "global gay" politics. Gender "queer" can refer to a range of sexual minority identities, but "queering" more typically refers to analytical processes and social practices that defy heteronormative and homonormative readings of social reality and performances of normative sexual practices and gender identity. Heteronormative "patriarchy" refers not only to male-dominated or masculinist rule, but also to rule that enforces heterosexual norms to achieve that end.

2 Key works include Said (1979, 1993), Spivak (1987), McClintock (1995), and Eisenstein (2004).

3 Cultural generalizations of enemy groups or nations typically feminized them, and European notions of ethnic/racial hierarchies permitted selective valorization of men identified with "martial races" and "warrior" cultures. Without conceding any sense of their military superiority, imperial governments selectively allied with soldiers of particular cultural identities to advance colonial interests. The British, for example, recruited Nepali Ghurkas to fight their wars and now recruit Fijian men. In the "war on terror," the George W. Bush administration selectively allied with ethnically and religiously differentiated groups—without exception extremely masculinist—that best served its short-term military objectives, with little attention to the hierarchies—especially of gender and sexuality—these exacerbate.

4 On women's rights and/as human rights, see Cook (1994), Peters and Wolper (1995), Peterson and Parisi (1998), and Ackerly (2008). For critiques of this approach, see, for example, Hesford and Kozol (2005) and Hua (2011).

5 See Web and Video Resources at the end of this text (and in the e-resource accompanying it at www.routledge.com/9780813350851) for the online locations and full texts of a host of UN documents, conventions, and protocols referred to in this text, including the Beijing Platform for Action, as well as a host of videos that can supplement and deepen engagement with this text. A list of acronyms and their referents is provided at the front of this text for handy reference.

6 See, in particular, Shepherd (2015) for a useful feminist IR reader with some important works, past and present, as well as Steans and Tepe-Belfrage (2016) for the breadth of contemporary feminist IR thought and research.

Suggested Questions for Discussion and Activities for Research

Each of the chapters in this text begins with questions that not only organize the discussion, but also can serve as questions for discussion. Here and at the end of subsequent chapters are additional questions for discussion as well as some suggested and adaptable individual and/or group activities to prompt further research and discussion and to better engage with the text per chapter and in relation to the list of Web and Video Resources provided (in this text and in its e-resource).

Chapter 1

Questions for Further Discussion

1 What is the power of gender? How is it disturbed by trans, queer, and intersectional feminist perspectives?
2 Why is it important to use both a gender and gendered lens on global politics? How are they differentiated, but also related?
3 Why do gendered divisions of power, violence, labor, and resources persist despite recent attention to gender inequality in international policymaking, and how are they implicated in the rise of new authoritarianisms?
4 What are the relationships between gendered divisions of power, violence, labor, and resources and the crises of representation, insecurity, and sustainability?

Activities for Further Research

1 Go online (or consult your local newspaper), and search for a sample of mainstream news stories about contemporary international relations between states. What gendered patterns (such as the absence or presence of women or men, the positions of power men versus women hold, the "masculine"/hard or "feminine"/soft nature of the issues discussed, and which states are featured as dominant or subordinate) do you notice in these stories? Consider in your gender analysis who wrote the stories, what the stories are about, which states they focus on, what state leaders are featured, how their leadership is characterized, and whether or not domestic populations are mentioned, who among them are featured, and how they are portrayed.

2 Read the text of CEDAW online (www.un.org/womenwatch/daw/cedaw/cedaw.htm), and consider why the US has not ratified it. Do you think the US needs gender (and even "diversity') quotas? Why or why not?

3 Watch this interview by Counter/Action Magazine with feminist IR scholar Cynthia Enloe entitled "Feminism in the Age of Trump"? at https://counteractionmag.com/current-issue/2017/7/12/feminism-in-the-age-of-trump-interview-with-cynthia-enloe. Why does she say it is important for feminists to focus not only on the Trump regime but also authoritarianisms elsewhere in the world and their interconnections? Find more examples of the gender and gendered effects of current authoritarian government actions in various parts of the world and how feminist and other social justice movements are responding to these.

2 Gender(ed) Lenses on Global Politics

Why do lenses through which we view the world matter? How do critical lenses in IR differ from conventional IR lenses? What are feminist lenses and how do they interact with other critical lenses? How is the power of gender operant in conventional IR lenses and thus in global politics? Why is it important to use intersectional feminist lenses in theory and research to see the consequences of and alternatives to this?

In Chapter 1, the concepts of a gender lens and more intersectional gendered lenses were introduced and elaborated on in terms of the immensity and complexity of power relations and structures we see in global politics when we use them and why it is important to not only attend to the masculine/feminine dichotomous and hierarchical dynamic at work in global politics past and present, but also the way this is enlarged upon and complicated by interrelated dynamics of racial, sexual, class, and nationality divisions and hierarchies. In this chapter, background is provided on why and how gender and gendered lenses emerged in the study of IR, how they challenge conventional IR lenses, and what significant understandings such lenses, and the research they have generated, have revealed about how the power of gender works in the study and practice of global politics.

As argued in the introductory chapter, the power of gender is an especially resilient and adaptive filtering and organizing mechanism, a meta-lens that produces particular ways of seeing, thinking, and acting in the world. Gender may feature in policymaking, women and men may be repositioned, and ideal forms of masculinity may shift, but as long as the power of gender as a meta-lens continues to operate, it will produce and reproduce inequalities, injustices, and crises of global proportion. Here the central case made is that *feminist lenses*, and particularly intersectional ones, often in concert with other lenses critical of conventional IR approaches, are necessary to reveal the extent of the power of gender to produce and obscure inequalities and the global crises that ensue from and sustain inequalities.

Feminist IR scholars, emerging in the discipline by the 1980s, generally do not subscribe to the conventional definition of IR as being the power struggles between sovereign states in an anarchic world in which there is no supranational government to control state behaviors through the rule of law. Rather, these scholars favor an alternative definition of IR: "the identification and explanation of social stratifications and of inequality as structured at the level of global relations" (Brown 1988: 461). In this sense, feminist perspectives on IR understand power in broader and more complex terms than more conventional IR scholars do, and have sought to put the relations of people, as agents and within social structures, back into IR. To do so, these IR scholars have relied on feminist sociopolitical theorizing in other disciplines, including the now well-developed (inter)discipline of women's, gender, and sexuality studies.

They have also relied on, and contributed to, an array of other IR lenses, arising prior to and after the emergence of feminist IR, that critique conventional IR for such things as assuming reality is given rather than socially constructed, centering the state and state elites as the main actors in world affairs to the exclusion of actors above and below the state, and failing to see or center how global power structures and relations immiserate the majority of the world's people and the planet. What connects what are broadly referred to here as *critical lenses* or perspectives on IR is the view that conventional IR, as a result of its focus on political and economic elites and state power, and its relative blindness to the deleterious effects of dominant political, economic, and social arrangements upheld by elites and states, is oriented to serving elites to maintain global power structures. Thus, conventional IR is not value-free. Critical perspectives, which maintain no knowledge is value-free and that scholars should acknowledge their always present values or normative commitments that invariably shape the questions they ask, are, in contrast, oriented to producing more "emancipatory" knowledge, which confronts global power structures and relations and their effects on peoples and the planet. Critical perspectives, however, do differ in terms of which global power structures and relations they highlight, how those structures and relations are understood, and what to do about them. Feminist IR perspectives center gender as a global power relation and structure. But as presented in Chapter 1 and expanded upon in this chapter, feminist intersectional analysis in IR goes beyond a gender lens to encompass a gendered lens that highlights the interconnections among global power relations and structures.

This chapter begins with an account of how lenses work and why they matter in a general sense. It then moves to a discussion of IR lenses. Despite the proliferation of such lenses, certain conventional ones still hold sway and take us down very narrow and problematic paths. Why this is the case is particularly explored through a discussion of more privileged positivist knowledge production in conventional IR versus more marginalized postpositivist knowledge production in critical approaches to IR of which feminist IR is a part. Feminist IR, and the multiple perspectives in and approaches to it, is the subject of the rest of the chapter. This discussion includes how feminist IR in particular challenges the power of gender that especially infuses conventional IR lenses and makes them hegemonic or dominant in unquestioned ways, and produces research that is dedicated to revealing and countering gender and gendered divisions of power, violence, labor, and resources in global politics. Such research informs the empirical findings and analysis presented in Chapters 3, 4, and 5, which examine gender and gendered divisions and their contributions to global crises in the contexts of global governance, security, and political economy.

How Lenses Work and Why They Matter

In simple terms, lenses focus our attention selectively. Selective attention is a necessary feature of making sense of any particular subject, practice, paradox, or social order. Because it is not physically possible for any human to see or comprehend everything at once, we rely on conceptual filters—lenses—that enable us to see some things in greater detail, with more accuracy, or in better relation to certain other things. Lenses simplify our thinking by focusing our attention on what seems most relevant. They "order" what we see and provide direction for subsequent actions. In this sense, lenses are like maps: they frame our choices, expectations, and explorations, enabling us to take advantage of knowledge already gained and, presumably, to move more effectively toward our objectives. Like maps, lenses enable us to make sense of where we are, what to expect next, and how to proceed. From the conceptual ordering systems available to us, we choose the lens we assume is most appropriate for a particular context—a lens that we expect will enable us to make sense of and act appropriately in that context.

Lenses are thus indispensable for ordering what we see and orienting our responses. But their filtering function is also problematic. Because we cannot focus on everything, any particular lens directs our attention to some features of a context, which unavoidably renders other features out of focus—filtered out—by that lens. In short, lenses both include and exclude, with important and often political implications.

By filtering our ways of thinking and ordering experience, the lenses we rely on have concrete effects. We observe this readily in the case of self-fulfilling prophecies: if, for instance, we expect hostility, our own behavior (acting superior, displaying power) may elicit responses (defensive posturing, aggression) that we then interpret as confirming our expectations. It is in this sense that lenses and "realities" are interactive, interdependent, or mutually constituted. Lenses shape who we are, what we think, and what actions we take, thus shaping the world we live in. At the same time, the world we live in ("reality") shapes which lenses are available to us, what we see through them, and the likelihood of our using them—or adjusting them—in particular contexts.

In general, as long as our lenses seem to work, we continue to rely on them. The more useful they appear to be, or the more accustomed to them we become, the more we are inclined to take them for granted and to resist making major changes in them. We forget that a particular lens is a choice among many alternatives. Instead, we tend to believe we are seeing "reality" as it *is* rather than as our language, culture, or discipline interprets reality. It is difficult and sometimes uncomfortable to reflect critically on our assumptions, to question their accuracy or desirability, and to explore the implications of shifting our vantage point by adopting a different lens.

We acquire our lenses, or learn our conceptual ordering systems, in a variety of contexts, but early childhood is especially consequential. From infancy on, we are socialized into and internalize ways of thinking and acting that enable us to perform appropriately within a particular culture. This involves acquiring an identity that constitutes subject formation—"who I am"—and assimilating cultural codes that provide meaning for "what I do." Socialization processes are embedded in wider social relations of power that determine which codes are dominant. These include familial, linguistic, cultural, economic, educational, religious, political, and legal institutions that stabilize particular symbolic and social orders and orderings. Dominant codes are infused with normative and ideological beliefs that constitute systems of meaning and valorization, and these can have significant effects on global politics. For example, in complex relationships with governmental, economic, and patriarchal power, religious institutions have historically promoted particular worldviews that guide human action in its most passionate expressions and normative investments—not least, the willingness to die and/or kill others in the name of a cause.

What we learn at an early age is psychosocially formative: the conceptual ordering system (language, cultural rules) we uncritically absorb in childhood is especially resistant to transformation. This is not simply a matter of accustomed habits but of psychic coherence and the security of "knowing" how to act appropriately and effectively in the world. Hence, we are intensely invested in identities and cultural codes learned in early childhood, and challenges to the meaning and order they afford are experienced as particularly threatening.

Of course, the world we live in, and therefore our life experiences, are constantly changing, prompting changes in our lenses as well. The modifications may be minor: from liking one type of music to liking another, from being a high school student in a small town to being a college student in an urban environment. Or the changes may be more profound: from casual dating to parenting, from the freedom of student lifestyles to the assumption of full-time job responsibilities, from Newtonian to quantum physics, from conditions of relative peace to the direct violence of war. To function effectively as reality changes, we must modify our thinking as well. This is especially the case to the extent that outdated lenses or worldviews distort our understanding of current realities, placing us in danger or leading us away from our objectives. As both early explorers and contemporary drivers know, outdated maps are inadequate, and potentially disastrous, guides.

IR Lenses on Global Politics

There are many IR lenses (or theoretical perspectives, explanatory frameworks) through which global politics has been viewed in history and in the contemporary context. How to label lenses is always controversial, and most lenses are continually changing in response to both analytical debates and real-world developments. Most at the center of IR inquiry have been (neo)realist lenses and (neo)liberal lenses, which largely constituted IR as it developed into a discipline from the early twentieth century on. The rise of IR as a modern discipline occurred in the tumult of world wars. It took as its mission to explain such wars in order to contain or reduce them in the absence of supranational governmental authority, thus differentiating itself from political science as the study of domestic government and its presumed legitimate authority to make and enforce laws and maintain order within nation-states. Neo(realist) lenses (see, for example, Morgenthau 1948; Waltz 1959; Mearsheimer 2001), most associated with the study and practice of global security, bring the conflictual behavior of states to the fore. Generally, such lenses start from the premise that the state has a monopoly on the legitimate use of force, define power as state power to amass economic resources and weaponry to use or credibly threaten to use force, see state action as motivated only by rational self-interest, center inter-state warfare as opposed to other forms of armed conflict and violence, and focus on great powers or superpowers as principal actors in global politics most able to, at lease minimally, contain global conflict and most interested in doing so to maintain the global order from which they most benefit.

In some contrast, (neo)liberal lenses (see, for example, Keohane 2005; Cohen 2008), most associated with the study of and practices in the global political economy, focus attention on interstate cooperation and organization. Although still centering states and their rational self-interest, (neo)liberals argue that because of the disruptions war constitutes, particularly to national economies, states have an interest in reducing them. Thus, states, and even the most powerful ones, are also motivated to enter into international institutions and agreements to try to minimize economic disruptions produced not only by military but also non-military conflicts, such as trade wars. The more that states participate in international organizations and agreements that set rules for, for example, "free" trade, which (neo)liberals presume enables all nations to prosper, the more likely they will agree on other matters. This produces norms about such things as the desirability of democratic rule (which some (neo)liberals argue is a prerequisite to peace based on some findings that democracies do not make war on each other). Thus, international organizations and the rules and norm-setting they spawn can come to constitute not world government, but rather global governance—a more diffuse and uneven form of cooperation, largely based on the economic interests of states, which (neo) liberal proponents argue can reduce armed conflict.

Contemporary neorealists now more often acknowledge that domestic non-state actors can also influence the resort to war, and contemporary neoliberals now recognize that international non-state actors, such as transnational corporations and NGOs, are significant participants in global governance and its norm-setting in a more globalized world. However, these still-dominant lenses in IR take states for granted as natural, necessary, and enduring political formations, assume they have unitary and self-evident interests (typically imbued, whether acknowledged or not, by notions of human nature that are ascribed to states), privilege them as actors in global politics, and prize state military and economic security with much less attention to whether these actually produce safety and prosperity for the majority of the world's people and the protection of the planet.

More at the margins of IR inquiry, but gaining increasing attention and use, have been a host of older and newer lenses that are critical of the inadequacies of (neo)realist and (neo) liberal lenses to understand how power works and for whom in the international system. (Neo)Marxist lenses (see, for example, Cox 1987; Wallerstein 1979; Harvey 2003) have their roots in nineteenth-century thought and action that resisted the rise of industrial capitalism and its construction and extreme exploitation of a laboring class (the proletariat) by a much smaller managerial class (the bourgeoisie) which came to own the forces of industrial production and worked with (and/or became) state elites to keep workers in their place, with no or little recourse for the minimal pay and miserable working conditions they endured to enable maximum profits for the few. Thus, (neo)Marxists direct our gaze primarily to class inequalities in global politics. Some (neo)Marxists continue to focus on class inequality within states and the not only material but also ideological and political mechanisms peculiar to capitalism in various forms over time that keep the basic structure of class inequality and exploitation in place. These include critical theorists of the Frankfort School and those known as Gramscians (proponents of the thought of Antonio Gramsci on hegemony as the way that oppression becomes accepted by those oppressed without coercive force), both of which revised classical Marxism to make sense of why workers have not risen up in revolutionary form globally against the capitalist system as Marx predicted and to look for more multiple forms of what are sometimes called "counter-hegemonic" resistances to capitalism. Others, such as dependency and world system theorists, have applied (neo)Marxist lenses to center, understand, and resist class inequalities among nation-states, pointing to how especially industrial capitalism set up the exploitation of the global South to enrich the global North, making global South countries producers of cheap raw materials for global North production, and then dependent on the global North for expensive finished goods, thus keeping global South countries "undeveloped" and in constant debt. (Neo)Marxist critics of globalization look to how capitalist relations have spread throughout the world through global industrial and financial capitalism, producing a global laboring class and a global managerial class across all countries in both the global North and the global South. Although the forms capitalist relations take can vary from country to country, certain patterns of exploitation cut across them under global capitalism, such as the flexibilization and informalization of labor (processes expanded on in Chapter 5). Thus, critics of globalization see some potential in the common cause that could be forged among workers across states to resist such global patterns.

Several newer critical lenses have emerged in IR since the 1980s (and earlier in some humanities and other social science disciplines), although most of their critiques, too, are based on long struggles against the inequalities most of them highlight. IR constructivists (see, for example, Onuf 1989; Wendt 1999) do challenge the (neo)realist and (neo)liberal assumptions that the state in particular is given rather than socially constructed, that state interests (in such things as sovereignty and the accumulation of power and wealth) are not fixed, and that the state structure in the international system is determinative of state behavior. Instead, constructivists argue that ideas held by and the agencies of decision-makers "make" states and, thus, the meanings given to states and their identities and interests can be quite varied. Constructivists, however, tend to be silent on unequal and unjust structures within, among, and across states and on non-elites. As a result, they tend to be more "accepted" within conventional IR. Still, their emphasis on the socially constructed nature of states and state relations provide somewhat of a wedge for far more critical lenses to be employed in IR.

Poststructuralist IR lenses (see, for example, Der Derian and Shapiro 1989; Campbell 1992) go beyond constructivist ones by focusing on the social production of what is assumed to be "objective reality" through symbolic ordering, language, and discursive practices that create it and make it seem true. Arising from the thought of European theorists in the latter part of the twentieth century in reaction to modernist ideologies (liberalism, Marxism) that resulted in oppressive systems even as they claimed to be liberating, it is oriented to deconstructing dominating truth claims about reality, seeing them as an effect of the relationship between power and knowledge. Power is not seen as a property of individuals and institutions, but rather as a dispersed system of power relations that produce subjects (e.g., man, the state, the economy) and confer meaning on them, typically in highly naturalized, essentialized, and binary ways. As a result, poststructuralists, who do not argue that material reality does not exist but rather that reality is always represented through interpretive frames deeply embedded in and (re)productive of power relations, are highly suspicious of binary thinking and grand theorizing that takes subjects as given and foundational to a coherent "common sense" representation of the world that forecloses seeing multiple realities and thinking otherwise.

Postcolonial and related decolonial IR lenses (see, for example, Sanjay 2016; Jones 2006; Agathangelou and Ling 2009) go beyond (neo)Marxist ones in calling attention to how colonialism and the racial hierarchies it instantiated underpins capitalism and racist and imperialist practices within, among, and across states. Such lenses, which arise from the experiences of peoples colonized in the global South and indigenous peoples colonized in both the global South and North (the latter known as settler colonialism), see the discipline of IR as a colonial project itself that privileges stories of the Westphalian state system as a mark of civilization and the Western Enlightenment and the capitalist order it promoted as bringing "progress," and "development" to the rest of the world. What is obscured by such stories are the brutalities of conquest, enslavement, territorial theft, resource extraction, and cultural destruction visited upon racialized peoples—racialized to justify colonization in the name of superior civilizational values, orders, and practices. Postcolonial and decolonial IR thought are concerned with decolonizing global politics by not only revealing how ongoing colonization and racialization is practiced in the study and conduct of IR, but also offering how global politics could be otherwise if we paid attention to and learned from the diverse cultural, sociopolitical, and economic values and arrangements of non-Western and indigenous peoples. Some of these can contain alternative and more just approaches to social life and human relations as well as relations between humans and nature.

Feminist IR lenses (see, for example, Tickner and Sjoberg 2011; Tickner 2014; Steans and Tepe-Belfrage 2016) focus on gender and its relation to other inequalities, and the political nature and effects of masculinist and other inequality-producing orders. As such, they are highly influenced by (neo)Marxist, poststructural, and postcolonial thinking in and outside of IR. More recently, queer and trans theorists in IR (see, for example, Weber 2016; Peterson 2014; Sjoberg 2012), many of whom are feminist, have directed greater attention to the implications of heteronormativity and gender conformity not only for sexual and gender minorities, but also for the further disruption of binaries in IR.

In general, gender analysts in IR operate from feminist perspectives, which, although varied (as discussed later in this chapter), share, minimally, a concern with the problem of gender inequality as a motivation for research. They have found in their examinations that individuals, institutions, and practices associated with masculinity (men, states, war-making, wealth production) remain highly valued (or valorized) in political and world political thought, whereas those individuals, institutions, and practices associated with femininity (women, local or international political formations, peacemaking, poverty reduction) have been more typically devalued (or devalorized) and even dismissed in such thinking until very recently. Again, this is key to what is meant in this text by the power of gender—the pervasiveness of gender as a filtering category, or meta-lens, that puts in motion the broad processes of masculinization and feminization. That is, gender-sensitive research does more than document the pattern of excluding or trivializing women and their experiences while inflating men's experiences and power. It documents how gender—characterizations of masculinity and femininity—can influence the very categories and frameworks within which scholars work.

Gender inquiry in IR began with the question "Where are the women?" in international affairs, as they appeared absent in typical accounts of the rise of great powers, their leaders, their weaponries, and their wars, as well as in dominant theories about the nature of and interactions among states and their economies. At first glance, activities associated with masculinity (e.g., competitive sports, politics, militaries) appear simply as those in which men are present and women are absent and only the men engaging in these activities need be attended to. Gender analysis, however, reveals how women are in fact important to the picture (enabling men's activities, such as providing reasons for men to fight), even though women and the roles they are expected to play are obscured when we focus only on men. Through a gender lens, we see how constructions of masculinity (agency, control, aggression) are not independent of, but rely upon, contrasting constructions of femininity (dependence, vulnerability, passivity). In an important sense, the dominant presence of men and the overvaluing of masculinity depend on the absence of women and the devaluing of femininity. Because of this interdependence, using gender analysis in IR does not merely reveal heretofore-unseen conditions and roles of women in global politics, but "transforms" what we know about men and the activities they undertake in international affairs. Hence, the study of gender alters our understandings of the conventional foci of IR—power politics, war, and economic control—by exposing what more deeply underpins them and why they are given such prominence over other ways of thinking about and acting in the world.

Thus, the seemingly simplistic question "Where are the women?" has yielded many insights. First, it has revealed that women are not absent in global politics, even though they are rarely present in the top echelons of states, corporations, and IGOs. Instead, they tend to play roles that

- grease the wheels of global politics, such as military or diplomatic wives who enable men to make war or peace by taking care of men's needs through freeing them for combat or creating social environments for men to negotiate, or sex workers who provide R&R (rest and recreation) to combat troops in service to sustaining militaries;
- produce the wheels of global politics by sustaining everyday life in households and serving primarily as low-paid workers in defense plants, assembly work, agribusiness, and domestic, sexual, social, and clerical service industries—thereby undergirding the world's production of weapons, goods, and services—while also being situated as the predominant consumers of goods for households; and/or
- derail the wheels of global politics through social movements and NGOs that protest global politics-as-usual, whether in resistance to dictators, global capitalism, nuclear weapons, or natural resource depletion and destruction (Enloe 1989).

Such observations have led to an understanding that women are, in fact, central to the operations we associate with global politics, but their centrality in relation to greasing and producing the wheels of global politics-as-usual rests upon their invisibility and conformity to "acting like 'women'"—that is, subservient to men. Second, the positioning of women in world affairs has also illuminated the positionings of men. Prior to gender inquiry in IR, the fact that men dominated positions of power in global politics remained unremarked upon. It was just assumed that men would hold such positions of power, and there was no interest in why or with what effects. Asking the "man question" in IR (Zalewski and Parpart 1998; Parpart and Zalewski 2008) draws attention to what "acting like 'men'" means for the conduct and outcomes of global politics.

Queer and trans IR lenses arising through feminist inquiry, in initially asking where sexual minorities and people with non-normative gender identities are in global politics, have not only extended the categories of women and men to include those who identify as either one, but also complicated and even exploded them. By drawing attention to the performative nature of gender (the acting out of gender identities makes them seem "real"—see Butler 1990) and the fluidity of gender and sexual identifications, even over individual lifetimes, which do not conform to the binaries of male and female, heterosexual and homosexual, they trouble the entire logic of hierarchically dividing people and assigning roles to them in these ways. They also reveal, however, how deeply invested the global political order is in maintaining gender and sexual conformity, for transgressing these is met with extreme forms of exclusion and violence.

As is discussed at more length later in this chapter, feminist IR scholars partake of a host of other critical lenses in their work to produce feminist gendered lenses through which to view and analyze global politics and which complicate gender lenses. Too often, however, other critical researchers still fail to include feminist, queer, and trans lenses in theirs. This is yet another consequence of the power of gender to render masculinist, heteronormative, and gender-normative orders and commitments invisible in other critical research.

As in all academic inquiry, differing IR theoretical lenses direct our attention and orient our research in particular ways. IR lenses shape, for example, our assumptions about who are the significant actors (states, transnational corporations, social movements), what are their attributes (rationality, self-interest, power, activism), how are social processes categorized (conflict, cooperation, division), and what are the desirable outcomes (national security, wealth accumulation, welfare provisioning, global equity). Thus, IR lenses have global political consequences. As has been discussed in this section, critics of lenses at the center of IR inquiry in general argue that these must be "decentered" because they perpetuate unjust consequences for much of the world's people:

> First, IR focuses primarily on and legitimizes the actions and decisions of the US and the global North/West. Second, IR privileges certain political projects, such as neoliberal economic policies, state-centrism, and Northern/Western liberal democracy. Third, IR legitimizes the most privileged socio-political players and institutions, in both the Global North/West and the Global South, to produce knowledge and make decisions about the rest of the world, thus replicating or maintaining certain unequal power relationships. Finally, IR examines certain understandings of political concepts (such as sovereignty) and particular narratives that can elide, distort, or completely miss multiple ways of understanding and living in the world.
>
> (Nayak and Selbin 2010: 2)

Indeed, it is no accident that the majority of IR scholars who engage (neo)realist and (neo) liberal lenses at the center of IR inquiry are primarily US/Western-based, white, heterosexual, and cismale. It is also no accident that many critics of these lenses are either non-US/ non-Western-based, of color, non-heterosexual, female, or have non-normative genders (or some combination of these). Those in IR who occupy the most privileged social locations tend to evince a top-down preoccupation with elite governance, international militarism, and corporate profits while rendering everything that underpins and enables these activities—and their power—irrelevant. Those in IR who do not occupy one or more privileged social locations tend to be more interested in and sensitive to the underside of elite power, militarized power projections, and bottom-up resistances to social injustice.

These fundamental differences are reflective of power relations not only in the wider world, but also within the discipline of IR. Indeed, IR has been likened to a heteronormative, patriarchal, and colonial household (Agathangelou and Ling 2004), with (neo)realism occupying the position of the white colonial father and (neo)liberalism acting as the white colonial mother and expecting loyalty from their offspring to remain and be nurtured in the household. Contending sons are either somewhat accepted (constructivists) and or seen as too rebellious ((neo)Marxists, poststructuralists), while contending daughters are seen as failing to be dutiful (some feminists) or as irredeemable (other feminists, queer, trans). Forced downstairs and outside the "house of IR" are racialized subjects (female, male, non-normative people partaking in postcolonial lenses in concert with other critical ones) who the colonial family has colonized to serve them or to be banished. Although metaphoric, such a deeply critical and disturbing description underscores the nexus between knowledge and power and the relationship between intimate relations (particularly in the family) and IR, both of which are shot through with power relations, and the highly problematic gatekeeping in IR that prevents a more diverse IR that thinks more seriously about global politics otherwise. Because who and what is centered and marginalized in IR (as summarized in Table 2.1) shapes and is shaped by global politics, we need to be attentive to what lenses we are using, why, and with what consequences for whom. We also need to become aware of the deeper forces at work that make opting for non-critical lenses at the expense of critical ones the path of least resistance. The following discussion elaborates on the central tension between conventional and critical IR—seeing reality as self-evident versus seeing reality as socially constructed—and

Table 2.1 IR Lenses

IR Lenses	*Focus*	*Normative Orientations*
Neorealism	Sovereign states	Maintaining order and stability
Neoliberalism	International organizations	Building cooperative order
(Neo)Marxism	Class relations	Critiquing classism within, among, and across states
Constructivism	Institutional identities	Exposing cultural state constructions
Poststructuralism	Power relations in knowledge	Deconstructing reality claims
Postcolonialism	Colonial and race relations	Decolonizing identities, thought, and relations
Feminism	Gender relations	Challenging gendered identities, thought, and relations
Queer	Sexuality/heternormativity	Queering identities, thought, and relations
Trans	Gender normativity	Resisting binary identities, thought, and relations

how the power of gender is implicated in dichotomous thinking that pervades and privileges conventional lenses.

Positivist and Postpositivist Thinking in IR and the Power of Gender

When considering different theoretical lenses and how some are deemed more central than others, it is helpful to distinguish between *what* objects (variables, topics, issues, levels of analysis) are focused on and *how* knowledge/truth about those objects is produced (empirically, analytically, comparatively, intuitively). Stated another way, the former refers to *ontology* (the nature of "being," i.e., *what* is reality?) and the latter to *epistemology* (the study of truth claims, e.g., *how* do we know?), and they are always intertwined because claims about what x is are necessarily also claims about how we know what x is.

Epistemological preferences cut across both normative/political commitments and substantive foci (objects of inquiry), though such preferences often go unacknowledged. As a starting point, the most salient epistemological distinction in IR lenses is between *positivist* (sometimes called modernist, Enlightenment, rationalist, and empiricist characteristic of neorealist and neoliberal inquiry) and *postpositivist* orientations (including critical, interpretive, reflexive ones found in varying degrees in neo-Marxist, postcolonial, poststructuralist, queer, trans and all feminist forms of these as well as some constructivist perspectives). There are at least two major assumptions associated with a positivist orientation: first, through the application of scientific method, facts can be separated from values; second, subjects (knowers, observers) and objects (the known, the observed) can also be categorically separated. Hence, positivists assume that the subject/knower is independent of—can stand "outside of"—the reality being observed, and that the observer can see this reality objectively (separating fact from value) by employing the scientific method to control for bias or other emotional investments. Similarly, positivists assume that social reality is "given" (separate from the knower) and is the product of identifiable "laws" of (human and physical) nature and rational action.

A key point is the extent to which positivists assume a referential view of language, understanding it as a neutral, transparent medium that corresponds to, and therefore simply reflects or refers to, the "objective" world "as it is." The claim here is that objects (states, rights, power) have some central essence or timeless form that can be captured and conveyed linguistically in a word, or signifier, that simply refers to that essence. This orientation tends to essentialize—to understand as timeless, unchanging, and independent of context—the meaning of terms (power, rationality, human nature) and, hence, what they refer to (capacity to enforce compliance; logically determined relationships; atomistic, self-interested, acquisitive). It assumes that the meanings of and the differences between terms can be clearly specified and will remain constant across contexts, thus suggesting order, continuity, and stability.

In contrast, postpositivists argue that "reality" is socially constructed in the sense that humans/subjects create meaning and intelligibility through the mutual constitution of symbols, languages, identities, practices, and social structures. Again, this is decisively *not* to argue that the physical world does not exist independent of humans/subjects, but rather that it has no social meaning independent of what is constructed through human thought and interaction. In other words, there is no pre-social or pre-discursive meaning (or essence) to things, only the meanings produced by social subjects inevitably reflecting their specific contexts, interests, and objectives. Recall the general discussion of lenses: humans depend on selective attention to make sense of and act in the world. Lenses are drawn from the conceptual ordering systems and languages available to us, and these do not predate culture and social relations but instead are produced by them. The conditions of human existence and the successful reproduction of social formations *require* some stable ordering—of meaning systems *and* of social practices. Yet we often forget that the conceptual systems, social identities, and institutionalized practices that humans have constructed are historically specific and contingent. They "lack any essence, and their regularities merely consist of the relative and precarious forms of fixation [stabilization, normalization] which accompany the establishment of a certain order" (Laclau and Mouffe 1985: 98). Moreover, power relations operating in all historical contexts have shaped which and whose ordering preferences dominate. Those who have more access to and control over symbolic and material resources have more opportunities and capabilities for stabilizing and institutionalizing particular symbols, meanings, lenses, norms, rules, and practices. In this sense, elites draw on particular lenses to construct more encompassing belief systems—or ideologies—to normalize, legitimate, and reproduce their privileged positions. As with all lenses, these reflect selective attention and interests that entail devaluing, marginalizing, or excluding alternatives.

The key point, and one that informs this text, is that knowers cannot stand outside of the reality they observe because their participation in that reality is a necessary condition for the object observed to have any meaning; both subject and object gain their meaning and intelligibility by reference to their locations in a system of meaning (language, discourse, norms, rules) that encompasses them both. In this view, subjects and objects are not categorically separate, but rather exist in a relationship and in a historically specific context that shape what we wish to know (what questions we ask, etc.), how we go about knowing (what methods we use, etc.), and whose knowledge counts (whose truth claims are included or excluded). When we as knowledge seekers question the positivist lens, we rethink objectivity, we see the centrality of the relationship between power and knowledge, and we understand that language is political insofar as it constitutes the meaning system of intelligibility and order.

Accepting that knowledge is socially situated and thus productive of, at best, only partial accounts of reality does not entail a position of absolute relativism—that "anything goes" or that no criteria for comparative assessments can be substantiated. That conclusion reflects a positivist lens where we have *either* "real truth" *or* complete relativism. But the either–or cage is rejected by postpositivists, who insist on thinking not oppositionally but relationally. Sandra Harding proposes an alternative lens: practicing "strong objectivity" that permits one

> to abandon notions of perfect, mirror-like representations of the world, the self as a defended fortress, and "the truly scientific" as disinterested with regard to morals and politics, yet still apply rational standards to sorting less from more partial and distorted belief
>
> (Harding 1991: 159)

In other words, we must give up the pursuit of an Archimedean standpoint, the "God's-eye view," or the illusion that certainty is attainable, and recognize instead that all perspectives, problems, and methods are context-specific and value-laden (shaped by power and commitments). This does not mean that they are all equally valid or that we cannot comparatively assess them. It does mean that all claims must be situated and, therefore, that any absolute, transcendent, universal claims—because they deny context and the politics of their making—are inherently suspect and politically problematic. Because inquiry is a social practice and so is always value-laden, it is incumbent on inquirers to critically examine their social locations and the values that arise from them. In this way, the normative commitments that underlie inquiry are made visible and can become the subject of political debate about what values inquiry should advance.

By denying the categorical separations (fact from value and subject from object) that are assumed by positivists, then, postpositivists—and especially poststructuralists—challenge conventional claims about scientific objectivity and spurn either–or thinking (dichotomies) as a distortion of social reality. But, as now argued, postpositivists who do not take the power of gender as a meta-lens seriously miss links between dichotomized gender and the status of dichotomized thinking in modernist, positivist orientations that remain present and dominant in the field of IR. The basic argument is that the essentialized binary of sex difference (which grounds and generates the dichotomy of gender differentiation) and the privileged status of dichotomies (which grounds rationality and objectivity claims) are *mutually reinforcing*. As a consequence, both are further naturalized (taken for granted), become constitutive elements of the power of gender, and operate systemically to shape conceptual and social orderings hierarchically. Exposing how this power operates to effectively move beyond it is necessary for any critical agenda that purports to be concerned with social justice.

On the one hand, poststructuralists and postcolonialists criticize the structure and status of dichotomized thinking that pervades modernist, positivist thought. They argue that dichotomies *structure* our thinking in ways that are stunted (reductionist), static (ahistorical), simplistic (decontextualized), and politically problematic (essentializing, disabling critical reflection). And the privileged *status* of modernist, positivist orientations sustains dichotomized thinking as a taken-for-granted and desirable outcome, obscures how dichotomies structure thought in extremely limited ways, and resists critical reflection on the politics of dichotomies and their divisive effects. As constitutive elements of ideological thinking, dichotomies essentialize particular group identities in oppositional, hierarchical terms; amplify and privilege the interests of elites at the expense of stereotyped "others"; and obscure the commonalities and possible shared interests of larger collectivities and longer-term objectives.

On the other hand, feminists, queer, and trans critics of heteronormativity and gender normativity have exposed the assumption of binary sex difference as stunted (reducing "sex" to paired opposites, precluding alternatives and commonalities), static (neglecting historical shifts in how "sex" is "seen" and responded to), simplistic (obscuring the complexity of "sex" and its relationship to gender), and politically problematic (unreflectively essentializing what is historically situated and socially constructed). Feminist research has additionally documented the deeply sedimented normalization of dichotomized gender (generated by essentializing sex as a binary) as a governing code valorizing what is privileged as masculine at the expense of what is stigmatized as feminine. Gendered socialization and social control mechanisms amplify individual and collective internalization of, and investments in, reproducing gendered orderings. Here it is argued that more adequate analyses of power require attending to and integrating the critical insights particularly of poststructuralist, postcolonial, feminist, queer, and trans lenses. In particular, to comprehend the resilience of hierarchical thinking and its reproduction of divisions and inequalities requires making sense of the power of gender as a hegemonic and pernicious but typically unacknowledged worldview.

Stated simply and based on the discussion of the power of gender in Chapter 1, the "naturalness" of sex difference becomes indistinguishable from the "naturalness" of dichotomized and hierarchical gender differentiation that we reproduce, consciously and unconsciously, as we act out gender in all areas of social life. Because of this interaction, gendered stereotypes have political significance far beyond their role in male–female relations. First, gender normalizes dichotomized thought as a deeply embedded practice reproduced throughout social orders. Second, the gender dichotomy is so taken as given that it lends authority to the binary logic that "naturally" divides terms and identity groups into polarized opposites. The naturalness of dichotomized gender then becomes indistinguishable from—and lends credibility and authority to—the naturalness of dichotomized thinking. Third, the normalization of dichotomized thinking reproduces not only gender hierarchy but also other relations of inequality as dichotomies are taken for granted and effectively legitimate hierarchical ordering.

At the same time and as argued earlier, the binary logic of positivist orientations normalizes and privileges thinking in dichotomies. The elevated status of this logic lends credibility and authority to the practice of essentializing categories as paired opposites, valuing one over the "other" term, and normalizing domination of whatever and whoever is "othered." In this sense, the normalization of dichotomies in modernist thought lends credibility and authority to the binary of sex and dichotomy of gender. Insofar as other familiar dichotomies have gendered connotations (culture–nature, reason–emotion, autonomy–dependency, public–private), when they are deployed in modernist thought, they buttress the stereotypes of masculine and feminine.

This is what is meant by mutually reinforcing: the dichotomy of gender gains its naturalness by being grounded in the assumption of essentialized sex difference; gendered orderings are normalized by being reproduced throughout social life; dichotomies gain their taken-for-granted and even desirable status by being privileged in modernist thought and acquiring credibility through the "reality" of pervasive gendered differentiation. The mutually reinforcing interplay of essentializing sex, dichotomizing gender, and the binary logic of positivism generates the constellation of dimensions of the meta-lens of the power of gender. Recognizing the power of these coding and filtering devices is crucial for improving our ability to see beyond essentialized identities and oppositional "wholes." Thus, feminists argue that dichotomized thinking cannot be adequately understood, critiqued, or effectively transformed without addressing how sex-differentiated gender grounds, naturalizes, and reproduces binary thinking.

These points are crucial to the arguments of this text because the perpetuation of dichotomized thinking and its gendered normalizations reproduces hierarchical divisions and, hence, antagonistic relations between groups. But the power of gender also operates to obscure intersectionality, and, thus, the gendered power relations and divisions discussed in Chapter 1. When the power of gender focuses attention on essentialized notions of gender—masculinity and femininity—we fail to see these as constructed and crosscutting dimensions operating within any particular group and across groups. This is among the problems with the way in which gender has been taken up by international policymakers, not as a matter of equality and social justice, but rather instrumentalizing women's empowerment to try to "fix" serial crises without addressing deeper ones that arise from not only gender but also gendered divisions. Similarly, when essentialized notions of group identities erase the differentiations within them, we fail to see the complexity of social orders and how inequalities are often sustained by pitting subordinated groups against each other. We are seeing this now in the rise of illiberal democracies resulting from the cultivation of ethno-nationalist and masculinist political backlash, associated with some (typically white, global North, working-class, and heterosexual) men falling down the economic ladder and "strong man" political rhetoric that places the blame for this on groups also in increasing and often greater precarity. Such blaming deflects attention from the global crises that are producing and are the result of vast and intersecting inequalities, while undermining the equality struggles of all subordinated groups. This militates against the potential for coalitions and more comprehensive resistances to unjust social and global political orders. Deploying intersectional analysis facilitates a more comprehensive notion of gender equality that is indivisible from racial, class, and sexual equality and equality among nations. It encourages contemporary feminist IR scholars to ask not just "Where are the women?" but also "Which women?" and "Where are the men and which men?"

The Multiplicity of Feminist IR Lenses

Masculinism is arguably the dominant mode of gender ideology: valuing what is characterized as masculine at the expense of what is feminine, with the material effect of elevating the positioning of men in general above and at the expense of the positioning of women in general. But masculinism also operates to materially exclude or marginalize all those who are feminized, whether women, men, or other genders, as well as intellectual and political commitments that are concerned with social justice. Understood as a key "move" in producing, reproducing, and naturalizing gender hierarchy, masculinism and masculinist lenses are political and deeply implicated in exclusionary practices.

Feminism, in contrast, is a more complicated and contested term. There are, in fact, many forms of feminism. It can be argued that the common thread among feminisms is an orientation valuing diverse women's (including all those who identify as women, cis or trans) experiences and taking seriously diverse women's interests in and capacities for bringing about social and political change for social justice. (Because ideologies are not given biologically but are socioculturally and politically constructed, it is noted here that masculinist perspectives can be held by women and feminist perspectives can be held by men, both cis and trans.) As an aspect of making change, many feminists advocate shifting attention away from men and their activities so that women and their lives come into clearer focus. The objective is to increase awareness of and take more seriously women's diverse ways of identifying, acting, and knowing, and especially women's agency. This may involve revaluing feminized characteristics—affect, connectedness, sensitivity to others and the self—that have traditionally (through masculinist lenses) been romanticized, trivialized, or deemed inferior. But the ultimate objective is not a simplistic role reversal in which women gain power over men or femininity becomes more valued than masculinity. Rather, a range of feminist individuals, organizations, perspectives, practices, and institutions seek an end to social relations of gender inequality in recognition that class, race, sexuality, and national origin inequalities exist among women and men and between them. Such recognition arose from the question of which men women want to be equal to, given the many inequalities among men. This, in turn, prompted the understanding that economically and racially privileged women can oppress less economically and racially privileged (or feminized) men. Thus, gender equality has been rethought to entail transforming the stereotypes and polarization of gender identities and contesting how masculinity is privileged in concepts, practices, and institutions. This also entails transforming the masculinist, racist, heteronormative, and colonizing or imperialist ways of thinking and acting that produce global crises of representation, insecurity, and sustainability. Doing so requires feminist lenses that reveal not only the (re)positionings of women in relation to men but also how the power of gender operates to reposition some women at the expense of other women and to continually disempower the majority of men—and women.

Over a half-century since feminist studies emerged and became institutionalized in the academy, feminist scholarship is now produced within and across most academic disciplines. Both within and outside IR, feminist critiques have altered disciplinary givens, challenged conventional explanations, and expanded the reach of intellectual inquiry. As noted earlier, feminists share a commitment to investigating gendered inequalities and to improving the conditions of women's lives. But neither feminists nor women constitute a homogeneous category, and there is no single meaning of feminism. Like theoretical lenses or perspectives in IR, feminist approaches vary and have been characterized in a number of ways.[1] Most importantly, endless mixing is the rule, not the exception, so assuming that lenses constitute discrete "boxes" misrepresents the diversity, the range, and especially the extensive overlap among many perspectives. Individuals make assumptions that may be common to various lenses, they may make different assumptions when focusing on different substantive topics or normative issues, and how assumptions are mixed is an effect of learning, objectives, experience, and context. With these thoughts in mind, the following presents a very brief introduction to feminist lenses, especially those applied in the context of IR work, though transgressing the conventional boundaries of it.

Compared with other fields of inquiry, for a variety of reasons feminist interventions in the disciplines of IR and, relatedly, economics emerged only in the late 1980s, and, hence, in the midst of debates throughout the academy regarding the nature and politics of knowledge claims. Their critiques of rationalism as masculinist positioned feminists as some of the earliest and most telling critics of modernist, positivist epistemologies. In IR, the "problems and pitfalls of positivism" featured in what has been called the discipline's "fourth debate" (Steans 2006: 22). As noted earlier, positivism is criticized for its dichotomizing assumptions (separating subject from object, fact from value), its essentializing (ahistorical and reductionist) tendencies, and how these generate an unreflective (acritical) attitude and, hence, conservative effects.

Feminist IR scholars adopt a wide range of positions and research orientations, but most identify with postpositivist epistemologies, in part because these permit a wider range of questions and afford more space for critical reflection on global politics-as-usual. Like the work of feminists in other disciplines, early efforts tended to focus on revealing how masculinist bias operated in, and hence distorted, the discipline's knowledge claims. This involved exposing androcentrism in fundamental categories, empirical studies, and theoretical perspectives; asking "Where are the women?" and making them visible; documenting mainstream constructions of the abstract "woman" as deviant from or deficient in respect to male-as-norm criteria; and incorporating women's activities, experience, and understanding into the study of global politics. These inquiries tended to rely on gender as an empirical category—in effect, as a reference to embodied sex difference—that permitted researchers to "add women" to existing scholarship. They also tended to reflect existing feminist lenses, which are briefly characterized in the following sections.

Feminist Lenses Employed in Feminist IR

Feminist lenses, even as they appeared at different points in time, are currently employed in mixed fashion by feminist scholars. Mixing them reveals how each uses elements of the others but also how they interrogate each other for what is foregrounded and backgrounded, made visible and invisible, and voiced and silenced. Thus, the various feminist lenses presented here (and summarized in Table 2.2) that are employed by feminist IR scholars should not be seen in isolation from each other, even though they foreground different aspects of gender and interrelated inequalities.

Liberal feminisms gained formal expression in the context of Europe's bourgeois revolutions that advocated equality but limited its application to (propertied) males. Built upon

Table 2.2 Feminist IR Lenses

Feminist Lenses	*Focus*	*Change Orientation*
Liberal	Equality between women and men	Ending sexism in global politics
Radical	Male domination and alternative perspectives of women	Challenging patriarchy, masculinism, and androcentrism in global politics
(Neo)Marxist	Class and gender oppression of poor and working-class women	Contesting capitalist patriarchy in global politics
Constructivist	Cultural constructions of gendered institutions	Exposing gender identities and ideologies in global governance institutions
Poststructural	Constructed categorizations of "women" and "men"	Deconstructing gender and other social categories to destabilize assumed foundations of global politics
Postcolonial/Decolonial	Racial and (neo)colonial oppression of women in the global South and indigenous women	Resisting gendered racialization and (neo)colonization through gender-sensitive decolonizing of global politics
Queer	Oppression of LGBTQ and other sexual minorities	De-naturalizing and de-normalizing heteronormativity and contesting homophobia and homonormativity in global politics
Trans	Oppression of gender minorities	De-naturalizing and de-normalizing gender as a binary and contesting transphobia in global politics
Intersectional	Intersecting and cross-cutting identities, oppressions, and inequalities	Coalition-building to resist patriarchy, heteronormativity, gender normativity, racism, capitalism, and (neo)colonialism in global politics

Enlightenment claims and shaped by its historical context, liberal feminisms tend toward positivist inclinations, decrying the exclusion of women from, and promoting their "addition to," male-dominated activities and power structures. In this sense, they seek to move women from private to public spheres. Socialist feminisms draw on Marxist traditions to foreground economic inequalities between women and men. They link capitalism and patriarchy to expose how gender hierarchy operates in the workplace *and* the home, and thus these feminisms challenge categorical boundaries between reproductive and productive spheres. Radical feminisms problematize the cultural denigration of femininity and link this to masculinist violence across all levels of analysis. They expose how experiences and activities associated with women and female bodies are devalued, how sexual violence is a form of social control of women, and how heterosexism reproduces the objectification of and violence against women (and feminized men).

Asking initially "Where are the women?" and subsequently "adding women"—and comparing their positions to those of men—were and remain productive orientations. They make embodied women (and men) visible in our picture of world politics, illuminate how women and men are differently engaged with and affected by international politics, and reveal women as agents and activists, as well as victims of sociocultural, economic, and political oppressions. But adding women to existing paradigms also raised deeper questions by exposing how the conceptual structures themselves presuppose masculine experience and perspective. For example, women/femininity cannot simply be added to constructions that are constituted as masculine: the public sphere, rationality, political identity, objectivity, "economic man." Either women as feminine cannot be added (e.g., women must become like men) or the constructions themselves are transformed (e.g., adding women as feminine alters the masculine premise of the constructions and changes their meaning). In this sense, the exclusions of femininity are not accidental or coincidental but rather are required for the analytical consistency of reigning explanatory frameworks.

The lesson that emerges from these studies is that we cannot systemically add women without rethinking gender—recognizing it not only as an empirical category or variable but also as an analytical category and governing code. Doing so requires acknowledging the constitutive power of language, which is most effectively addressed through a feminist poststructuralist (sometimes referred to as postmodern) lens. This redirects our attention from adding women and deploying sex as a variable to analyzing gender as a category of mental ordering that produces masculinity and femininity as hierarchical power relations. In effect, examining "the woman question" leads us to examine "the man question," which, as argued in this text, leads us to examine questions of "race," "class," "sexuality," and "nationality" as well. Doing so requires acknowledging intersectionality, derived from anti-racist and postcolonial feminist thought, as a necessary analytic, which is also further illuminated through poststructuralist lenses. As used in this text, poststructuralist lenses in general reject essentialized categories, unitary meanings, sovereign claims, universalizing solutions, and presumptions of (foundational) objectivity associated with positivist and modernist commitments. Moreover, feminist poststructuralists criticize the residual essentialism that haunts references to "women" and other "identity-based" groups, rendering them homogeneous, undifferentiated wholes and erasing hierarchies within as well as across all groups.

As in other disciplines, we have seen that diversity among women has forced feminists in IR to reflect critically (and uncomfortably) on the meaning of feminism, definitions of "woman," the politics of representation, and the dangers of universalizing claims. "Sisterhood" aspirations have always been in tension with differences of ethnicity, race, class, age, physical ability, sexuality, and nationality and are especially fraught in a global context marked by stark inequalities among women. Intersectionality approaches attempt to address these issues by rejecting ahistorical and essentialist identities and recognizing "complex or hybrid subjects" (Grewal and Kaplan 2001: 669). These lenses owe much to women of color in the North, women of the global South, and postcolonial critics.

Postcolonial feminists criticize the presumption and privilege of Western feminists and insist on the importance of local and "Third World" agency in identifying problems and negotiating remedies (Mohanty 2003; Chowdhury and Nair 2002). They expose how the ideologies of racism and imperialism continue to reproduce the subjugation and exploitation of "women of color" worldwide. They draw attention to the economic, political, and sociocultural forces of contemporary recolonizations and to nationalist and/or religious fundamentalisms that are dominated by men and deployed to discipline women. When viewed through a postcolonial feminist lens, globalization is both a continuation of colonizing practices that span centuries and, through neoliberal capitalism, an intensification of the exploitation of women in the global South (which includes poor and migrant women in the North). Feminist postcolonial critics challenge the binary "othering" that Eurocentric discourse invokes as a perpetual explanation for and justification of hierarchical power in world politics. They put into sharp relief how gender, race, class, nationalist, and imperialist hierarchies are interwoven in ways that particularly undermine the lives of women (and men) in the global South—physically, politically, economically, and culturally.

Most recently, queer and trans theorizing has emerged, both out of feminism and in some tension with it. Queer theorists and researchers expose how heteronormativity operates to pathologize sexual minorities and reduce their life chances throughout much of the world where political, or state-sponsored, homophobia is fomented by (neo)conservative elites to deny rights, and even life in some places, to them. Queer lenses (which are generally post-structuralist in orientation but also employ postcolonial and other critical analysis) have also shown how sexual minorities, particularly among the poor, people of color, and people from the global South, are rendered invisible by economic and social development, entitlement, and immigration programs that are designed only for supporting heteronormative families. As a result, these lenses challenge the heteronormative family as the foundation of the state and seek to enable other family and social arrangements for human intimacy, care, and welfare to emerge. In doing so, queer lenses disrupt even further the dichotomizing power of gender and further shift feminism from a focus on "women" to a focus on resisting gender and sexual normativities that disallow or constrain multiplicitous social formations and relations. They have also countered moralizing approaches to sexuality and sexual expression that can be found in some feminist work, particularly in relation to sex trafficking, calling instead for a "sex-positive" orientation in feminist thought and activist agendas that foregrounds multiple forms of sexual agency and pleasure for women and men. And they have also critiqued homonormative approaches that advocate "conservative" strategies for "fitting into" the heteronormative order through, for example, traditional marriage rather than countering that order for everyone. Trans theorizing challenges both feminist and queer theory to go beyond the dichotomies of male/female and heterosexual/homosexual that still can infect those lenses. Taking seriously the lived experiences of trans people who are uncomfortable with their assigned sex and/or gender (or, in the case of intersex people who wish to remain so, comfortable with the ambiguous sex organs with which they were born), trans theorizing argues that sex and gender are not just social constructions, but neither are they fixed or reducible to male/female and masculine/feminine polarities. Instead, trans theory directs us to "gender diversity," intersex bodies and identities, and the ability to actually change gender and/or sex assignments, sometimes surgically,[2] in ways that do not line up with "sex as a dichotomy" (Sjoberg 2012: 341). This has major implications for breaking down not only dichotomized identities but also dichotomized thought entailed in the power of gender.

Research Through Feminist IR Lenses

As feminist IR lenses have shifted, combined, and recombined through a greater multiplicity of theoretical voices and orientations—creating their own productive tensions—subjects of feminist IR inquiry have also shifted. Tickner (2006) expresses this in generational terms: first-generation feminist IR scholars tended to focus on deconstructing key concepts in IR—sovereignty, the state, security, development, and the economy—exposing or unpacking their masculinist bias and underpinnings. Through these openings that put gender inquiry on the IR map, second-generation scholars have applied gender analysis—often in more intersectional ways—to a range of global politics topics both familiar (alliance constructions, state militaries, peacekeeping, peace agreements, trade agreements, UN conventions) and unfamiliar (sex tourism and sex work, homework and domestic service, migration, social movements, and even world art, popular culture, and the cruise industry).[3] In doing so, these scholars have not only greatly expanded what global politics inquiry entails but also have rethought earlier approaches to gender theorizing in IR.

In the contemporary period, feminist IR is characterized as consisting of two major and interactive areas of inquiry—feminist security studies (FSS)[4] and feminist international (or global) political economy (F(I or G)PE) studies.[5] FSS scholars engage with and critique conventional, state-centric understandings of war, peace, and security that remain at the center of the discipline of IR and challenge the everyday as well as international violence they leave in place. They re-theorize such concepts as states, just war, the democratic peace, and human security through a gender(ed) lens while emphasizing the role of "subjectivities," human "agency," and "discourses" (or narratives) as well as bodies and emotions in the production and experience of direct violence, from the intimate to the global (Hudson 2018: 129). F(I or G)PE scholars focus most on "economic insecurities" produced by neo(colonialism), (capitalist) economic development, and globalization and the gendered nature of these processes (Hudson 2018: 129). They apply more materialist analyses to reveal how conventional accounts of the global political economy and its global governance structures fail to understand how the political economy of gender—from the sex, domestic labor, and beauty trades to the reliance on women's unpaid reproductive labor to make up for declining wages, public services, and environmental protection standards under global (and financial) capitalism—underpins unjust global economic relations. As a result, they are more focused on structural violence. However, FSS and F(I or G)PE scholarship often intersect, such as in studies on the political economy of peacekeeping in rural societies that disregards women's economic roles in the gathering of food and fuel far away from homes and refugee camps, making them most vulnerable to attacks, or in studies on the privatization of security forces, either as subcontracted or mercenary labor, which is implicated in greater direct (including sexual) violence being perpetrated on local populations (particularly women) with less accountability than state militaries (Hudson 2018: 135). Although FSS inquiry is highlighted in Chapter 4 and F(I or G)PE inquiry is highlighted in Chapter 5 of this text, as is argued throughout the book, there are strong connections made between direct and structural violence and discursive and material forms of violence in much current feminist IR scholarship.[6]

As interrelated FSS and F(I or G)PE research has burgeoned, scholars working in these areas have multiplied the methodologies used in IR inquiry in order to get at the multiple ways in which global politics is gendered. In contrast to conventional positivist IR research, feminist IR scholars (and other transnational feminist scholars who engage with and contribute to feminist IR thought) have often utilized such qualitative approaches as ethnographic fieldwork to learn about the lives of the non-elite, social action research through participant observation of social movements, and discourse analysis of classic IR texts, world leaders' pronouncements, (inter)governmental policies and documents, NGO campaigns, and local group articulations of social problems. In doing so, they consider the role of emotion and bodily experience in the production and reproduction of global political actions and reactions. They thus participate in what is referred to as the "affective" turn in IR inquiry, which destabilizes rational actor claims in IR and takes seriously how global politics thought and practice are embodied phenomenon. They also plumb cultural sources, such as popular culture images on the airwaves and the Internet and even literature, art, and poetry, to find expressions over time and space of resistance to global politics-as-usual in unusual places (Ackerly, Stern, and True 2006). As a result, feminist scholarship, as well as, increasingly, other critical scholarship, also engages in what has been referred to as the "visual" or "aesthetic" turn in IR inquiry, which examines such things as images, mediascapes, places, and cartographies to better understand how global politics is embedded in, shaped by, productive, and reproductive of cultural construction and processes.

Such practices seek to reveal the underside of global politics, simultaneously exposing the gendered dynamics that underlie and infect the thought, language, structures, and practices of it and privileging dissident and alternative voices about how it might be rethought, rearticulated, and rearranged. These practices also require reflexivity about the power relations between the researcher and the researched. In cases of "studying down"—such as working with non-elite actors—feminist IR scholars aim to be cognizant of their privilege and, thus, their responsibility to allow such actors to represent themselves in their own ways so as not to impose Eurocentric/Orientalist, heteronormative, gender normative, or classist interpretations on the motivations, nature, and outcomes of their struggles. When "studying up"—or dealing with elite or more privileged actors—feminist IR scholars aim to be cognizant of how such actors limit access to researchers engaged in critical scholarship and mystify their power through bureaucratic language. Discourse analysis is thus especially productive when studying up because it enables reading between the lines and catching how the powerful consistently represent themselves and how they consistently represent "others" to justify their policies and actions. In these ways, feminist IR scholarship itself seeks to counter the crisis of representation both in the field of IR, in which the study of people and especially non-elite people has historically been absent, and in global politics, which has historically operated as if people and especially non-elite people did not matter. Moreover, it has ignored how bodies, embodied experiences, and embodied thought are integral to producing and understanding global political phenomenon

Recent generations of feminist IR researchers (some of whom have worked in or with international agencies) also engage in a significant amount of quantitative research to have a greater and more meaningful impact on international policymaking (Den Boer 2016). Although feminist IR scholars have long relied on governmental, non-governmental, and UN gender-differentiated data produced during and continuously since the UN Decade for Women (which are also used in this text), but knowing how incomplete and insufficient this most often statistical information can be, some are now producing extensive and continuously expanded and updated databases, such as WomanStats (see Box 2.1). Some have also engaged in large-scale studies, drawing upon existing, and creating new, databases, on the impact of international policymaking on women and the relationship between women's status and global problems. For example, in the last decade, such research has showed that women's literacy, access to reproductive health services, and employment have increased in states that have ratified and observed CEDAW, most markedly in secular states with effective legal systems (Simmons 2009), and that the higher the level of violence against women within a state, the higher the likelihood it will engage in war, with violence against women rates being more significant than levels of democracy, religion, wealth, and racial disparities as predictors of state peacefulness or bellicosity (Hudson et al. 2008/9). Such research is positivist to the degree that it treats gender (as well as race, class, nationality, and so on) as a variable, operationalizing it often as female sex and women's rights in relation to a host of other variables. While this has yielded major findings which tell us gender not only matters, but centrally matters in global politics, feminist IR researchers cannot control if and how policymakers make use of such findings, nor does it particularly challenge the preference for positivist, quantitative measures in international policymaking.

Box 2.1 WomanStats

WomanStats (www.womanstats.org/), led by feminist IR scholar Valerie Hudson of Texas A&M University and involving faculty investigators across the US and beyond, is an open-source multidisciplinary database that provides quantitative and qualitative data on women's security in 175 countries. It employs 350 variables on topics ranging from violence against women to women in governments and militaries, which enable researchers to engage in single-country inquiry and cross-country comparisons across one or more topics and variables. Its website also includes a great array of worldwide maps and infographics on such topics as:

- women's property rights
- child marriage
- trafficking in women
- rape (including infographics on such topics as rapes of Syrian refugees)
- femicide
- national equality programs

There has been a veritable explosion at the international level in the collection of quantitative indicators by which to rank states not just by power and wealth, but also by their performance with respect to a range of human rights, democratic and non-corrupt governance, and sustainable development. This is the latest feature of the shift to more global governance discussed more in the next chapter. This multi-dimensional attention to how well or poorly states are subscribing to emergent human rights, security, and development norms, discussed at greater length in subsequent chapters, is, on the one hand, a welcome development, partially ushered in and making space for more feminist IR research, activism, and impact. On the other hand, we must not assume that this is dislodging global politics-as-usual with all the divisions and inequalities upon which it is based because "indicators do not stand outside of regimes power and governance but exist within them" (Merry 2016: 21). Among the dangers of reducing the world to numbers is that global crises are treated as "technical" problems to be solved by (almost exclusively quantitatively-oriented) experts, rather than through inclusive, equitable, and thus more transformative political processes. Moreover, we can see the power of gender operating in the masculinization (or over-valorization) of positivist lenses and methods and the feminization (or devalorization) of postpositivist lenses and methods. Thus, while the quantitative work performed within feminist IR is very informative, as well as informed by a social justice orientation, and is rarely pursued in isolation from qualitative research or unmindful of the problematics of positivism, we must always be attentive to how any knowledge production, but especially that which is most privileged and/or conducted by the most privileged, can feed into sustaining global power structures and relations in which it is embedded.

In sum, as we move across the array of feminist IR lenses and the array of actors and subjects they reveal as operative in global politics, attention focuses both on women as an empirical variable and on gender as an analytical category and the power of gender as a meta-lens that (re)produces positivist presumptions and systemic difference construction. In subsequent chapters a range of feminist IR lenses are employed to examine repositionings of women and men and the power of gender in global politics, drawing from the extensive and

variant feminist IR and transnational feminist literature that now exists. The very extent and diversity of contemporary feminist IR work reveal that it is not engaged in static, monological, or universalizing analyses that deflect debate. Feminist IR lenses, through their interactions, share a critique of positivism's essentialized and homogeneous categories, oppositional dichotomies, and universalizing narratives. This text especially foregrounds feminist postcolonial lenses on global politics to emphasize gendered divisions, arising particularly out of earlier colonizing and continuing imperialist practices, while employing feminist queer and trans IR insights to further complicate gender divisions discussed in the next three chapters. In the final chapter, such lenses also particularly inform a more transformative response to gender and gendered divisions and the crises of representation, security, and sustainability.

Notes

1 For feminist lenses in IR, see, for example, Tickner and Sjoberg (2011), Tickner (2014), and Steans and Tepe-Belfrage (2016).
2 Trans analysis argues that among cisgender or gender-normative privileges is a certain abhorrence among some feminists of surgical procedures performed on the "female" body, thereby unjustly vilifying desired trans-sexual surgeries and upholding naturalistic constructs of sex and gender.
3 See multiple issues of the *International Feminist Journal of Politics*, the journal devoted to feminist IR scholarship and emerging from the Feminist Theory and Gender Studies Section of the International Studies Association.
4 For the breadth of current scholarship in FSS, see Gentry, Shepherd, and Sjoberg (forthcoming 2019).
5 For the breadth of current scholarship in F(I or G)PE studies, see Elias and Roberts (2018).
6 See Parashar, Tickner, and True (2018) for a strong example of how feminists in IR are presently analyzing the gendered nature of states in both a globalizing and securitizing world.

Chapter 2

Questions for Further Discussion

1 What are the differences between positivist and postpositivist approaches to knowledge production in IR? Why are most feminist approaches postpostivist?
2 Why is it necessary to be attentive to inequalities among women and among men when advocating for gender equality?
3 How do feminist lenses differ and why is it useful to mix them?
4 What various kinds of methodologies do feminist IR scholars use, and why are they so varied?

Activities for Further Research

1 Interview a few friends and/or family members, asking them how and when they were first conscious of being "male" or "female," if they felt comfortable with and accepting of their sex and gender assignments, and what they learned early on about the differences between how boys and girls should behave and what life directions/occupations they should pursue. Consider how resisting the hierarchical dichotomies or binaries of sex and gender could change not only those oppositional relations, but also help to change others.
2 List the ways in which you are privileged or disadvantaged by your gender, race, class, sexuality, and nationality. Consider how the ways you are disadvantaged affect your life choices,

such as aspiring to national or international office or becoming a corporate elite. Consider as well how your lenses are different when you view global politics or a global issue from positions of disadvantage as opposed to privilege. Watch the video of Kimberly Hutchings on "International Relations: Feminism and International Relations" at www.youtube.com/watch?v=ajAWGztPUiU to help you think about the links between subordinated perspectives and rethinking how global politics work (often to the detriment of most).

3 Explore the WomanStats Project (www.womanstats.org) by visiting its "First Time Users" page at www.womanstats.org/first_time_users.html. There are tutorial videos available to view and you can set up a free account to access the database through this link. Navigate the database where you can choose from countries around the world and select different issues to explore such as abortion, education, age of marriage, divorce, citizenship, and many other issues. Look up three countries in three different regions of the world on three different issues. Did anything strike you about what you found out?

3 Gender and Global Governance

How does the power of gender affect "who rules the world"? What do gendered divisions of power tell us about how the world is ordered politically and for what purposes? What is the relationship between the gendered divisions of power and the crisis of representation? How are women and men positioned and repositioned in and by global political structures and with what effects? What is the new global politics of gender equality, and why did it arise? How has neoliberal governmentality captured and depoliticized feminist politics for gender equality? How are neoliberal governmentality and the related anti-equality political backlash deepening the crisis of representation?

This chapter focuses on the relationship between gendered inequalities and global governance. As noted in the last chapter, there is no world government, and much conventional IR thinking continues to see states as the central actors in world politics. However, in recent years the term *global governance* has come to refer to a constellation of global actors including states; IGOs such as the UN bodies and agencies, the World Bank, the International Monetary Fund (IMF), and the World Trade Organization (WTO); regional governments such as the EU and regional IGOs such as organizations of African, American, and Asian states and free-trade regimes like the North American Free Trade Agreement; and global market actors such as transnational corporations (TNCs) and transnational NGOs (Rai 2008: 22). States make up IGOs, and the wealthiest and most militarily powerful states hold primacy in them. At the same time, states are variously subordinated to IGO rules made by state representatives (with increasing input by NGO actors), which range from international laws and regulations to agreed-upon norms. Thus, although this chapter especially focuses on the *power of gender* to shape the meaning of state power in world politics and the relative positionings of women and men as state actors in world politics, other gendered institutions are looked to at the global level as are the new global gender equality, or, more accurately, women's empowerment, norms that are emanating from some of them and that are having impacts on states and the *repositionings of women and men*.

Another feature of global governance, beyond the multiplicity of actors in it, is its organization around the ideology of *neoliberalism*. This is often referred to as an ideology that "disseminates the *model of the market* to all domains and activities—even where money is not the issue—and configures human beings exhaustively as market actors" (Brown 2015: 31). It is implicated in turning states into firms which reduce democratic decision-making to technical cost-benefit analyses driven by quantitative indicators (as noted in the previous chapter) and transforming humans (and nature) into capital, citizens into stakeholders, consent into "buy-ins," and collective responsibility into personal responsibility (Brown 2015). It is also implicated, as discussed in Chapter 5, in the privatization of the public sphere (thereby defunding social welfare), the flexibilization and informalization of work, and, thus, the expansion of global economic inequities, particularly between elites and non-elites. Thus, neoliberal governance or *neoliberal governmentality* depoliticizes, or empties out, public institutions and public life and leaves the "management" of global problems to the experts. But even as it reduces global governance to a technocratic exercise at the top, in not fundamentally disturbing power relations and, in fact, expanding inequalities while reducing public capacities to ameliorate them, it also is producing a particularly "toxic" politics—"full of ranting and posturing, emptied of intellectual seriousness, pandering to an uneducated and manipulable electorate and a celebrity-and-scandal-hungry corporate media" (Brown 2015: 39). Such not only illiberal but also anti-democratic patterns that have emerged in some places are both a reaction to, but more significantly a result of, democratic deficits and market logics of neoliberal global governance. Thus, this chapter concludes that emergent women's empowerment norms associated with the new global politics of gender equality are tenuous and even being threatened in some places because they do not seriously disrupt gendered divisions of power and leave intact the power of gender and the *crisis of representation* it sustains.

Before examining the gender distribution of global power, this chapter begins with the gendered nature of the idea of "power" itself. As introduced in Chapter 1, the definition of power conventionally favored in IR, as in political science generally, is one of "power-over." Power-over is captured in Robert Dahl's (1961) classic definition: the ability of A to get B to do something that B would not otherwise do. Defining power in this way emphasizes control of material—especially military—resources and a willingness to use them in order to enforce one's preferences. It is power-over in the sense of being top-down (those on top, where the most resources are concentrated, are determined to have the most power) and coercive (the ability to force compliance is presumed to be the surest sign of power). When we use only this narrow definition of power to study global politics, however, we neglect investigating how other dimensions of social reality—moral commitments, religious beliefs, ethnic allegiances, disciplinary practices, sociopolitical ideologies—shape how power works and who rules the world. Finally, and particularly relevant to this text, this definition of power is masculinist when it presupposes androcentric notions of strength, competition, aggression, and coercion and because it focuses on power understood only in terms of public-sphere activities dominated by elite men who embody these traits and exercise power-over strategies that are assumed, particularly in realist thinking, as endemic to states.

One aim in this chapter is to examine where women are positioned relative to men as political elites in formal global power structures. In doing so, the following questions are addressed: Where are the women who wield power in global governance? Why have women and gender issues been so underrepresented in global power structures, how may this be changing, why, and with what effects? This chapter further demonstrates how the power of gender remains systematically at work through an apparent paradox. On the one hand, women gaining positions of power challenges gender stereotypes that portray women as uninterested in or unfit for political leadership, and greater attention to gender equality in global governance could be read as a success story. On the other hand, gains in women's power positions in global governance do not eradicate gender stereotypes, and gender-oriented policies are more an effect of neoliberal restructuring and governmentality than of commitments to gender justice. These realities preclude fundamental change in the conduct of global politics and its priorities. The gendered concept of power as power-over—accompanied by the co-optive power of neoliberalism—maintains gender, race, class, sexual, and national hierarchical dichotomies (gendered divisions of power) that continue to be productive of global crises, even as more women are represented in, and gender equality gets on the agenda of, global power structures.

The maintenance of gender(ed) divisions of power and the crises they promote have also enabled anti-equality agendas to arise that deepen the global representational crisis.

As intimated in the first chapter, these *gender(ed) divisions of power* include dichotomies of political–apolitical, reason–emotion, civilized–uncivilized, active–passive, freedom–necessity, autonomous–dependent, public–private, citizens–non-citizens, and leaders–followers (see Table 3.1). Those who are feminized—including most women and many men—are generally denied the status of independent and rational agency and leadership qualities in the public sphere and are reduced to the ground upon which real men act, thus enabling political man to be released from and unmindful of the necessities of everyday life. At the same time, these divisions narrowly define rationality as instrumentalism in the service of power-over and control, disregard the intertwining of private life with public life and domestic politics with international politics, and mistake acting together (or interdependent action) and refraining from harmful actions as signs of weakness, passivity, and lack of autonomy. Autonomy (or reactionary individualism devoid of affective relationships and concern) becomes privileged as the "true" meaning of freedom, which sets in motion a zero-sum game. The overall effect of the power of gender to dichotomize thinking about power and privileged power-over identities and actions is a crisis of representation whereby large numbers of people, peoples, identities, and perspectives remain un- or underrepresented in formal and informal positions of power, and those who supposedly speak for "others" misrepresent them, their issues, and their aspirations in service to the priorities and desires of the few at the top of whatever hierarchical structure. This crisis of representation, in turn, feeds crises of insecurity and sustainability that, in turn, silence or marginalize alternative or engaging dissident voices, all of which sustains the crisis of representation. This vicious cycle sets up the dynamic of reducing responses to bureaucratic "problem-solving" rather than efforts toward transformation of the cycle itself. Thus, the power of gender remains relatively undisturbed even as there are some shifts in the gendered divisions of power.

Table 3.1 Gender/ed Divisions of Power Productive of the Crisis of Representation

	Masculinized	*Feminized*
Gender (Male–Female Dynamics)	Political	Apolitical
	Reason	Emotion
	Public	Private
	Leaders	Followers
	Active	Passive
Gendered (Intersectional Dynamics)	Elite	Non-elite
	Power-over	Power-to
	High politics	Low politics
	Hard politics	Soft politics
	Civilized	Uncivilized
	Freedom	Necessity
	Autonomous	Dependent
	Citizens	Non-citizens

Feminist Approaches to Politics

Prior to the rise of feminist IR, feminist interventions had been made in a host of disciplines, primarily in the humanities and social sciences, since at least the 1960s. The general trajectory of these interventions was also to initially ask, "Where are the women?" The women first identified as missing were "women worthies" (Harding 1986), or those women whose outstanding contributions to literature, art, history, and social, political, and economic thought were overlooked or hidden because they were produced by women in patriarchal societies that could not imagine women as capable of great things. In political science more generally, this meant recovering histories of women political thinkers and leaders (Smith and Carroll 2000) to make the case that women have always been fit for politics and have generated significant and original political thought, despite ideologies to the contrary. This was an important insight, but it still did not yield significant change in women's representation in political office or significantly increase women's access to and participation in formal politics more generally. Such a focus on "women worthies" also limited feminist interventions to getting relatively few women into relatively few positions of formal power. This led feminist political theorists to question the very definition of politics and the standards by which political behavior is judged.[1]

That public-sphere, formal politics is only one form of politics was revealed by showing how the private sphere and everyday life are shot through with power relations and negotiations ("the personal is political"). This also drew attention to the ways in which women engaged in non-formal political action to turn practices assumed to be natural and unchangeable (such as rape and domestic violence) into "political" (and thus changeable) "issues." Feminist political theorizing also revealed that formal politics was defined, and political behavior judged, on the basis of (hegemonic) male norms that privileged notions of politics as winner-take-all affairs, effectively necessitating individualist and aggressive traits to be successful in such politics. This problem is magnified in the case of international politics, which could be defined as hypermasculinist when compared with masculinist domestic politics. Feminists have also shown that domestic politics, as not only national but also local, household, and interpersonal politics, is not separate from international politics, arguing that "the personal is international" (Enloe 1989).

These points suggest how this shift in analysis, in turn, shifted strategies: from "adding women" to formal power structures to valorizing feminine traits in order to redefine politics from "power-over" to "power-to" (also known as "power-with" or enabling power) and change the standards of political behavior in favor of interdependence and cooperation. Still, this left intact a lingering and limiting referent to "women" that did not de-homogenize the category to recognize power differentials among women and the power some women hold over some men. It also left intact the association of embodied women with feminine values, which, on the one hand, led to essentialist assumptions about women as cure-alls for social (and global) ills and, on the other hand, positioned certain embodied men (largely non-Western, non-white, and/or lower class) as the villains of the piece. In the process, attention is deflected from the complicity of both women and men—particularly those with the most power and privilege—in contributing to global ills. It also misrepresents feminist politics as exclusively about women rather than about resisting gender and gendered hierarchies and the ills they cause globally. This is not to say that raising the status of women and other subjugated people—in politics and other facets of life—is not necessary to increase formal representation and better equalize voice, but to note that it is insufficient if there is no attendant ideological shift away from politics as power-over to politics that enables resistance to and transformation of global politics-as-usual, which the power of gender sustains.

This chapter follows the general trajectory of "adding women," to disturbing gender and gendered assumptions, to complicating gender, and, finally, to expanding feminist politics beyond the issue of women in politics. This leads to the matter of contemporary global political force of neoliberal governmentality, which effectively disciplines us all by securing our consent to disciplining ourselves and—through acquiescence to surveillance, fear, and anti-democratic oppositional politics—each other. It also has the capacity to manage or depoliticize feminist critiques and resistances. As this chapter concludes, the antidote to this is repoliticizing demands for more thoroughgoing political equalities and social justice.

Women Actors in Global Governance

Given that (cis)women's empowerment has been the focal point of international policymaking on gender over the past few decades, this section presents data on women's political representation in global governance to provide a picture of some gains (and losses) in this. As argued in subsequent sections, the still relatively low representation of women in formal power structures of global governance can be explained by a variety of gender-based impediments, but the new global politics of gender equality that is being constituted by and through international institutions and policies has also translated into some significant increases in women's representation at state and global levels, which are tracked annually by a host of global governance actors, from the UN and national governments to NGOs. However, as also addressed, simple increases in the numbers of (primarily cis, heterosexual, and elite) women in formal power structures does not mean that either gender or gendered divisions of power have relented.

State and National Leaders

Heads of states and/or governments are among the world's most powerful political actors, and a number of women have held these powerful positions over the past century and into the current one. Heads of state are key executive decision-makers and policy implementers within the nations they lead. At the same time, their power within the state has external, international consequences to the extent that the military, political, economic, and cultural priorities they establish extend beyond territorial borders. Additionally, heads of government "represent" their states culturally as well as politically: in varying ways, such leaders come to symbolize the values of the country they represent. Female heads of state and government are no exception.

Individual elite women have, throughout history, wielded considerable political power and influence. Consider such legendary hereditary rulers as Cleopatra, Queen Elizabeth I, and Catherine the Great, and such well-known twentieth-century leaders as Indira Gandhi, Golda Meir, and Margaret Thatcher. However, they have so far proved to be more the exception than the rule (Martin and Borelli 2016) when we recognize that in early 2017 only 16 women were serving as prime ministers, presidents, or chancellors beyond the six ceremonial monarchs and governors-general (Worldwide Guide to Women in Leadership 2016; IPU 2017b) and one of them has since been impeached and removed from office. The majority of female heads of state entered office recently, from the 1960s onwards, most after 1990 (Skard 2015: 53). The fact that women have led states on most continents over time suggests, however, that women can achieve such power across a range of political systems and cultures. Still, as Gunhild Hoogensen and Bruce Solheim note, certain patterns do persist—namely, the continued importance of dynastic political family ties that enable women to play on their names to downplay their gender, the continued paucity of women leaders at the top in most of the most powerful countries in the West and the global North compared with the global South, and the contemporary trend of more women coming to power in conflict or postconflict areas of the global South (with the exception of much of the Middle East), where women leaders "might be perceived as being less corruptible, mother figures, and often tap into the power of martyred husbands and fathers" (Hoogensen and Solheim 2006: 16, 128–132).

This latter trend can particularly be seen in parliamentary statistics on women assembled by the Inter-Parliamentary Union (IPU 2017b). As of January 2017, postconflict Rwanda still tops the world in the percentage of women elected to parliament, standing at 56 percent women members of parliament (MPs), after becoming the first country in the world with more women than men in a national legislative body in 2008. Forty-six other countries have reached or transcended the minimal threshold of 30 percent women in national legislatures that was called for in the 1995 BPA, including Bolivia, which has reached 53 percent women in its national legislature. Others include the Nordic countries that were among the first to do so as well as much of Western Europe. However, Cuba, Nicaragua, Senegal, Mexico, South Africa, Ecuador, and Namibia are also all over 40 percent, while a host of other Latin American, African, Caribbean, and Asian states interspersed with Western and Eastern European states as well as New Zealand are at or above the 30 percent threshold. Compare these with the US, which continues to fall in the ranks, standing at 104 with only 19.4 percent women in its national legislature as of 2017 (IPU 2017a). In the IPU's 2015 special report "Women in Parliament: 20 Years in Review," it was observed that women's representation in national assemblies nearly doubled from 1995, the year of the BPA, to 2015, going from 11.3 percent to 22.1 percent. The Americas as a region have seen the most significant growth in the last 20 years (IPU 2015: 1, 4). Much of this relatively dramatic rise in numbers of women can be accounted for by the increased use of legally required or voluntary quota systems and proportional representation (PR) electoral systems, practices which in some cases were stimulated by gender equality advocates working at international and national levels who have used the BPA for leverage (UNIFEM 2008: 20; IPU 2015: 1, 12). Likewise, the adoption in 2000 of the UN Millennium Development Goals (MDGs), which included Goal 3 that promotes gender equality and women's empowerment, and the subsequent 2015 adoption of the UN Sustainable Development Goals (SDGs), particularly Goal 5, to achieve gender equality and empower all women and girls, has also influenced the numbers of women in office (UNIFEM 2008: 20; UN 2017). (These goals are discussed in more detail later in this chapter.) Hoogensen and Solheim note one other particularly significant feature shared by those countries with the highest proportions of women in national legislatures: a strong separation between church and state (Hoogensen and Solheim 2006: 17).

As reported in "Women in Parliament: 20 Years in Review Report" produced by the IPU, 12 of the 15 countries that in 2015 featured lower house legislatures with 30 percent or more women represented used some form of legal or voluntary quota system (2015: 5). Moreover, as quantitative research conducted to account for the rise of women's representation in national legislatures between 1945 and 2006 has found, quotas, whether voluntary or less often used compulsory party quotas or reserved-seat quotas, are among the most statistically significant predictors of increased women's representation and tend to be "contagious" within regions—that is, it is more likely that once one country in a region adopts one kind of quota system, others tend to follow (Thames and Williams 2013: 126–128). In contrast to 1995 when only a few countries used quotas, most of which were voluntary and adopted by political parties themselves, gender quotas are now being used in some form in every region of the world, in 120 countries in every region of the world (IPU 2015: 4).

According to the UN Development Fund for Women's (UNIFEM) 2008 report, other strategies that appear to promote women's numerical representation in national public office-holding include (1) seeking parity in executive positions in political parties (such as in the rare case of Costa Rica); (2) further developing women's parties that have existed in such countries as Iceland, Sweden, the Philippines, and Afghanistan and that circumvent mainstream parties to bring gender equality issues to the fore; (3) campaign finance reform that provides equitable public financing and is tied to developing or sustaining party quota systems; (4) more women's political action committees that raise money for women candidates; and (5) combating sexism in media coverage of women candidates (UNIFEM 2008: 23–26). According to the IPU's "Women in Parliament: 20 Years in Review" report, the top five deterrents that continue to limit women's political representation are women's domestic responsibilities, cultural attitudes concerning women's social roles, lack of support from their families, lack of confidence, and lack of financial ability (2015: 4). But, as Thames and Williams (2013) also found in their statistical study, there is no substitute for women's active engagement in politics as voters, office seekers, and activists to increase their political representation (131). Thus, women's unprecedented but still relatively low gains overall, as 22.8 percent of the world's legislatures in 2016, are in jeopardy should there be any let-up in efforts on any of these scores. Moreover, the gendered divisions of power that portray—and internalize in women—the sense that women are unfit for politics, the masculinist construction of power as aggression and confrontation, and the separation between public and private that leaves women leaders (most of whom are mothers) responsible for the family on top of political responsibilities remain strong countervailing forces. These and other barriers to women's representation are discussed more fully in this chapter.

Gains have also been seen in the percentage of women in national cabinets. According to the 2017 Women in Politics map (IPU 2017a) compiled jointly by UN Women and the IPU, 31 countries have reached the goal of women occupying 30 percent of their ministerial positions, with Bulgaria, France, Nicaragua, Sweden, and Canada having more female ministers than male ministers and Slovenia having reached female/male parity. Following the Nordic countries with the highest representations of women ministers (on average 43 percent), are Europe as a whole, the Americas, and sub-Saharan Africa (ranging between 26 and 19 percent), trailed most by Pacific, Arab, and Asian states (ranging from 11 to 9 percent). Cabinet ministers are appointed and, thus, not subject to quota systems for parliamentarians that some countries have adopted, but Thames and Williams have found that the existence of parliamentary quotas of all types does increase the likelihood that more women will gain executive power (2013: 128). In the absence of quotas, but sometimes even with them, increases in this area must rely on enlightened heads of state and government backed up by gender equality advocates within and outside government. Despite some notable gains in this area (including three female US secretaries of state since the 1990s, one of whom was African American), cabinet appointments that go to women still tend to be clustered in domestic-focused social welfare agencies, while men far more routinely head foreign affairs, military defense, and finance ministries that have far more influence internationally as evidenced by the UN Women in Politics map (IPU 2017a).

UN and Other IGO Officials

As IGOs have become more significant actors in global governance, more attention has been given to women's representation in these bodies. In 1995, the UN committed itself to increasing the number of women on its professional staff to 30 percent by 1990, which it achieved in 1991. In 1998, the General Assembly further committed to the 50/50 goal of gender parity in all posts in the UN system (UN 2000: 167). In the last decade, the UN has come closer to reaching gender parity. According to the 2016 UN Women report on the Status of Women in the United Nations System, five entities, including UN Women, the International Court of

Justice (ICJ), the Joint United Nations Programme on HIV/AIDS (UNAIDS), the UN Educational, Scientific, and Cultural Organization (UNESCO) and the UN World Tourism Organization (UNWTO) actually have more women than men working within them (2016a: 8). However, even as of 2016, women remained concentrated in the lowest levels of the UN professional staff. The recent report notes that there is a negative relationship between women and seniority in the UN where women hold only 32.1 percent of senior positions, so as job status increases, the proportion of women found within higher-ranking levels decreases (UN Women 2016a: 8). On a positive note, the majority of UN agencies are within reach of gender parity, with most being within 10 percentage points (UN Women 2016a: 8). Yet such progress has been slow-moving. For example, only the lowest of the UN professional levels have achieved gender parity, and the percentage of women in the top-ranking UN positions actually dropped from 2010 to 2015, from 31 to 27 percent (UN Women 2016a: 11).

A major factor that contributes to the lower proportion of women in seniority is the role of location. Women at Headquarter agencies are more likely to move up than at non-Headquarter locations (UN Women 2016a: 9). Regionally, there are differences in women's representation in the UN system. Women from Western and Central Africa and Arab states are least represented at the UN at only 25 percent and 35 percent respectively, while women from the Americas and Caribbean and Europe and Central Asia are best represented at 49 percent and 46 percent (2016a: 10).

It was in response to the need identified by NGOs and IGOs with gender equality portfolios for a more coordinated UN response to gender inequality in the world and in its ranks that UN Women was formed in July 2010.[2] With revenue totaling a meager $319 million in 2015–2016, UN Women was charged in 2012 with overseeing the new UN-SWAP (or System-Wide Action Plan)[3] for gender equality and women's empowerment to mainstream gender perspectives across all UN bodies and activities through standardizing and measuring performance indicators of progress being made (or not) on instituting gender equality in representation and as a matter of substantive concern in relation to all UN-sponsored events, agreements, and issue areas (UN Women 2016b: 44). In the 2016 *Report of the UN Secretary-General: Mainstreaming a Gender Perspective into all Policies and Programmes in the United Nations System*, it is noted that whereas only 55 UN agencies reported on gender mainstreaming in 2012, in 2015 that number jumped to 64, which represents over 90 percent of the bodies that make up the UN system, demonstrating the increased commitment to gender mainstreaming and empowerment by the UN (UN 2016: 4). The report also revealed that 57 percent of UN agencies have either met or exceeded expectations on gender mainstreaming, which is a jump of 26 percentage points as compared to 2012 when the UN-SWAP program began tracking gender mainstreaming and gender equality progress (UN 2016: 5).

Member state performance with respect to women's representation of their countries as Permanent Representatives at the UN has been increasing. In the last few decades, there has been a rise in the number of women ambassadors, who now account for 25 to 40 percent of diplomats in some countries. For example, in Finland, 44 percent of ambassadors are women, and in the Philippines and Sweden, 41 and 40 percent of ambassadors are women. In Norway, 33 percent of ambassadors are women, and in the US, 30 percent of ambassadors are women, while Canada and Colombia are at 29 percent and 28 percent respectively (Towns and Niklasson 2016: 1). However, these percentages do not hold true for all countries as there are noticeable regional differences. Worldwide, Nordic countries have the highest percent of female ambassadors, at 35 percent. Oceania and North America each have a 25 percent female representation among their ambassadors, while Latin America and Africa stand at

18 and 17 percentage points respectively for women ambassadors. Europe has 14 percent female representation among ambassadors, with Asia at 10 percent and the Middle East at 6 percent (Towns and Niklasson 2016: 10). However, because women's numbers overall still remain comparatively small in diplomatic and foreign policy circles, women have organized lobbying and policy groups (such as the Associates of the American Foreign Service Worldwide and Women in International Security (WIIS)) that both expose and influence gender dynamics in ministries, departments, and committees dealing with foreign affairs. Of special note, however, is a recent proliferation of special rapporteurs and envoys for women's issues representing states and regional commissions and within UN agencies. For example, the Obama administration created the Office of Global Women's Issues in the US State Department in 2009 when the first US Ambassador-at-Large for Global Women's Issues was appointed. Despite banning US funding for foreign aid organizations that provide or discuss abortions, the Trump Administration has not (as of yet) shut down the Office of Global Women's Issues (McGinley and Goldstein 2017; Office of Global Women's Issues 2017), although the Ambassador-at-Large position remains vacant.

What has been most problematic until very recently was the relative lack of women in IGOs that have real enforcement power. Three women are now (as of 2017) serving as judges on the ICJ, constituting 20 percent of this judicial branch of the UN that adjudicates state behavior (ICJ 2017); however, the more recently formed International Criminal Court (ICC), which tries individuals for crimes against humanity, including genocide and war crimes such as sexual assault, when national courts fail to do so, now has six women, constituting one-third of ICC judges (ICC 2017). What remains more disconcerting is the relative paucity of women on the governance boards of international financial institutions (IFIs), which have much say in the workings of the global economy. Of the 49 members of the top leadership of the World Bank, 14 (28.5 percent) are women (World Bank 2017). Women constitute only 11.1 percent (six positions out of 54 filled ones) of the executive directors of the IMF and 18.8 percent of senior officials overall (IMF 2017a, 2017b). The WTO's five top leadership positions are held exclusively by men (WTO 2017). Still, it is notable that Christine LaGarde, former Minister of Finance for France, became the first woman director of the IMF in 2011, succeeding Dominique Strauss-Kahn who became the subject of a sexual assault scandal involving a hotel maid that tarnished his reputation even though he was eventually acquitted.[4] Also of note is that women make up the majority, at 60 percent, of the top leadership of the International Trade Center, a joint agency of the WTO and the UN for promoting the economic competitiveness of developing countries through small and medium-sized business exports as part of meeting the UN SDGs (ITC 2017).

Global Market and NGO Actors

Many observers of the global political economy see global market actors such as TNCs as rivaling state power on the world stage, particularly since the 1990s. But just as women are heavily underrepresented in economic decision-making within state and IGO bodies, so too are they poorly represented in the top echelons of global business entities. As of 2017, women constituted less than 6 percent of the Chief Executive Officers (CEOs) of the Fortune 500 (Catalyst 2017) and less than 7 percent of CEOs of Fortune 1000 companies (Darrow 2016), and as of 2016, women held 19.7 percent of all board seats in Fortune 1000 companies (2020 Women on Boards 2016). In 2015 in the EU, women constituted, on average, only 21.2 percent of the largest public companies' boards. Only Latvia, Finland, France, UK, Sweden, Denmark, Germany, and Italy have achieved at least one-quarter female representation on corporate boards (European Commission 2015: 1). In November 2012, the European Commission made balanced representation of women and men in public companies a legislative aim (European Commission 2015: 2). From 2010 to 2015, there was an increase in women board members in 24 of the 28 EU countries, with Italy, France, Belgium, Germany, UK, and Slovenia seeing the greatest rise, ranging between 21.2 and 12.4 percentage points (European Commission 2015: 3). Norway, not an EU member, mandated in 2002 that state-owned companies and in 2006 that private companies have at least 40 percent women on their boards, which increased female board membership to 42 percent by 2009, where it has remained (UN DESA 2010: 123–124; EIGE 2017). Since then, Austria, Belgium, France, Germany, Greece, Italy, the Netherlands, and Spain have introduced varying quotas, some mandated, some optional, with varying requirements, with some only applicable to state-owned businesses (European Commission 2015: 6–7).

For a period immediately following the 2008 financial crisis, the world's corporations began to take notice of studies that linked high-risk and volatile trading with men and more careful and even financial management of stocks by women. Still, women were not represented on the G20 expert committees that attempted to deal with that crisis and avoid future ones through new regulations (Marchand and Runyan 2011: 246). Nevertheless, the World Economic Forum (WEF), a Swiss-based independent forum of worldwide business, government, and civil society leaders who gather periodically to shape global economic agendas, has developed an interest in closing the global gender gap as a matter of economic efficiency and competitiveness, issuing annual reports on it since 2006. Its 2016 report found that despite narrowing gaps primarily in education and health, and secondarily in economic participation in many countries, the least progress has been made in empowering women politically overall (World Economic Forum 2016).

At the other end of the spectrum of women's representation in global governance are transnational NGOs. Few formal statistics exist on women's participation in NGOs, but it is estimated that women constitute the majority of members of NGOs, particularly at the local, grassroots level, but also through the transnational level given that they have much more access to and voice in them when compared with their prospects for participating in formal political office-holding and decision-making. This is the case for in-country studies conducted on the non-profit sector in Canada and Poland (Zieleńska 2012; HR Council 2017). Although women constitute the majority of rank-and-file members of most NGOs, particularly those concerned with human rights, labor, social justice, and environmental causes, but also more conservative issues, women exercise the most NGO leadership in women's NGOs. Although women's transnational NGOs have a long history (consider, for example, women from warring countries gathering at The Hague during World War I to form the still-extant Women's International League for Peace and Freedom), most contemporary women's transnational NGOs, sometimes referred to as transnational feminist networks (TFNs), began forming during the UN Decade for Women and proliferated particularly in the 1990s. Margaret Keck and Karen Sikkink (1998) have hypothesized that such TFNs are part of a generalized rise of transnational social networks (TSNs) that emerged in response to their causes being blocked at the state level and the political opportunity structures the UN provided (through conferences, consultations, and so on) that enabled them to air their issues at the international level to pressure states to act. Valentine Moghadam (2005) divided up TFNs that have been most active and influential in international forums and policymaking contexts into five issue areas: women's human rights; peace, antimilitarism, and conflict resolution; ending violence against women; reproductive health and rights; and economic critique and justice. What can be added to these is the issue area of environmental protection and sustainability. TFNs also tend to interconnect these issue areas (discussed in subsequent chapters). But the main point here is that women participate most in global governance through these channels, albeit exercising little masculinist "power-over" but significant "power-with," a feminist conception of power that stresses shared, collective, bottom-up empowerment.

Barriers to Women's Participation in Global Governance

As can be seen from this brief review of women's contemporary numerical representation in global governance, women's recent, highly uneven, and fragile gains in this area have been largely due to the institutionalization of particular gender equality, again, more accurately, women's empowerment, measures at international and national levels advocated primarily by TFNs and national women's movements. Such measures as gender quotas were advocated to address persistent and otherwise intractable barriers to women's political participation at almost all levels, but particularly the highest, and in all arenas of government and governance. Factors such as "the level of development within a country, the existence or absence of a tradition of political participation and labor force participation by women, the type of electoral or selection system, the characteristics of the institution, and [political] ideology all have strong and significant effects" on the level of women's representation (Thames and Williams 2013: 130). But two other conclusions have emerged repeatedly from the extensive research done on women's political participation and slow progress on this. First, women do not lack interest in or motivation for political action: studies of women's participation in grassroots organizing, community politics, election campaigns, and political organizations suggest that "women are as likely (if not more likely) to work for political causes or candidates as are men" (Lips 1991: 91). Second, a point related to the first, women's underrepresentation in political office and leadership positions is linked to gender-differentiated patterns still pervasive in today's world. Joni Lovenduski (2015) identifies these as institutional constraints, including institutional masculinity and sexism that structurally pervade political parties and their ideologies and recruitment, and attitudinal sexism and racism. The following examines such factors and additional ones by addressing how gender socialization and gendered situational constraints, structural obstacles, and institutional impediments interact in favoring men (especially those associated with hegemonic masculinity) and discriminating against women (in varying degrees depending on their social locations) as formal political actors (Randall 1987: 83–94; Henderson and Jeydel 2010: 12–22).

Gender Socialization

Early studies tended to focus on the effects of sex-role stereotyping—that is, on the enduring consequences of childhood socialization of girls and boys into mutually exclusive gender roles. Presumably, socialization into appropriate "feminine" behavior makes women less likely than men to pursue traditionally defined political activities. For example, feminine identity formation is inextricable from cultural expectations that motherhood is the primary role of women, that women's domestic role is antithetical to public-sphere activities, and that traits associated with political efficacy (ambition, aggression, competitiveness, authority) are distinctly unfeminine. To the extent that women internalize these stereotypical norms, then, they are less likely to perceive themselves as political actors or aspire to public office.

As a corollary, socialization into appropriate "masculine" behavior makes men more likely than women to identify with political activities. Just as important, gender stereotypes, because they are held by men and women, create a climate that encourages male participation while discouraging female participation in politics. Thus, individual women who seek leadership positions must struggle not only with their own internalized stereotypes but also with the fact that gender stereotyping in general fuels resistance to women as political actors. Finally, for women who do achieve positions of power, expectations of appropriately "feminine" behavior are often in conflict with qualities required for successful leadership. In short, gender stereotypes suggest that appropriately feminine women (passive, dependent, domestic, engaged in meeting private, familial needs) are by definition inappropriate political agents (active, autonomous, public-oriented, engaged in meeting collective, not personal needs).

This picture is further complicated by men's and women's positions in relation to race/ethnicity, religion, sexual orientation, ability, age, and so on. Masculinities and femininities vary along these dimensions, and not all men are socialized to desire or expect political participation or leadership. These variations matter significantly in terms of who actually enters and/or succeeds in politics. But despite hierarchies among men, the consistency of gender stereotypes is so strong that within particular groups more men than women will be associated with public-sphere activities, political participation, and corporate power.

Situational Constraints

Gender socialization produces different male and female orientations toward political participation. Also, gender stereotyping produces behavioral patterns that result in different concrete living situations for women and men that also constrain women's participation. Hence, we are better able to explain gendered political participation if we look at the *interaction* of stereotypes (for example, how women are assigned domestic and mothering responsibilities) and gender-differentiated living situations (for example, how the gendered division of labor limits women's involvement in traditional or formal politics). In masculinist societies, it is women who confront the time and energy demands of having primary responsibility for family and home care—what UN Women (2011) refers to as "time poverty." Family care includes child-rearing and/or care of the elderly or infirm as well as the emotional maintenance work required to sustain intimate and extended family relationships—responsibilities that disproportionally fall on women regardless of their sexuality or the family form in which they live. Worldwide, home care involves ensuring that food is secured and prepared for all and that the household is physically maintained. For millions of women, the latter entails arduous efforts to secure water and fuel. For most women, it means responsibility for cleaning, laundry, upkeep, and adequate performance of household functions. Even for affluent women, it means a great deal of shopping, scheduling, and transporting family members. Not surprisingly, because these demands are placed on women more than men, women are constrained in terms of how much time and energy they have for political participation, especially the pursuit of political office. When this reproductive work is coupled with productive work for an income that most women in most of the world perform, whether in formal or informal sectors, women's energy and time are further constrained. It is not simply the double workload of reproductive and productive labor that inhibits women's participation in politics; it is also women's lack of control over when they will be available and whether (or how) family obligations will interfere with political pursuits. These problems persist once women hold political office because "national capitals are often quite far away from people's homes, the hours are unorthodox, and there are often no on-site daycare options" (Henderson and Jeydel 2010: 21).

Men are typically not forced to make these choices because their political activities are considered separate from their domestic relations. Women, in contrast, are so closely identified with the domestic sphere that when they take on political activities, this is considered in combination with, not separable from, their role in the family. It is also important to note that globalization or global economic restructuring (see Chapter 5) for the most part exacerbates this gender imbalance. Men increasingly confront un- and underemployment. But this change in their workday still rarely translates into their making greater contributions to family and home care. At the same time, withdrawal of social and welfare services by the state disproportionally hurts women, who (in their role of family and home caretakers) are assigned responsibility for "taking up the slack."

Decreased public spending on education, health, and food subsidies means that increased costs must be borne by women, who work longer hours, look for less expensive food, spend more resources on basic health care, make difficult choices about which children will get an education and which will work to sustain the family economy, and face lower wages or fewer job opportunities as the wages in female-dominated industries decline or as the returns to agricultural labor are not sustained (Chowdhury et al. 1994: 6).

Hence, insofar as political participation requires time, resources, and control over them, capitalist and masculinist conditions make women's participation exceedingly difficult. For women of non-dominant race/ethnicity and of subordinate classes, the obstacles are multiplied.

Structural Obstacles

Clearly, stereotypes and situational constraints shape the gender of political activism, but the recurring differences in women's and men's participation must also be examined in relation to large-scale, interacting, and enduring social structures. Here these are referred to broadly as sets of power relations and/or social-cultural institutions that determine the boundaries of individual behavior. Understanding why so few women hold political power requires understanding how social structures and their interaction make it much more difficult for most women (than for most men) to seek and secure political office. Although primary gender socialization occurs in childhood, the hierarchical dichotomy of masculine–feminine is enforced throughout our lives. The gender dimensions of multiple social structures interact and in effect "discipline" individual behavior to conform to stereotypes.

For example, traditional religious belief systems and institutions play an important role in perpetuating images of women that deny them leadership positions. All too frequently, women are portrayed as either the source of evil (the uncontrollably sexual whore) or the model of saintliness (the self-sacrificing virgin). Neither is an appropriate identity for political leadership. In addition, the vast majority of religious institutions themselves exclude women from top leadership roles. No matter how this exclusionary practice is legitimized, it in fact sends a clear and unequivocal message that reinforces gender stereotypes: that women are not equal to men and that they cannot be trusted with or lack the qualifications for positions of authority and power.

Religious beliefs interact with and may reinforce other cultural sources of gender stereotyping. This is generally the case in regard to identifying the heteronormative home/family as woman's sphere and the public/politics as man's sphere. It can also be quite explicit, as in the seclusion of women (*purdah*) practiced in many Islamic countries, or in Western ones where neoconservative policies (sometimes inspired by Christian fundamentalism) seek to return women to the home and to reconstructed patriarchal and heteronormative families. Religious, educational, and judicial institutions tend to reproduce the ideological—and gender—division of public and private. And both informal and formal public–private separations affect women's political participation negatively by identifying women exclusively with the private sphere.

Thus, our expectations of different behaviors for men (appropriate for politics) and for women (inappropriate for politics) make it difficult, first, for women to see themselves comfortably in conventionally defined political roles and, second, for men and women generally to see and accept women as political agents. Attitudinal changes are occurring, however, with younger generations showing more acceptance of women in politics, and women within younger generations the most likely to advocate for women's increased representation (Henderson and Jeydel 2010: 21). But to the extent that the stereotype of "a woman's place is in the home" (or in the bedroom) is held, women will be seen as "out of place" in political office.

The horizontal and vertical segregation of both men and women in the workforce affects women's access to political power. Horizontally, women are concentrated in fewer occupations than men and in jobs where women are the majority of workers—clerical work, elementary teaching, domestic maintenance, daycare, nursing, waitressing. Moreover, these are not occupations from which political candidates are traditionally recruited. In general, the work women do for pay is an extension of the feminine role assigned to women (and feminized others) and replicates work that women, according to both gender and heterosexual norms, are expected to do as mothers and wives: caring for dependents, serving the needs of others, providing social and physical necessities, and being docile, flexible, emotionally supportive, and sexually attractive (Macdonald and Sirianni 1996). Not only are women (and feminized others) clustered in certain jobs, but they are also expected to be "feminine" in whatever job they hold.

The workplace is also segregated vertically, with women concentrated in pink-collar jobs (men in blue-collar ones), in domestic services (men in protective services), and in light industry (men in heavy industry). Vertical gender segregation (the higher, the fewer) occurs both within and across industries: women generally are concentrated in part-time, temporary, non-organized, lower-status, lower-paying, and less powerful positions (Henderson and Jeydel 2010: 106). As a result, women earn less money, have less secure jobs, and rarely climb into powerful executive ranks. Race, ethnicity, and class discrimination interact with gender discrimination to exacerbate the self-perpetuating cycle of elite males holding onto power at the expense of all other groups.

Gendered divisions of labor affect women's political participation in multiple ways. Most obviously, women's structural disadvantage in the labor market translates into their having fewer resources, less status, and less experience wielding power when competing with men for political office. And when it comes to recruiting and promoting people for political office, educational and occupational structures interact to exacerbate women's disadvantage. Women receive not only a different education from what men get but also, until very recently, a good deal less education than men. Because education is so closely related to occupational opportunities, lack of educational training fuels the gender segregation of the workforce and its negative consequences for women. Moreover, certain professions have historically been associated with or appear particularly compatible with achieving and maintaining political power: law, military, career civil service, big business. It remains the case that women are underrepresented in most of these occupational areas and are especially few in number at the top levels from which political leaders are often recruited.

Other obstacles to women's political participation are direct and indirect legal barriers. It is only in the past century that most women secured the rights to vote and to hold political office, which are prerequisites to seeking formal power. Women in some of the Arab world as well as some women (and men) elsewhere continue to be denied these rights, either due to their gender, race or ethnicity, or sexuality. Military experience has also been a traditional path to power not only in authoritarian states but also in democracies such as the US. To the degree that women remain small percentages of state militaries, are legally prevented from holding combat roles, and/or are excluded from being in such militaries because of their sexuality or ethnicity, this avenue is effectively blocked. Moreover, as long as military experience is perceived as a requisite criterion of manliness for high political office, women may be pressured to "out-macho" their male counterparts and sublimate any "feminine" concerns that they might bring to high office.

For women who do gain power as the result of family connections and, specifically, the death of a father or husband who is in office or in the midst or wake of a conflict situation where symbols of unity, compromise, or conciliation are sought, being a woman and expressing traditional femininity can be an advantage. But when women act "like women," even though they are at the helm of national governments, the traditional picture of gender is not disturbed. Similarly, when women assume national leadership as a result of their success in grassroots activism, their association with "soft issues" (the environment, peace, feminism) can reinforce the traditional disassociation of women with "hard issues" (national security, economic competition) and the masculine traits assumed necessary for dealing with them (fearlessness, calculative reason). It is not surprising, then, that women who achieve national-level leadership positions "on their own" are often identified as especially masculine, but this also brands them as "deviant or abnormal" (Henderson and Jeydel 2010: 20).

The overall picture remains one of continued gender dichotomies creating no-win situations: women succeed through their identification as "traditional" (feminine) women facilitating male-defined projects, as trivialized "soft leaders," or as perversely man-like leaders by playing down any association with feminine "weakness." As long as female political actors are perceived either as traditional (or "hypervisible") women or "invisible women" (because they are acting "like men"), hierarchical gender expectations are not really disrupted. Paradoxically, even when women wield the highest state power, by continuing to behave in gender-stereotypical ways, they often reinforce, rather than challenge, the politics of gender. Even though the power of gender is at work here (shaping pathways to and the exercise of power), it remains "invisible" to observers of world politics. In other words, by appearing as traditional women or honorary men, and often rejecting any identification with feminism or the history of the feminist struggles that often paved the way for them (Hawkesworth 2012: 204), female politicians do not challenge the categorical distinction between femininity and masculinity and do not politicize this gender dichotomy. Their conformity to traditional gender stereotypes in fact works to reproduce them.

The pervasive bias of androcentrism in political science and international relations operates to produce this no-win situation. One effect of this bias is the assumption that political actors are men. Another is the narrow definition of politics as exclusively public-sphere or governmental activities. Yet a third effect is the narrow definition of power as the capacity to enforce one's will (power-over in contrast to an alternative feminist conceptualization of power, namely, empowerment or power-to).

These effects are not simply an academic concern, because the definitions they take for granted are promoted outside of academic disciplines as well. Consider the focus of television news on "spectacular" (rather than everyday) events: wars, weapons, violence, crises, men as leaders/legislators/protectors, and women as dependents/victims. The leaders we see tend to be heads of government of countries that are geopolitically powerful or significant at the level of foreign policy. Otherwise, international news is almost exclusively viewed through the lens of various crises: seemingly hopeless extremities of governmental, military, economic, refugee, population, health, food, water, fuel, and/or ecological breakdown, all seemingly emanating from the global South. Such images sustain gender, race, class, and nationality stereotypes, denying political agency to women and people of the global South and the roles of men and the global North in precipitating such crises.

In these accounts, gender operates but remains invisible in various ways. Attention to wars and spectacles is at the expense of everyday maintenance activities that are, in fact, a precondition of the world's continuing to function. The latter are largely ignored, yet they are the activities occupying women's—indeed most people's—lives. To the extent that women appear in depictions of politics, they tend to be acting "like men" (paradigmatically Margaret Thatcher) or functioning in supporting roles to the main/male actors (for instance, as wives, secretaries). Although there are increasing exceptions to this among women leaders who identify with feminist principles and thus see a greater repertoire for women's behavior and action in politics, gender conformity in positions of power remains the rule. In depictions of crises, women (or what Cynthia Enloe (1990) terms "womenandchildren") remain the ever-present victims in need of protection by men or through male-defined programs. Not inconsistent with the crisis picture, women occasionally appear as saints and crusaders (Mother Theresa, Princess Diana, Angelina Jolie), whose model of sacrifice and commitment spurs men on to greater feats of protection (or competitive performance), thereby strengthening male roles.

Again, not only are women and their activities depicted as secondary to (or merely in support of) men's public-sphere pursuits, but also the way in which women make an appearance tends to reinforce, rather than challenge, conventional gender stereotypes. From manner of dress and demeanor to lifestyle and sexual orientation, we rarely observe any blurring of rigid gender boundaries in the mainstream media. Left in place are androcentric accounts that obscure women as powerful actors and leaders across a spectrum of political activities, that deny the politics and societal importance of ostensibly private-sphere activities, and that mystify the role of masculinism (ideologically and structurally) in the continued subordination of women and perpetuation of multiple social hierarchies. In short, the gender dynamics of politics—especially international politics—remain in place yet invisible as long as women "appear" only when they adopt masculine principles or epitomize feminine ones.

Institutional Impediments

From another angle of vision, political institutions themselves can be seen to impede women's participation. Over three decades ago, Vicky Randall identified three institutional barriers to political recruitment and promotion that still hold true today (Randall 1987: 92–94). First, at each level, political advancement requires "appropriate" political, leadership, educational, and/or occupational experience: as already noted, these criteria discriminate against women who are structurally likely to have different and fewer resources and/or who start later in their pursuit of office. They also ensure that women's campaigns are typically far less financed than men's (Henderson and Jeydel 2010: 13).

Second, the institutions associated with politics and power and the norms and practices of these institutions are those of "a man's world." Exclusively male until recently and still dominated by men, they are hegemonically masculinist in the following senses: behavior traits deemed suitable, sometimes essential, for political success are stereotypically masculine (ambition, leadership, rationality, competitiveness, authority, toughness); meeting times and locations as well as socializing (networking) activities are, in practice, convenient for men's (not women's) schedules and geographical mobility; and issues of central importance are not those most immediately relevant to most women's lives ("women's issues" have been treated as peripheral to conventional politics until very recently) (Henderson and Jeydel 2010: 17, 20–21).

Third, there is outright prejudice and discrimination against women. Forms of discrimination in the workplace vary, but the presence of gender hierarchy and sexism (complicated further by racism and/or heterosexism for women in racial and sexual minorities) creates a less favorable environment for women, who must then struggle harder than their male counterparts to be successful. As long as the workplace and political office are identified as "male terrain," women constantly confront and must deal with resentment of their unwanted presence. Women are most frequently reminded of their outsider status when they are viewed not as colleagues but through their gender and sexuality. Subtle and not-so-subtle references to women and sexuality produce an atmosphere of male dominance in which women must either become "like men" or become invisible. These are not trivial aspects of power. The pervasiveness of masculinist assumptions, of androcentric worldviews, and of sexist and heterosexist humor poses formidable obstacles. Because we are so saturated with gendered assumptions, these obstacles typically go unrecognized or are not taken seriously as the pillars holding up male privilege and power—at the expense of women's participation. At times, sexual harassment in governance (and other work sectors, such as the media, factories, and so on) has been catapulted to a national and even international issue, as in recent scandals in not only the US but elsewhere, resulting in and from the global twitter campaign, #MeToo (see Box 3.1). But while some heads are rolling, some governmental representatives and ruling parties are being weakened, and some more concerted anti-sexual harassment programs are being instituted in some quarters, it remains to be seen if the status quo is returned to as the scandals of the moment disappear on the world mediascape.

Such obstacles continue when women do achieve high political office. Study after study has found that women across polities have proven to be just as effective as men as legislators and leaders, and are, in fact, more effective, particularly when it comes to working across

Box 3.1 #MeToo Global Campaign

Began by Tarana Burke in the US in 2006 to call attention to sexual abuse of women of color, the **#MeToo** campaign went viral and global in Fall 2017 after many sexual harassment and assault allegations by women and men against high-profile men in the media and politics, not only in the US, but also in many parts of the world. It is credited with exposing the silences, silencing, and economic costs that gender violence in the workplace produces and the bringing down of many very powerful men. The following are examples of the campaign in some other languages:

- In French: #BalanceTonPorc (DenounceYourPig)
- In Italian: #QuellaVoltaChe (TheTimeThat)
- In Spanish: #YoTambién (MeToo)
- In Arabic: #أنا_كمان (MeToo)
- In Chinese: #我也是 (MeToo)
- In Russian: #Ятоже (MeToo)

parties and putting social welfare generally and gender equality measures more specifically on the legislative and policy agenda. However, their often-greater efforts not only to become state actors but also to serve constituencies-at-large, as well as to "substantively" represent women through greater attention to so-called women's or gender issues, are met with resistance at every stage. Androcentric norms and outright hostility to women as undeserving political interlopers translate into lack of party and male counterpart support for women's legislative proposals, trivialization of any gender-based reforms, and paternalistic or sexualized treatment of women officeholders by their male counterparts (Hawkesworth 2012: 206–214).

In sum, long-entrenched gender stereotypes and the interaction of gendered situational constraints; domestic responsibilities; religious, educational, economic, legal, and military structures; and gendered institutional impediments have so discriminated against women's political participation and, especially, their access to and room to maneuver in high political office and global power structures that feminists have long concluded that major policy interventions must be launched even to hope to level the playing field.

Institutionalizing Global Gender Equality

As indicated earlier, the 1995 BPA arising out of the UN Fourth World Conference on Women, which was unanimously supported by UN member states, provided a major impetus for the widespread adoption of a range of gender equality policies and measures at national and international levels. These include not only gender quotas, but also the institution of women's policy agencies, the practice of gender mainstreaming, the inclusion of women's empowerment in first the MDGs and then the SDGs, and the creation of a host of global measurement systems to track gender (in)equality and rank states on the basis of them. As noted in Chapter 1, prior to these instruments, CEDAW was adopted. It is binding on the vast majority of states that have ratified it (with the still notable exception of the US). CEDAW's objective is, among other things, to ensure that gender equality, as defined by CEDAW, is enshrined in and enforced through state constitutions and laws to achieve equality outcomes. Far fewer countries have signed onto the CEDAW Optional Protocol that makes them liable for complaints made to the CEDAW committee (of which there have so far been very few formal ones), and many countries ratified CEDAW with reservations that reduce its intent and enforceability (Zwingel 2016). However, CEDAW has also been the basis of an international women's human rights movement that has added to the definition of human rights certain previously unrecognized rights, such as reproductive rights, sexual rights, and rights to be free from domestic and sexual violence. Although such women's human rights are unevenly accepted by states, they are reflected in the BPA as a norm-setting document.

These are significant developments that bear testimony to the success of the power-with strategies of national women's movements and TFNs working in concert with UN women's agencies to hold the international community accountable for gender equality. Kara Ellerby (2017) has amassed a compendium from UN reports and large-scale quantitative studies of achievements in state policymaking to advance women's empowerment as a result of TFN organizing and global governance policymaking and norm-setting. For example, education gender gaps have been closing in recent years, with gender parity in primary school being reached by two-thirds of states; at least 86 percent of states now have equal pay laws and laws that increase women's access to employment, credit, and property; two-thirds of states have laws on violence against women, with 42 percent having legislation on "sexual violence, domestic violence, sexual harassment, and trafficking of women" and an additional 26 percent addressing at least three of these (Ellerby 2017: 28–32).

However, as indicated in the following review of aspects of institutionalization of women's rights and women's empowerment measures carries not only rewards but also risks in terms of uneven implementation, co-optation, and deepening divisions among women. It can also maintain the power of gender by institutionalizing gender difference while depoliticizing it, shifting attention away from a broader feminist critique of gendered power relations that uphold global politics-as-usual in favor of simply increasing women's (and only certain women's) participation in those politics.

Gender Quotas

A quota is typically seen as an affirmative action measure designed to redress to some degree (ranging from setting minimum numbers or thresholds to creating representative balance) the political underrepresentation of a particular group, which can include women, ethnic minorities, indigenous peoples, and even geographical groups. There are three distinct kinds of gender quotas. One is reserved seats in the legislature for women, which means women have a certain number of seats ensured for them. A second type of quota is a legal one, which ensures a percentage of women are nominated as candidates by law. The last type of quota is a voluntary one adopted by a political party to make a percentage of the candidates it runs women (Gender Quotas Database 2017). So widespread have gender quotas become as instruments for strengthening democracy that the Stockholm-based International Institute for Democracy and Electoral Assistance (IDEA) has compiled and maintains a Gender Quotas Database. However, as Torlid Skard, former Norwegian politician and former chairman of the UN Children's Fund (UNICEF), explains, furthering women's representation requires additional institutional changes within political culture and political parties. Also essential to inclusive democracies is an emphasis on mass-level participation, along with a state that is accountable to upholding human rights and social justice. Crucial to furthering women's representation in politics is ending patron–client networks, abuses of power, and male-only public spaces, but so too is market regulation to lessen inequalities since global economic justice is a prerequisite for women's rights and political participation (Skard 2015: 498–499).

Party quotas were first adopted in the Nordic countries of Western Europe by leftist political parties in the late 1970s and early 1980s, but it was only after women had secured between 20 and 30 percent of parliamentary seats, in part due to robust feminist movements, political cultures oriented to social welfare values, and PR systems. These party quota systems have remained voluntary and representative of what is called an "incrementalist" approach to women's empowerment (Friedenwall, Dahlerup, and Skjeie 2006: 49–50). Even though Nordic countries have not used legal or constitutional quotas to reach consistently high numbers of women in political office, the Scandinavian case has been cited as an example of what can be achieved with some form of quota system, especially a more "fast-track" one that is legally or constitutionally mandated. This is particularly the case in those countries where women's share of political power has been persistently low and incrementalist change is unlikely to alter that anytime soon.

Feminists have long made the argument that getting more women into political office is not only a matter of fairness but also crucial for having any true democracy. The quota argument gained significant traction in the 1990s when a range of countries were undergoing transitions to some form of democracy and entering into the rising global capitalist economy.

This was the same period in which UN agencies and IFIs began to take up the argument that gender equality was necessary as part of democratization and of a modern market economy and good governance. The conflation by IGO actors of gender equality with democratization and mature market-based economies accelerated the top-down institution of legal or constitutional gender quota systems, particularly in the South. The assumption was that such commitments to gender equality would help to legitimize the countries that adopted them as modern, democratic, and market-oriented (Matland 2006: 277; Squires 2007: 29). At the same time, most older democratic nations have tended to resist legal quotas on the assumption that they have already achieved democracy, regardless of the current statistics on women's representation.

As noted earlier, some form of gender quotas had been adopted by 120 countries as of 2015 (IPU 2015: 4). Most of the 40 countries with legal quotas are heavily concentrated in Latin America and sub-Saharan Africa but also including countries like Afghanistan, Pakistan, Iraq, and Nepal, which are not part of the OECD to which mostly Western democracies belong (Dahlerup et al. 2014: 24–25). Moreover, most legal quotas (including reserved seats systems that can be found in parts of the Middle East, Africa, and Asia) were adopted after the Beijing women's conference in 1995 or in the wake of the institutions of MDGs in 2000 and SDGs in 2015. In contrast, voluntary party quotas are more typical in OECD countries with parliamentary systems that include social democratic or other left-leaning parties. The US has remained hostile to quotas (with the exception of their use by the Democratic Party in the early 1970s), although the two major political parties are mindful of the need for some women's (and racial minority) representation and thus exercise informal or "soft" quotas (Squires 2007: 26–28). Democratizing Eastern and Central European countries were more resistant to gender quotas that are seen as smacking of old forms of central control (Dahlerup 2006a: 197–198) despite the post-Communist downward plunge in women's relatively high formal political representation (albeit not in the most powerful echelons) during the Communist period. Recently, as outlined in the 2016 Council of Europe's report "Women's Political Representation in the Eastern Partnership Countries," more countries in the region have been adopting voluntary quotas, including Belarus, Moldova, and Georgia, while Armenia has a mandatory legislative gender quota, and civil society movements are working to gain legislative gender quotas in Ukraine, Moldova, and Georgia (Council of Europe Regional Study 2016: 35, 41, 46). Even the states that emerged from the violent breakup of the former Yugoslavia have all adopted gender quotas in recent years (Gender Quotas Database 2017).

Tunisia is also among the countries that have adopted mandatory electoral list quotas for women, requiring parity in the numbers of women and men on those lists. Thus, the Arab Spring that cut across wide swaths of the Middle East and Northern Africa and most notably brought down dictators in Tunisia, Yemen, and Egypt in 2011 through massive popular protest by men and women (as opposed to armed conflict as in Libya the same year) is another factor in the increase of gender quotas, although Tunisia is alone in adopting them so far given the collapse of democratic rule in Yemen and Egypt. Surrounding countries that did not see any Arab Spring action, including Jordan and Morocco, have also adopted gender quotas, which is linked to the regional effects of the Arab Spring. Such recent cases arising from political upheaval, the regional diffusion (or "contagion") effect of quotas, and the documented success of quotas for fast-tracking women into high office has led to such wide adoption of them. However, recent research (Rincker 2017) indicates that quotas must be accompanied by women's policy agencies and gender mainstreaming (including gender-responsive budgeting) to not only get women into office, but also for legislative responsiveness to women's rights and needs.

Women's Policy Agencies

It was following the UN First World Conference on Women, held in Mexico City in 1975, which called for the adoption of state machineries to advance the status of women, that the first women's policy agencies were instituted. Since that time, as a result of continued TFN lobbying using CEDAW and UN women's conference documents as leverage, coupled with pressure from UN women's agencies, 165 countries had created some form of national women's policy agency by 2004 (Squires 2007: 33). These range from "stand-alone government ministries" and "offices within the head of state's department" to "quasi-autonomous state agencies such as national commissions or divisions for gender equality within ministries for labour, social welfare or national development, parliamentary commissions and delegations" (Squires 2007: 34). Women's policy and gender equality units have also been formed within regional and supranational entities, such as the EU and its constituent executive, legislative, and judicial bodies. Although these units vary considerably in terms of resources and functions (ranging from policy formation or input to mere reporting) and thus influence, they have been productive of what is termed "state feminism," with insider "femocrats" working to advance women's representation and issues not only in elective arenas, but also in bureaucratic ones (Squires 2007: 33).

In the midst of the initially laudable and rapid institutionalization of women's policy agencies, feminist "outsiders" have questioned to whom femocrats are really accountable (typically governments rather than women's movements), how they can effectively represent diverse women (as they are largely elite women), and what women's issues they tend to advocate (typically those that are digestible by a government in power, leaving more radical demands by the wayside) (Squires 2007: 119). At the same time, economic restructuring pressures, particularly during the last decade and in the wake of the 2008 global financial crisis which ushered in austerity programs in the global North as well as the global South, have led to some defunding and privatization of these entities, which are then essentially reduced to NGOs without state support (Hawkesworth 2012: 227). Moreover, since the mid-1990s, those agencies that remain have been charged with the advocacy of gender mainstreaming, which shifts attention away from women, women's movements, and women's issues. Instead, the focus is on what is seen as a more expert-based, bureaucratic exercise that has been adopted, like gender quotas and women's policy agencies, less because of any commitment to gender equality and more because of states' desires to appear more modern and market-oriented.

Gender Mainstreaming

Although the BPA calls upon governments to engage in gender mainstreaming, it is largely a creation of IGOs. Conceptually developed by the World Bank and the UNDP in the early 1990s, gender mainstreaming has been globalized through its adoption by the UN, the OECD, Northern development agencies (which also disseminate it to the South), and, especially, the EU since 1995 (Squires 2007: 41–42). Somewhat differing UN and EU definitions of gender mainstreaming share the following in common: the goal of integrating the experiences, needs, and concerns of both women and men into the design, planning, implementation, monitoring, and evaluation of all policies (economic, political, and social) with the aim of achieving gender equality (Squires 2007: 39–40).

At first blush, gender mainstreaming constitutes a significant improvement in how to bring about gender equality in that it attempts to decenter the male norm upon which policymaking has rested and within which women have to fit. Moreover, it represents a more thoroughgoing application of gender equality norms to all spheres of policymaking and makes all government agencies accountable for this application. Gender mainstreaming need not await parity in women's political representation that is still a long way off, nor is it the sole responsibility of typically under-resourced and more lowly women's policy agencies. Plus, its focus on gender moves away from constructing "women" as the problem toward tackling the problems that have arisen as a result of gender inequalities, such as poverty and violence. Thus, TFNs and femocrats in state and UN agencies have supported it.

However, studies have found that the rapid adoption of gender mainstreaming by states and IGOs appears to be yet another attempt to conform to "favoured international norms such as modernization and good governance" rather than a desire for "gender justice" (Squires 2007: 48). As a result, not only is it quite unevenly enforced where it has been adopted, but also it is most often engaged in through an "expert-bureaucratic model" rather than a "participative-democratic model," thereby cutting out consultations with and accountability to social movements and relying on femocrats (Squires 2007: 41). It has also had the effect of pulling back commitments to women's policy agencies on the assumption that they are less needed under this diffused approach, and reducing a transformational political struggle for gender equality to a management technique whereby gender audits and assessments are performed through largely quantitative approaches that are seen to adhere to the social science ideals of objective truth and rationality (which are also most associated with masculinity and masculinist commitments to positivism) (Squires 2007: 143; Caglar 2013: 338). Those social movements and NGOs that do not present their claims through such language and filters are dismissed. This has spawned cadres of NGO gender experts, typically at the transnational level, who can speak in the language of gender mainstreaming bureaucracies at the cost of being further separated from the struggles of the movements they claim to represent (Squires 2007: 145–154; Caglar 2013: 340).

Gender Equality Indices

There has been a veritable explosion in the creation of, tracking of, and reporting on gender equality indices. Beginning in 1995, the annual UNDP's *Human Development Report* began issuing Gender-Related Development Index (GDI) and Gender Empowerment Measure (GEM) statistics by country. The GDI was an adjustment of how countries rank on the Human Development Index based on gender differentials in life expectancy, adult literacy, and primary, secondary, and tertiary education. GEM measured opportunities by gender based on relative numbers of women in parliament, official and managerial positions, and professional and technical work, as well as women's earned income relative to men's. But amid criticisms of these tools for insufficiently capturing gender differences in quality of life and improvements in this in low-income countries, in 2010 the UNDP introduced the Gender Inequality Index (GII), which determines how much is lost in terms of achieving full labor force, education, and political participation, as well as reducing teenage fertility and maternal mortality as a result of gender inequality in countries and regions. The aforementioned WEF Global Gender Gap Index measures gaps between women and men in terms of health, education, and economic and political participation gleaned from UN statistics, while the World Bank, through its GINI index, measures income inequalities among individuals and households within countries. A number of other UN agencies and NGOs use similar, other, or additional indices to track gender (in)equality in relation to a range of issue areas. What emerges from the plethora of these statistical measurements and the annual reports that are spawned by them is some commonality in results: OECD countries, particularly Nordic ones, rank the highest in gender equality and gain the most from this economically and socially, and Arab states rank the lowest and lose the most from this. As indicated earlier, UN Women is also now charged with introducing and monitoring more standard indices across the UN system to track gender (in)equality and mainstream gender equality in all UN activities.

On the one hand, the gathering of such data on the relative "female friendliness" of states and the seriousness with which it is now taken by forming these global indices are welcome. On the other hand, such measurements are representative of the kind of quantitative policy world to which gender equality politics has been reduced. In what Sally Engle Merry (2016) calls the global "indicator culture," only those things that can be more easily measured are counted, enabling complicated social realities to fall from view and disabling public debate on what they mean and what to do based on such data (219). Similarly, even though these indices have no doubt facilitated the contagion of states institutionalizing gender quotas, women's agencies, and gender mainstreaming, they also tend to set up gender equality as a feature of modern progress and development rather than as a matter of gender justice. Finally, although such statistical rankings are helpful to social movement and NGO actors seeking leverage to advance gender equality, they, along with other bureaucratic practices like gender mainstreaming, are "a technique of power" (Caglar 2013: 341). For example, they can also be used by powerful states and IFIs to punish less powerful states, through such actions as decreasing aid or trade on the basis of their gender equality failings. At the same time, more powerful Western states that underperform on gender measures relative to expectations and resources (like the US, which keeps falling relative to other OECD states and even a number of global South states on some indices) are not subject to such "discipline." These latter two concerns also relate to UN development goals, starting with the MDGs and morphing into the SDGs, which constitute "the new aid agenda" (Antrobus 2006: 39).

Sustainable Development Goals

In September 2015, the UN General Assembly approved the 17 Sustainable Development Goals (see Box 3.2), ideally to be achieved by 2030, as part of the Transforming Our World: The 2030 Agenda for Sustainable Development. The SDGs were an update of eight Millennium Development Goals (MDGs), which were launched in 2000 as the basis of the international development agenda ideally to be achieved by 2015. Relevant particularly to women's political empowerment was Goal 3 in the MDG ("promote gender equality and empower women") and Goal 5 ("achieve gender equality and empower all women and girls"), although such goals ultimately rest on the fulfillment of all the other ones. But while the considerable expansion of these goals signals recognition of a greater multiplicity of factors that translate into a highly unequal world, gender equality itself becomes more marginalized amidst the proliferation of goals.

Nevertheless, there has also been an expansion of what must be done to achieve gender equality in the SDGs compared to the MDGs. Beyond increasing females in all levels of education, women's employment in non-agricultural sectors, and women's representation in national legislatures that were the targets in MDG Goal 3, SDG Goal 5 includes eliminating all forms of discrimination against women and violence against women, recognizing the value of and supporting women's unpaid labor through public resources and shared responsibilities in the home, and ensuring women's full participation in political decision-making and equal opportunities for political leadership. Disturbing, however, is the fact the UNDP declared that MDG Goal 3 had been achieved by 2014, despite the facts that "fewer than

Box 3.2 Sustainable Development Goals

The **UN SDGs** (www.un.org/sustainabledevelopment/sustainable-development-goals/) consist of 17 goals, which have 304 indicators for 169 specific targets. Goal 5: Gender Equality is related to almost all the other goals (from zero hunger, good health, and quality education to reduced income inequality among and with states, sustainable communities, climate action, and peace, justice, and strong institutions), but there are specific targets attached to it, including, for example:

- Ending all forms of discrimination against women and girls everywhere
- Eliminating all forms of violence against women and girls
- Valuing unpaid care and domestic work through public provisioning and shared household responsibilities
- Full participation in leadership in public life
- Universal access to sexual and reproductive health services
- Equal rights to economic resources

25 percent of states have 30 percent of women in national parliaments" (Ellerby 2017: 49), greater educational parity between females and males tells us little about the quality or type education enjoyed (or not enjoyed) by females relative to males that leads to occupational segregation, and there are still wide gaps in pay, labor force participation, and poverty rates between men and women. While the (global) gender wage gap lessened (dropping slightly from 28 to 26 percent) between 2000 and 2010 in 45 of 50 countries with available data, a substantial wage gap nevertheless exists in most countries. In fact, the gender pay gap has actually widened recently in several countries including Colombia, Australia, Finland, Paraguay, and Mongolia (UN Women 2015: 96). Women constitute 63 percent of the most vulnerable workers, as informal workers in family businesses and in agriculture (UN Women 2015: 102). Given these considerable shortfalls in any semblance of gender equality, it is hard to see how the elimination of it will occur by 2023.

Another problematic aspect of the SDGs (and all other women's empowerment or inclusion policies labelled as gender equality measures) is that nowhere are men addressed as part of the agenda. As a result, measurements of gender gaps fail to reveal growing gaps "between rich and poor women, between rich and poor men, between rural and urban areas, and between high-income and low-income countries" (Roberts 2016: 64). They also fail to account for the facts that some decline in gender gaps in labor participation (at 50 percent for working age women and 77 percent for working age men in 2016) is the result of declining male labor participation globally, while pay gaps have increased among women and among men and are the widest in well-paid and the lowest in poorly paid occupations (Roberts 2016: 65). UN Women, in its "2015–2016 Progress of the World's Women" report, does acknowledge small declines in the gender pay gap are the result of men's falling labor participation, which it attributes to the continuing legacies of the 2008 global financial crisis (UN Women 2015: 12).

The sources of massive and growing class inequalities that gender gap measurements hide are attributable to many factors prior to and since the global financial crisis as discussed in Chapter 5, but suffice it to say here that masculinist neoliberal constructions of and commitments to the global capitalist economy have loosened little in the wake of the MDGs and the

SDGs, which do not call for a transformation of global economic structures controlled primarily by the North, particularly the West. Under such circumstances, SDGs, which ideally are goals that all countries should work to achieve through cooperation and a massive redistribution of resources not just within but also across countries, can also be used as "conditionalities" to withhold the distribution of aid more in the interests of power politics than of social justice. Relatedly, as discussed next, gender equality itself can be used as a pawn of power politics, sustaining neoliberalism and provoking backlashes to it (covered in the next section) and excusing neocolonialism or (neo)imperialism (covered in the next chapter).

Neoliberal Governmentality, New Authoritarianism, and the Politics of Gender (In)Equality

As indicated by the preceding analysis, the recent gains made in women's representation in global governance and global governance attention to gender equality have been cause for some celebration but also significant suspicion among feminists. Postcolonial feminists in particular have pointed to these advances as the "neoliberal governmentalization" of gender equality. This refers not just to the co-optation (and attendant depoliticization) of gender equality by global governance bodies, but, more significantly, also to the way in which gender equality (and, more generally, women's human rights) has been made coterminous with neoliberalism. In this view, it is no accident that gender equality becomes (at least a rhetorical) priority in global governance precisely at the time that neoliberal ideology is globalized.

This critique stems from another conceptualization of power put forth by Michel Foucault (1991), who coined the term "governmentality" to refer to how individuals and populations "could now be controlled, administrated, empowered, or disciplined through certain governmental techniques" (Woehl 2008: 69). Governmentality pertains not only to state and suprastate bureaucratic apparatuses and policies but also to civil society institutions (including NGOs) that enable governing on the basis of rational, scientific, and statistical calculations and produce human subjectivities that are amenable to being "managed" or "regulated" and even participate in self-management or self-regulation in conformance with rationalized approaches to "problem-solving," now associated with "good governance" (Woehl 2008: 65–66). Power in this sense is more diffuse and both repressive and enabling, but it rests upon "hegemony," or the inculcation of "the right order" that brooks no deviation. As noted in the introduction to this chapter, neoliberal governmentality refers to the ascendance of the global capitalist economy and "economic rationality" as "the sole criteria for governance" (Woehl 2008: 69). Under neoliberal governmentality, the state is reduced primarily to the promotion of the "free market," leading to the privatization of social welfare and the "marketization" of political and social life, whereby populations are to be

> free, self-managing, and self-enterprising individuals in different spheres of life—health, education, bureaucracy, the professions, and so on. The neoliberal subject is therefore not a citizen with claims on the state but a self-enterprising citizen-subject who is obligated to become an "entrepreneur of himself or herself."
>
> (Ong 2006: 14)

In this scenario, gender equality becomes the technique to "free" women to be these free-market actors, taking care of their own needs without resort to the state for their welfare. The male (and class-based) norm of free-market actors, devoid of dependents and interdependencies, and an androcentric construction of states as not responsible for the welfare of their citizenries, are strengthened by this reduction of gender equality to the production of "economic woman" in the form of "economic man."

Thus, the traction that gender equality has gained in the context of global governance can be read more critically and most cynically as just a neoliberal strategy, with NGOs, TFNs, and femocrats being turned into agents of neoliberal governmentality. Indeed, the very proliferation of these NGOs and TFNs can be seen as a feature of neoliberal governmentality, taking on roles of states to "manage" (depoliticize) populations and their problems and even providing services, albeit in far more under-resourced ways, that states used to provide. This has implications as well for women gaining public office in states, for if the reigning ideology is that states are to withhold public service in favor of privatization that makes individuals solely responsible for their own welfare, then it is difficult to mount more expansive public commitments and garner more public resources for changing negative conditions for women (as well as children, non-elite men, and even the planet).

There is little question that IGOs and, especially, IFIs frame gender equality as a matter of modern economic efficiency. States have been most responsive to this framing, and TFNs have often made their own arguments in relation to it. However, it is also the case that local, grassroots, and national women's movements have drawn on these instruments of neoliberal governmentality to make claims on states, although NGOs, TFNs, and state feminists, to varying degrees, continue to critique the insufficiencies of governmental responses. Thus, there are contradictions in this process that open up opportunities for resistance to neoliberal governmentality and for more radical demands than it typically allows (addressed most in Chapter 6).

However, neoliberal governmentality has also opened up ultraconservative resistances to it that are distinctly anti-democratic and anti-equality. Scholars (see, for example, Diamond, Plattner, and Walker 2016) have recently observed that despite the growth in countries categorized as democracies (119 by 2005), in the last decade or so, authoritarian ideologies and leaders have been on the rise in several democracies in many world regions. Although some authoritarian regimes came to power through military takeovers (such as in Egypt), others have been elected (such as in Turkey, Venezuela, Russia, Iran, Hungary, Ukraine, and the Philippines). But ultraconservative and ultranationalist leaders have also been highly competitive or have won presidential and/or parliamentary elections in the West (in, for example, the US, UK, Austria, France, The Netherlands, and Germany). While there is debate as to whether these can be classified as authoritarian (or even fascist), there is some sense that the 2008 financial crisis and the trends in the neoliberal global political economy that led up to it made such leaders attractive to certain segments of the population resentful of stagnant or declining wages (Baker 2016) in the midst of fraying social safety nets under post-financial crisis austerity programs. While such authoritarian regimes as Russia have been implicated in stealth campaigns to destabilize democracies in the West in the hopes of expanding efforts to roll back international democracy and human rights agreements and norms, "homegrown" xenophobia, (white) nationalism, racism, sexism, heterosexism, and Islamophobia are also at work. Such ideologies have long been present, to varying degrees, in some or many elements of Western civil society, enabling clearly fascist regimes to rise to power in parts of Europe and extreme anti-immigration, segregationist, and discriminatory policies in North America during the twentieth century. Thus, at some level, it is not surprising that these can be called forth, especially in a time of economic dislocation and an unending "war on terror," both of which are also dislocating people on a massive scale.

Despite the fact that the global North, and particularly the West, is far more insulated from the current unprecedented amount of forcibly displaced persons in the world (65.6 million as of 2016), given that 84 percent are located in the global South (UNHCR 2016: 2), fears of refugees and other (racialized) "outsiders" have been stoked by far-right parties and party leaders. Such fears have contributed to the 2016 vote in the UK (primarily in England) to exit from the EU (known as Brexit) so as to better control its borders through harsher immigration and refugee policies, the building of a border wall by Hungary, beginning in 2015, to stop refugees in contravention EU law, and the 2017 election of Sebastian Kurz, leader of the anti-immigration and anti-EU Peoples Party, to the post of Prime Minister of Austria. But it was the 2016 election of Donald Trump to the US presidency that constituted the most ominous shift, whether momentary or not, to illiberal democracy in the West.

Particularly relevant to this chapter is the fact that his opponent was Hillary Clinton, who would have been the first female US President had she not lost the electoral college vote (having won the popular vote). Moreover, in some sense, she is paradigmatic of the (new and neoliberal) global gender equality agenda as a major architect of it. She is highly identified globally with placing the improvement of the lives of women and girls at the center of US foreign policy and global governance while US Secretary of State, a policy dubbed the "Hillary Doctrine." Initially developed while she was First Lady, following her "women's rights are human rights" speech at the UN Fourth World Women's Conference in Beijing, she co-founded the President's Interagency Council on Women, the incubator for evolving US domestic and foreign policy around women's issues (Hudson and Leidl 2015: 18). She brought the Hillary Doctrine into full expression as former President Obama's Secretary of State. As she proclaimed, the central focus would be on the "smart power" of "sustainable economic growth, food security, global health, climate change, democracy and governance, and humanitarian assistance. In each area we will invest in women and girls at every turn, with the goal of empowering them" (quoted in Hudson and Leidl 2015: 18). Obama made permanent and tripled the budget of the Office of Global Women's Issues (formerly known as the State Department's Office of international Women's Issues under Bill Clinton) while appointing a record number of female US ambassadors. At the same time, Secretary Clinton made heads of missions 30 percent women. In addition to requiring gender analysis in all US Agency for International Development (USAID) programs and gender mainstreaming in every bureau and embassy, she put forth in 2012 alone a Counter-Trafficking in Persons Strategy; a Policy on Gender Equality and Female Empowerment; a National Action Plan for Women, Peace, and Security; a Strategy to Prevent and Respond to Gender-Based Violence Globally; an Equal Futures Partnership; and a Vision for Ending Child Marriage and Meeting the Needs of Married Children (Hudson and Leidl 2015: 54).

By contrast, Trump has been described as an "inveterate liar and authoritarian narcissist" who flaunts "democracy, the rule of law, and the authority of fact" (Bordo 2017: 182–183). As reported widely in mainstream press and chronicled in recent scholar-journalist accounts (see, for example, Dionne, Ornstein and Mann 2017), he also has exhibited sexism, not only bragging about "pussy-grabbing" on the campaign trail but also reinstituting and expanding the global gag rule on US publicly and privately funded organizations to prevent them from offering even information on abortion as an option; transphobia by attempting to ban trans people from the US military; Islamophobia by instituting an (ultimately partial) ban on visitors, immigrants, and refugees from many majority Muslim countries; white nationalism in his support of and the support given to him by such groups within the US as well as his "zero tolerance" policy to dehumanize, criminalize, and detain all who enter the US on its southern border without immigration papers, including asylum-seekers and their children; and militarism in his provocations directed at North Korea and Iran while dropping the "Mother of All Bombs" in Syria and dramatically increasing the US military budget. He has also significantly cut funding for the State Department, withdrawn the US from UNESCO and the UN Human Rights Council, sought to renegotiate or end a host a multilateral trade agreements, and begun exiting the US from the Paris Climate Change agreement to reduce greenhouse gases. While possibly more of an opportunist than an ideologue, his pronounced hostility to a free press and his warm relations with a host of authoritarian leaders on the world stage has signaled a deep retreat from human rights norms and major resistance to such things as the SDGs, not to mention other internationally adopted mechanisms for increasing women's empowerment.

But as serious a regression from liberal (and liberal feminist) values the Trump presidency represents, we also need to remain mindful of the neoliberal governmentality that has infused global gender equality policymaking, including that of Hillary Clinton. In reducing gender equality to (cis and heteronormative) women's empowerment without regard for deep class, racial, sexual, and national inequalities among diverse women and among diverse men and making it a technical, depoliticized matter that sidelines social justice movements, gendered divisions of power remained significantly in place and reactionary forces gained traction. As masculinist as they are, they have included quite a few women and some "strong man" women leaders; thus, in the final section a distinction is made between the goal of just getting women into global governance politics and enabling intersectional feminist politics for transnational social justice to actually address the crisis of representation.

Women in Politics Versus Feminist Politics

There is no one-to-one relationship between the presence of women in politics and the extent of feminist politics. Women cut across the political spectrum and can just as easily hold antifeminist views or very narrow feminist commitments that justify the opening of doors for women like themselves to be in power but do not translate into supporting policies that improve conditions for all women or "other" women. Contemporary far-right women leaders like UK Prime Minister Theresa May and Marine Le Pen of the French National Front Party are cases in point. Moreover, despite findings in the UNIFEM 2008–2009 report on the progress of the world's women that women in public office tend to diminish corruption (UNIFEM 2008: 27), two female heads of state have been recently ousted from office on corruption charges—South Korean President Park Geun-hye and Brazilian President Dilma Rousseff. The current leader of Myanmar and former Nobel Peace Prize laureate Aung San Suu Kyi is also implicated in driving out hundreds of thousands of Rohingya Muslims from her country, leaving female refugees particularly susceptible to sexual assault. There are self-identified feminist leaders who have held or hold high positions, including not only Hillary Clinton, but also, for example, current President of Chile Michelle Bachelet (who formerly headed UN Women), Prime Minister of Iceland Katrin Jakobsdottir of the Left-Green Party, and Swedish Foreign Minister Margot Wallstrom, who is advancing a feminist foreign policy and labelled as such (see Box 3.3).

But while some women leaders (as well as some male leaders such as Prime Minister of Canada Justin Trudeau) are associated with advancing women's issues and even feminism (and meet annually under the auspices of the Council of Women World Leaders), many feminists have begun to question the very notion of some universalist constructions of "women's issues" or "women's interests" or even "women's human rights," especially in light of the co-optation of such concepts by neoliberal governmentality (Stern 2016; Chappell and Hill 2006; Hesford and Kozol 2005). Jennifer Chan-Tiberghien (2004) expresses this as the tension between the "gender boom" in transnational feminist organizing and "gender

Box 3.3 Swedish Feminist Foreign Policy

In October 2014, the government of **Sweden**, which defines itself as a feminist government, became the first country in the world to launch a **Feminist Foreign Policy** (www.government.se/government-policy/feminist-foreign-policy/). Its six broad objectives for 2014–2018 include:

- Strengthening the human rights of refugee and immigrant women and girls
- Combatting intimate violence against women and girls
- Promoting women and girls in conflict-resolution processes
- Promoting women and girls' political participation to strengthen democracy and reduce vulnerabilities
- Strengthening women and girls' economic empowerment, including ending discriminatory policies
- Intensifying support for reproductive and sexual rights for everyone

skepticism" in postmodern or poststructural feminist thought. The latter sees dangers in essentialist assumptions about the nature and very category of "women." Negative and even valorized constructions of "women" as some kind of undifferentiated group seen only in relation to the undifferentiated category of "men" sustain a "gender hegemony" or meta-lens (referred to in this text as the power of gender) that entraps, conforms, excludes, and manipulates human subjectivities and actions. The key to resisting this is to resist rigid categorizations of "women" and "gender" altogether, seeing them rather as fluid and unstable signifiers that cannot be pinned down and, thus, not subject to control. From another angle, as repeatedly pointed out in this text, postcolonial feminists (see, for example, Agathangelou and Turcotte 2016) argue that universalist categorizations of "women" and "gender" obscure differences and, more importantly, power relations among women who are differentiated by race, class, sexuality, nationality, physical ability, age, and so on (which are productive of gendered divisions not only between women and men but also among women and men) and that these categorizations fail to recognize that women (and men), in fact, have a range of "genders" as a result of these other infinitely varied combinations of social locations and identities. When these multiple genders go unrecognized, policies made in the name of women or gender tend to be based on a particular hegemonic construction of women (e.g., racially privileged, Western, heterosexual, middle-class, able-bodied, and so on) and their interests. At the same time, "other" women are lumped together (often statistically) under various "victim categories" within which women constitute the majority—such as the poor, the diseased, refugees, the hungry, and the raped and battered in war and peace—and targeted as problems to be solved through outside intervention and rescue (whether by Western-dominated IGOs or NGOs), thereby not according women in these categories agency themselves. These are important critiques, but gender skepticism carries the danger of undercutting political claims made by and for women, whether by movements, NGOs, or state feminists, even though such claims are necessarily based on a fluid and unstable category.

As Chan-Tiberghien observes, one effect of not seeing women as a highly diverse category at the level of global governance is that the 1965 International Convention on the Elimination of All Forms of Racial Discrimination (ICERD) has long been seen as separate from CEDAW, as if racial discrimination had nothing to do with gender discrimination (Chan-Tiberghien

2004: 465). This has been changing since the 2001 UN World Conference Against Racism (WCAR) where UNIFEM and women's NGOs made this link in official ways, getting reference to gender into "forty-one paragraphs of the NGO outcome documents and sixteen in the IGO documents" as well as additional references to "multiple forms of discrimination" and even "intersectionality" in these documents (Chan-Tiberghien 2004: 468–469). "Sexual orientation," even though also prominent in NGO documents, was excised in IGO documents (Chan-Tiberghien 2004: 469).

While IGOs in general continued to prefer "adding women" and to resist more radical and complex notions of gender beyond a male–female sex binary, what emerged especially from the Women's Caucus in the NGO Forum held alongside the WCAR was an insistence that "women's issues" be expanded to include "globalization, colonialism, slavery, foreign occupation, caste, HIV/AIDS, etc., in addition to the theme of intersectionality of gender, sexuality, and race" (Chan-Tiberghien 2004: 468). Yet, states and IGOs were (and still tend to be) silent on many of these because they consider them improper women's issues (Chan-Tiberghien 2004: 467). This "gender in intersectionality approach," as Chan-Tiberghien terms it, has also affected how women's NGOs and TFNs are using CEDAW to highlight the conditions of ethnic minority women (including undocumented migrants) who are typically left outside of narrow gender policymaking (2004: 477–478). Judith Squires found, at least within the EU, that some attention was being given to "diversity mainstreaming" to address race and disability as well as gender discrimination (2007: 163–164). However, progress on this has been slow and contested (Prügl and Thiel 2009), and the additive approach of IGOs continues to pit gender inequality against race inequality in terms of which should get priority and resources, as if many women did not experience both (Squires 2007: 165). Indeed, ethnic quotas still remain separate from gender quotas, translating into extremely low numbers of minority women in office (Ellerby 2017: 120). Meanwhile, class inequalities continue to mostly divide women not only on the ground but also in global governance insofar as only the most privileged from North and South can participate most directly in it (Ellerby 2017: 119), albeit still in numerically fewer, more marginal, and subordinated ways. Although such divides among women within countries are increasingly statistically tracked, widening inequalities between rich and poor associated with the poor regulation of capitalist accumulation remain largely unaddressed in state and IGO constructs of diversity under neoliberal governmentality.

Discrimination against sexual minorities and non-normative gender identities has only recently become a part of the global governance agenda. In 2006, two international human rights conferences led to the drafting of the Yogyakarta Principles that created a framework for the human rights of sexual and gender minorities. By 2008, after years of organizing by such NGOs as the International Gay and Lesbian Human Rights Commission (IGLHRC) and the International Lesbian, Gay, Bisexual, Trans, and Intersex Association (ILGA), the Declaration on Human Rights, Sexual Orientation, and Gender Identity (or SOGI Declaration) was put forth at the UN General Assembly, meeting with a polarized response (one-third of states for, one-third against, and one-third abstaining) (D'Amico 2015: 60). There has been some shifting since, and sexual and gender minority principles continue to be put on UN agency agendas, but polarization continues (D'Amico 2015: 64, 66). Notably it was not until 2009 that the first openly lesbian head of government worldwide was elected—Johanna Sigurdardottir, then Prime Minister of Iceland. More typically, the actual illegalization of non-normative sexual and gender identities bars many more women, men, and other sexes/genders from public power and can even cost them their lives. As of 2016, same-sex relations were illegal in 65 countries and punishable by death in all of or parts of ten countries

(Cameron and Berkowitz 2016). However, 71 countries have banned employment discrimination on the basis of sexual orientation, 40 countries now penalize hate crimes based on sexual orientation, and 14 national constitutions prohibit discrimination on the basis of sexual orientation (ILGA 2016). A growing number of countries, now 24 in total, offer marriage equality, including Argentina, Brazil, Belgium, Canada, Denmark, Estonia, Finland, France, Greenland, Iceland, Ireland, Luxembourg, Netherlands, New Zealand, Norway, Portugal, Slovenia, South Africa, Spain, Sweden, Uruguay, the US (Cameron and Berkowitz 2016; Out 2016), and, most recently (December 2017), Australia.

Thus, the meta-lens of the power of gender continues to operate in terms of sorely limiting whether women, and which women (and men and others), can gain power in global governance, in what contexts do "women's" or "gender" issues get attention and why, how such issues are framed and through what mechanisms, and how they are acted upon (if at all). Despite recent progress of the type detailed here—mostly as a result of considerable "insider" and "outsider" feminist, LGBTQ, and anti-racist organizing—the continued power of gender largely keeps gendered divisions of power intact, which, as discussed in subsequent chapters, also leaves relatively undisturbed gendered divisions of violence and labor and resources. These all contribute to the crisis of representation that un-, under-, and misrepresents citizens as well as non-citizens, including those defined as stateless. The power of gender also ensures that when formal representation is achieved, it is circumscribed and often co-opted by neoliberal governmentality (Caglar, Prügl, and Zwingel 2012; Hozić and True 2016). Even more ominously, whatever (neo)liberal human rights and equality norms have been achieved can be quickly eroded by illiberal forces. Even though such forces rail against international institutions and law, democratic institutions, human rights, equality, and environmental protection, they remain deeply committed to the marketization of public and social life, privatizing (or simply excising) public goods and services and valuing only what can increase the amassing of private capital for elites. Nevertheless, these interconnected processes are being countered through feminist and interrelated social justice struggles to deepen democratization within global civil society upon which democratization of formal politics depends. This includes democratizing feminist movements through the hard work of forging shared interests through politics, which, at its best, is an open process for debate and the expression of differences and dissent through which shared and conflicting interests can be declared, worked through, and aggregated to make change (Vickers 2006: 32–33). As argued throughout the text, but particularly in the concluding chapter, a repoliticization of commitments to social justice is key to resisting the crisis of representation and its related crises.

Notes

1 For examples of early and influential contemporary challenges by feminist political theorists to conventional constructions of politics and political actors, see, for example, Okin (1979), Jagger (1983), Benhabib and Cornell (1987), Pateman (1988), Brown (1988), and Phillips (1991).

2 UN Women (www.unwomen.org/en) was the creation of merging the following UN agencies that predated it: Office of the Special Adviser to the Secretary-General on Gender Issues and Advancement of Women (OSAGI); UNIFEM; UN Division for the Advancement of Women (UNDAW); and the UN International Research and Training Institute for the Advancement of Women (UN-INSTRAW). UN Women is on Twitter @UN_Women.

3 See www.unwomen.org/en/news/stories/2012/4/un-women-welcomes-a-landmark-action-plan-to-measure-gender-equality-across-the-un-system/.

4 See Enloe (2013) for analysis of the Strauss-Kahn scandal and its relationship to masculinist financial power.

Chapter 3

Questions for Discussion

1 What are the differences between power-over and power-with or enabling power approaches in global politics?
2 What does "global governance" refer to, what are its features, and how does it open up but also circumscribe women's and other marginalized actors' political participation at the global level?
3 What are some major impediments, associated with the gender(ed) division of power, to women's political leadership at all levels, but especially at national and international levels?
4 Why is merely "adding women" to existing global power structures through various international policymaking mechanisms insufficient for addressing the crisis of representation?

Activities for Further Research

1 Visit the UN Women's Web site (www.unwomen.org/), enter the IKNOW Politics portal (under Resources tab), and join to participate interactively in international online discussions on increasing women's political participation. What would you recommend?
2 Find a list of recent and current (non-ceremonial) female heads of state and government (such lists of women world leaders are available online), choose two such leaders, and research their paths to power and support (or not) of "women's issues" through their public pronouncements and the policies they have promoted.
3 Explore the Gender Quotas Database at www.idea.int/data-tools/data/gender-quotas. Click on various countries. Did anything surprise you in terms of the numbers and types of countries and regions with and without quotas?

4 Gender and Global Security

What is security, and how is it obtained? Whose security are we talking about? At what expense and at whose expense are national security and global security pursued? How are men, women, and even feminism militarized? How are peacemaking, peacekeeping, and peacebuilding gendered? Can security be disarmed?

Chapter 3 examined how gendered divisions of power marginalize women's (and other feminized people's) status in conventionally defined politics, as well as how the power of gender sustains the crisis of representation even in the face of recent gender policies aimed at increasing women's formal representation and attention to gender inequality as a source of world political problems. This chapter examines how *gendered divisions of violence* and the *power of gender* that produces them construct and reproduce massive insecurities, or the *crisis of insecurity*. To organize the discussion, three interacting components are identified: (1) the gendered security ideology at work (its underlying assumptions and expectations); (2) the differential effects of this ideology on differing men and women (the roles they are assigned in relation particularly to militaries); and (3) the systemic consequences of these intersectional gender dichotomies (exacerbating global insecurities even as the frequency of wars has diminished and violence against women and women's exclusion from peacemaking, peacekeeping, and peacebuilding have been identified as major impediments to peace and security). The patterns identified through the examples offered (which are, by no means, exhaustive) paint an overwhelmingly negative picture of the gendered effects of violence pursued in the name of security. However, it is necessary to understand the highly negative impacts of the gendered divisions of violence and put them in relation to the negative impacts of the gendered divisions of labor and resources that are covered in Chapter 5 in order to appreciate the varied struggles against these interrelated processes that are documented in Chapter 6.

To review, what is meant by the gendered divisions of violence are the hierarchical dichotomies of strength–weakness, aggressive–passive, war–peace, soldier–victim, and protector–protected, superior–inferior, civilized–barbarian, self–other, and us–them that divide the world into masculinized offenders and defenders and feminized populations over which they fight and seek to conquer or defend (see Table 4.1). This has long been the main story of IR, although only recently has this been understood in gender terms within IR. Moreover, although IR was founded ostensibly to address how to end war, its masculinist bias and imperialist commitments—born of its creation initially by elite, Eurocentric men who made it a useful tool for elite, Eurocentric statesmen—have made it less about ending war and more about controlling it and using it more effectively in the interests of those in power. Given the masculinist construction of politics as aggressive and combative power-over practices, it was an easy leap to argue, as Carl von Clausewitz (2004) did in the nineteenth century, that war is the extension of politics by other means.

Table 4.1 Gender/ed Divisions of Violence Productive of the Crisis of Insecurity

	Masculinized	*Feminized*
Gender (Male–Female Dynamics)	Aggressive	Passive
	Strength	Weakness
	Battlefront	Homefront
	Life-taker	Life-giver
	Soldier	Victim
	Protector	Protected
Gendered (Intersectional Dynamics)	Self	Other
	Us	Them
	Superior	Inferior
	Civilized	Barbarian/terrorist
	Violence	Non-violence
	Fighter	Civilian
	War	Peace

However, if, as argued in the last chapter, politics is seen as enabling power, then politics is the opposite of war, which shuts down debate in the face of the raw power of might makes right. Similarly, for war to be contemplated and waged "effectively," those against whom it is waged must be dehumanized (typically through feminization and racialization) in order for aggressors to feel superior and righteous in their actions. At the same time, both offenders and defenders need to justify their actions by waging war in the name of those who cannot fight and, thus, are in need of and worthy of protection (typically, a nation's or group's "own womenandchildren"). Indeed, recent feminist IR statistical research on civilian victimization underscores this central dynamic (Sjoberg and Peet 2011). Such rationales for war are disturbed by the realities that "womenandchildren" are now rarely protected from direct violence in most contemporary wars and that the structural violence of homelessness, hunger, disease, and so on visited by war, particularly in the global South, and war spending affects especially civilian populations the world over. These inconvenient truths also redirect attention to the most historically frequent reasons for war and conquest—namely, the colonizing practices of the extraction of wealth and resources through the brutalization of populations in order to destroy communities and, thus, the will to resist such extraction. But the power of gender covers up this inconvenient (and currently politically unpalatable) truth and sets up the dynamics, in the forms of the gendered divisions of violence, that justify war and other forms of violence with which it is connected.

There have long been critiques of and resistances to war by women for the harm it does—ranging from the (male-authored) fifth-century BCE fictional play *Lysistrata*, which (comically) portrays women withholding sexual servicing from men until they stopped fighting, to such an actual action by Iroquois women in the seventeenth century, which opened the way for the long peace of the Iroquois Federation and to the writings of pacifist women (such as Christine de Pizan, Bertha von Suttner, and Virginia Woolf) from the Middle Ages through the world wars (and to the present day). But it was only in the past few centuries that there has been organized resistance to war in the form of peace movements. We argue, however, that the association of peace with the (hyper)feminine and the association of war with the (hyper)masculine have disadvantaged and marginalized calls for and analyses of how to bring about peace, not only as the absence of war and other forms of direct violence but also as an end of structural violence. Only by addressing both direct and structural violence can the crisis of insecurity be reversed.

Feminist Approaches to Security

Feminist IR approaches to war and violence and peace and security, as reflected in FSS scholarship, have their roots especially in the thinking of nineteenth- and early twentieth-century women peace theorists and activists. Many of these early thinkers and activists based their arguments against war on women's maternalist desires to protect their children from the ravages of war, neither wanting their sons to become cannon fodder nor their daughters to suffer from the destruction of families and communities (Pierson 1987). For those who were steeped in the biological determinism characteristic of nineteenth- and early twentieth-century thought, these maternalist desires were seen as innate, making women "natural" peace supporters and peacemakers. Maternalist arguments continued through the Cold War, when women's peace organizations sought to protect future generations from the threat of nuclear war, and into the present day, but more recent feminist peace researchers and activists have argued that maternalism is not innate but rather the result of women being made largely responsible for "maternalist practices" or caring work, whether or not they have children (Ruddick 1984). This makes them more likely to have empathy for "others" and the world's children and to be against war and its destructive power. Contemporary feminist IR scholars examining maternalism in national and international politics (Carreon and Moghadam 2015) refer to this as "political motherhood" and make a distinction between grassroots motherhood politics, which seek to emancipate the nation from unjust rule and/or to bring peace through increasing women's political voice and agency, and state-led, patriarchal motherhood politics which advocate keeping women in the home or expecting them to uphold heteronormative patriarchal family values to serve as conservative symbols of the nation.

Both kinds of political motherhood are at work in the fact that women have historically supported wars (both imperialist wars and wars of national liberation) and fought in them, often in the name of maternalism. Sending sons and daughters to war can be seen as a patriotic motherly duty, and fighting in wars can be seen as a form of motherly protection of the homeland or mothering in a new nation (Elshtain 1987). At the same time, many women have become soldiers out of economic necessity or sought gender equality in soldiering as a ticket to full citizenship and a path to public power for women. Thus, the idea that women are either naturally or socially geared for peace has been put in question and can be an impediment, particularly in cases of state-led political motherhood, to women seeking gender equality because it bars them from or marginalizes them in militaries that control significant resources and are particularly valorized in the stories of nations and the fabric of national life. This produces a "gendered nationalism" in which only men who forged a nation in blood get to define what that nation is, regardless of whether women spilled blood for it or on its altar as (fewer) combatants or (many) non-combatants, and regardless of the many other contributions that women make to (re)producing and sustaining the life of a nation (Enloe 1989: 63). When women are seen only as the symbols and the reproducers of the nation, not as agents in its narratives, then they become subject to an array of controls over their bodies and their beings by men of the nation (Kaufman and Williams 2007: 16–18; Yuval-Davis 1997).

Nevertheless, still other contemporary feminists have shown, most recently quantitatively as noted in Chapters 1 and 2, that there is a powerful and direct relationship between international violence and domestic violence, which gives women particular interests in resisting warfare and war preparedness because it produces men who do not visit violence only on the "enemy" but also on their own wives, partners, and children. But men, too, feminists have argued, can develop interests in resisting war because of the harm it does to their bodies and psyches, leading to the destruction of their loved ones and their own selves. What keeps more men—particularly those in subordinate military positions whose bodies are most on the line—from developing such interests is the valorization of war as the penultimate masculine activity through which men can prove they are "real men" (Whitworth 2008). As pointed out in Chapters 1 and 2, heteronormative masculinity is an elastic construct, but it is also an extraordinarily fragile and unstable one. Men are never sufficiently masculine simply when they have the appropriate genitalia, and establishing masculinity is never a done deal: males face relentless pressures to demonstrate they are real men by exhibiting unequivocally masculine qualities and distancing themselves from what is defined as feminine (Kimmel 2008). Thus, masculinity is an identity that leaves men having to prove repeatedly that they have "it." They are put in constant fear and anxiety that they will be dubbed less than "real men" and, therefore, be demoted down the gender hierarchy and be subject to greater violence by other, higher men.

But even though there are high costs for subordinated men who participate in or who resist war, feminists have particularly focused on the fact that women pay high prices for its valorization and conduct. Militarized violence makes them more subject to gender violence (whether they are combatants or non-combatants) in the forms of militarized domestic violence, rape, and prostitution, and more subject to the structural violence of dislocation, poverty, and disease that war leaves in its wake. Military spending also extracts resources needed for social welfare, shredding social safety nets, which leads to the violence of desperation. But even beyond this, postcolonial feminists in particular point to the costs of women's and subordinated men's support of imperial warfare and violence, typically in the name of national security and, increasingly, global security (Eisenstein 2007). As long as wars of extraction, most typically waged on the soil of the South, are cloaked as "civilizing," "pacifying," and "liberating" missions to protect national and global security, women and subordinated men in states with imperialist ambitions can be drawn in to support them and do the work of violence associated with them. This is at the expense of forming solidarities among women and less privileged men across the North and South to resist war and the violence that most harms them. Such solidarities can be built on the recognition that exclusivist and violent ethnic nationalisms (whether of the imperialist or anti-imperialist variety) are "'integral' to globalizing processes," with "opportunistic" nationalist movements "seeking statehood in some instances" while not being able to legitimately provide for the welfare of citizens under globalization and others "sustaining their power through the market economy" (Giles and Hyndman 2004: 18).

As argued in this chapter, the power of gender obscures and militates against the potential alliances between diverse women and men and among them across borders to resist war and other forms of violence. In the process, this chapter problematizes dominant constructions of security, examines the strategy of "adding women" to security structures and policies, destabilizes assumptions undergirding the gendered divisions of violence, and takes on contemporary forces that are expanding the crisis of insecurity. It is critical of "solutions" that put peacemaking and peacebuilding solely on the backs of poorly resourced and marginalized women and vilify only certain men to deflect attention away from elites (including some women) who promote militarism and war in the name of security. But it also sees some value in what has been called "strategic essentialism" (Spivak 1987), which refers to the way groups of people like "women," who are, in reality, non-homogeneous, have diverse experiences, and have multiple and even conflicting interests, can still make political claims as a group on the basis of what they perceive as their shared perspectives and conditions on the understanding that the commonalities they identify and strategically mobilize to make political demands for change are not timeless or the result of innate traits. As such, strategic essentialism constitutes a political strategy for diverse women to articulate interests in and paths to peace and act together (with supportive men) to bring about disarmed security.

Gendered Security

War—its causes and effects—animated and has long dominated the study of IR. Since the Cold War period, war has been studied in IR under the rubric of "security" studies. In (neo) realist security studies, the maintenance of security is understood as controlling and containing, but not eliminating, direct violence between state militaries through balances of military power and nuclear terror as well as collective security measures that rely on sustaining both credible threats to use force and the actual use of force. Ironically and problematically, this ensures the continued growth of militaries and the continuation of war to promote security—but only the security of the state, not necessarily of people within or across states, and certainly not of the planet.

The early post-Cold War period of the 1990s brought more interest within the discipline in wider definitions of security, ranging from economic to human, environmental, and even food security. These redefinitions occurred in the face of new "threats" to state security (such as globalization and global warming, discussed in the next chapter), but also newly recognized notions of security arising from critical perspectives (including feminist ones) entering the field, which pointed out that state security often compromised the welfare of people and the planet. Nevertheless, conventional security studies enjoyed somewhat of a resurgence in the post-9/11 period because decisions to engage in interstate and intrastate conflict and the globalized "war on terror" once again spiked militarized violence. The resurgent interest in direct violence has once again been at the expense of attending to structural violence and the insecurities generated by structural inequalities. We must be mindful that direct and indirect (structural) violence are not separate but interdependent. The inequalities of the latter shape the expression of the former. As dire as are the effects of direct violence, indirect violence shapes the lives of all of us all of the time—and especially injures women and other subordinated and marginalized people.

Hence, feminists argue that to understand violence and insecurities, we must look not only within particular "levels" but also at the linkages among them. According to Ann Tickner,

> Feminist perspectives on security would assume that violence, whether it be in the international, national, or family realm, is interconnected. Family violence must be seen in the context of wider power relations; it occurs within a gendered society in which male power dominates at all levels . . .. Any feminist definition of security must therefore include the elimination of all types of violence, including violence produced by gender relations of domination and subordination.
>
> (Tickner 1993: 58)

But as argued here, gender violence must also be seen in combination with racialized, sexualized, and class violence to reveal the interconnections between relations of domination and subordination that are present across all levels and constitute the conditions (structural violence) and goads for war (direct violence) as well as the effects of war or militarized conflict. Unless these are taken seriously, even rival notions of (non-disaggregated) human security to state security will fail to recognize all the sources of insecurity (bred of the injustices of structural violence) and their differential effects.

At the same time, a more poststructural feminist view of security is that it is always "elusive and partial" because the quest for absolute security is in itself productive of violence: it relies on the eradication of all threats, real or imagined, and thus sets up a never-ending defensive and offensive posture (Tickner 2001: 62). Such a posture is emblematic of the "sovereign man" (Ashley 1989), who, like the sovereign state that is fashioned upon this construct of hegemonic masculinity, thwarts connection and interdependence in fear of engagement with difference that might break down walls between the sovereign "self" and the "other" on whom is projected all that one denies in oneself (Eisenstein 2007: 13).

On this point, Susan Faludi's *The Terror Dream* (2007) continues to be quite instructive. Not only does this work document the resurgence in the US of a state security discourse proffered across the airwaves, almost exclusively by military men (to the almost absolute exclusion of female and particularly feminist voices representing alternative views), in the first few years of the post-9/11 period, but it also analyzes the resurgence of older sexist and racist mythologies from America's past called up to cover up the chink in the sovereign man's armor. Faludi asks us to consider the lionizing of male rescue workers at "ground zero" (and the attendant silencing of female rescue workers long discriminated against, as well as widows who questioned the US military response, because neither conformed with adulating male protection and security at any cost), the ersatz "rescue" of US soldier Jessica Lynch supposedly from rapacious Iraqi captors (who turned out to be caring medical personnel), or overblown (and in most cases untrue) claims about women opting out of the workplace to return home to raise babies and become "security moms" in support of war. She argues that these convenient "fictions" have roots in earlier frontier stories, captivity narratives, and Cold War hysterias. These get trotted out whenever there are fears of "masculine insufficiency" because hegemonic masculinity cannot countenance "vulnerability" (Faludi 2007: 280).

When we look more closely at the events behind these earlier narratives, we find that white male frontiersmen (such as Daniel Boone) were, in fact, undistinguished as providers or protectors and more often relied on the provisioning and protective skills of their wives, children, and indigenous peoples to survive, and the majority of white women taken captive by indigenous peoples either preferred to stay with their newfound families into which they were adopted or won their release from their captors on their own (Faludi 2007: 212, 256–262). Nevertheless, Faludi argues, insecure times in patriarchal cultures ratchet up the need for elaborate mythologies that "measure national male strength by female peril," requiring that "women be saved from more and more gruesome violation to prove their saviors' valor" (2007: 262). In the US white patriarchal cultural imagination, that peril is limited to concerns for white women and symbolized most by racialized men, whether they be indigenous "captors" of old and newer Iraqi ones, the "yellow" and "Hun" hordes of World War II, or the "red" communist threat of the Cold War. In each case, fears of "alien" invasion required the "securing of American domesticity," which conjured images of (white) women (re)confined to the home front, obsessions with "women's sexual purity" supposedly at risk from racialized men, and a summoning of "John Wayne and his avenging brethren" (Faludi 2007: 282–283, 286).

Thus, in each case, we also see a "remasculinization of America" (Jeffords 1989). A number of periods of this have occurred since the 1980s. Seeking to put behind them the defeat in Vietnam that led to a more chastened view about the value of military conflict to solve problems and secure geopolitical objectives, Reagan-era neoconservatives—through public discourse and policy and even popular culture—rehabilitated the Rambo-esque masculinist and militarist values of might makes right, unfettered by "feminine" considerations about the costs and usefulness of war. The post-9/11 remasculinization of America under yet another neoconservative government was justified with resort to the necessity of war arising from some inevitable "clash of civilizations" in which one ethnic and religious fundamentalism must combat another (the West/Christianity against the East/Islam), but also with resort, at least for a short time, to the claim that the war in Afghanistan was about civilized men (in the West) saving women from barbaric men (the Taliban). Today, under a far-right regime that claimed the previous more liberal one was "weak" on security (despite a record of massive deportations and drone warfare in the midst of troop drawdowns in Iraq and Afghanistan), has reignited obsessions with "homeland security" now entwined with discourses of "America first" that justify, for example, wall-building on the basis of such specious arguments as keeping Mexican "rapists" out.

In such times, Faludi reminds us that the constant replaying of this "security myth" and the remasculinization of leadership and civil society it entails disables an alternative response. Such a response "involves learning to live with insecurity, finding accommodation with—even drawing strength from—an awareness of vulnerability" (2007: 286) in order not to create sacrificial altars, but instead to create space for multiple and less vitriolic voices and ways of acting and being.

The too easy devolution of security into continual justifications for violence has also led to feminist wariness of new processes of "securitization" associated with a widening security agenda. On the one hand, the application of the term *security* to an issue elevates it to a matter of "high politics," as security (matters of war and peace) has traditionally held pride of place in IR theory and practice. Thus, relatively new conceptions of human security and environmental security, and even more recently, food, water, energy, and health security, have brought welcome international attention to sources of structural violence that undermine the well-being of people and the planet. On the other hand, there is also a tendency to reduce these once again to state security matters to be handled not through more collective and more non-violent means, but more typically through war or some approximation of it. Resource wars, wars on terror, wars on AIDS, wars on drugs, and so on all follow a similar logic. As Zillah Eisenstein argues, the logic of war of any kind is "opposition, differentiation, and the othering of peoples" (2007: 25). Thus, gendering, racialization, classing, and sexualizing go on unabated (and become even more pronounced) in order to affix blame and control, contain, and quarantine these "new" threats. For example, racial profiling becomes a weapon in the "war on terror," targeting sexual minorities and sex workers becomes the focus of the war on AIDS, and peasant farmers become casualties of the war on drugs. Still, some feminist IR scholars see value in employing such concepts as human and environmental security through an intersectional gender lens that reveals the interrelationships between a range of insecurities produced by and through state security (Tripp, Ferree, and Ewig 2013; Detraz 2012, 2015).

The logic of war also entails resort to military means, and as more and more issues are securitized, more and more of daily life is militarized. As Cynthia Enloe (2007) points out, anyone, any group or institution, and anything can be militarized.

> To be militarized is to adopt militaristic values (e.g., a belief in hierarchy, obedience, and the use of force) and priorities as one's own, to see military solutions as particularly effective, to see the world as a dangerous place best approached with militaristic attitudes. (2007: 4)

Thus, militaries are only a small part of the actual "security" apparatus. They rely on wider civilian cultures to enact militarized values, whether in the form of wearing "fashionable" camouflage clothing, joining militaries, working for defense industries, supporting national security over civil liberties, calling for closed borders and more prisons, and so on (Enloe 2007: 4–5). As a result, although "security," perhaps more than any other activity, has been constructed as "men's" business, its logic and enactment must be shared widely to shore up the elevation of militaries as the pinnacle of masculine endeavor. As we shall see in the following sections, the price of this elevation is too high for both women and men and for the planet.

Women, Militaries, and Political Violence

Although it is often assumed that women serving in militaries is a relatively recent, "modern" phenomenon, throughout history women have fought in wars. In *Women Warriors: A History*, David Jones provides an account "of the female martial tradition in a pan-historical and global perspective" (Jones 1997: xiv). He documents how women warriors have had an important presence across cultures and throughout history. They have led armies, constituted women's battalions, passed themselves off as male soldiers, rallied the troops as symbolic leaders, defended family and community structures in the absence of men, and exhibited the same courage, loyalty, steadfastness, heroism, and even bloodthirstiness that we associate with male warriors. Jones argues that "from the beginning women shared the qualitative experience of the warrior; everything men have ever done in warfare, women have also done, and, in many instances, they have done it better" (1997: xiii). Despite such evidence and the fact that even in the US it is increasingly more commonplace to hear references to "men and women" in the armed forces and the gender-neutral term "troops" (not to mention now ubiquitous Hollywood images of heroic and villainous women who engage in extreme and supernatural violence), there is still discomfort with—and even a desire to reject—the image and, indeed, the reality of *women warriors*. Still lingering and still powerful gendered divisions of violence account for this.

Gendered Divisions of Violence at Work

With modern state-making, gendered divisions became codified in particular ways. Liberalism in political theory favored divisions of power into public–private, government–household, whereas capitalism in economic theory favored divisions of labor into paid–unpaid, productive–reproductive. Interacting with these developments, modern state-making promoted particular divisions of violence. Masculinity involved not only heading the household and earning a "family wage" but also being prepared to defend "home and country." As Jean Bethke Elshtain notes,

> War is the means to attain recognition, to pass, in a sense, the definitive test of political manhood. . . . The man becomes what he in some sense is meant to be by being absorbed in the larger stream of life: war and the state.
>
> (Elshtain 1992: 143)

Femininity involved not only bearing and rearing children and maintaining the home front, but also serving, symbolically and literally, as the object that required protection. Whereas men served their country in combat as "life-takers," women served their country as mothers, as "life-givers" (Elshtain 1987).

In recent centuries, most male-dominated societies have constructed elaborate sanctions and even taboos against women as warriors, especially against women bearing arms and initiating violence. As a result, men gained almost exclusive control over the means of destruction worldwide, often in the name of protecting women (and children), who are either discouraged from or not allowed to take up arms to protect themselves or to be warriors protecting others. It is, therefore, not surprising that war—which remains the centerpiece of IR—is seen as *men's* deadly business. As argued here, however, war has always involved women as well as the power of gender to promote masculine characteristics—typically, as already noted, at the expense of cooperation, interdependence, and conflict resolution (Grant 1994). Moreover, the identification of war with men and peace with women completely unravels in the face of war practices over time in which civilians, not just combatants, have been subject to a significant direct violence and even more to structural violence.

As life-givers, women are not only prevented from engaging in combat but are also expected to restore "life" after a death-dealing war is over. Women are expected to mourn dutifully the loved ones who fell in war and then to produce new lives for the nation to replace its lost members. Thus, after the devastation, they must "pick up the pieces" and create the conditions for repopulating society. These conditions include creating more men, who too often serve as soldiers, and more women, who bear sons only to lose them too often through war. The work of men as life-takers thus creates perpetual work for women as life-givers.

In this sense, women are not separate from either the production or the consequences of war, even though they are often prevented from engaging in direct combat. Yet, in spite of their participation, women remain associated with war's opposite—peace. By denying the historical construction of gender stereotypes, the characterization of "woman" as passive and submissive is often translated into the idea that women are pacifist by nature. This reinforces the stereotype of women as life-givers and portrays them as insufficiently fit or motivated to be life-takers. The assumption that women have a natural revulsion against war also makes them undesirable partners in combat: how can women be trusted on the battleground if they are unwilling to fight and kill? Men, in contrast, are stereotyped as naturally aggressive and competitive, which presumably prepares them to kill or be killed. In addition, through heteronormative lenses, it is assumed that the presence of women on the battlefield will distract men from fighting successfully, perhaps by turning their aggressions away from fighting and toward sexual conquest or by tying them down to protect "weaker" female comrades, thereby endangering the pursuit of body counts. In this view, men might lose the war by pursuing or protecting women on the battlefield rather than fighting successfully to protect women at home.

After the battle, women are expected to take care of returning soldiers, salving their wounds and psyches as well as meeting needs—for food, clothing, and shelter—previously met by the military. When the "boys come home," women are expected to serve them and to do so with gratitude for those who fought and took life on behalf of their women and their nation. If women fail in these duties, then male protectors are often given tacit approval to "discipline" their women, through physical violence if necessary. Such physical violence is learned on the playground when boys "play" war in preparation for their adult roles as potential soldiers. The role is honed when men are actually trained by militaries and participate in "real" wars. Life-takers have no responsibility for "unlearning" these skills when they leave the war front; global statistics on domestic violence suggest that men may use these skills against the women and children they protected in wartime if the latter do not please them in the home. Thus, those who are denied access to the means of destruction to protect themselves during wartime also have little protection against the wartime protectors who may turn violent in the home (Sharoni 1995: 127; Nikolic-Ristanovic 1996).

As Faludi's (2007) study of the continuation of the security myth previously discussed shows, gender dichotomies such as the following are still powerfully at work in reproducing ever-expanding variations on the gendered division of violence: soldiers–mothers, protectors–protected, aggressive–passive, battlefront–home front, batterers–victims. However, it is becoming harder to sustain these dichotomies in the face of women's greater visibility in the armed forces and their activities as perpetrators of political violence (that is, sanctioned or extralegal violence against or in the name of the state) in recent years. These still constitute in relative terms what Elshtain (1987) refers to as the "ferocious few," but they nevertheless challenge the old story to a degree.

Military Women

Just as conforming to rising UN-sponsored gender equality norms (at least in terms of rhetoric and formal policy if not in terms of actual enforcement and results) is motivated by states' desires to appear modern, the presence of women in a state's armed forces is increasingly seen as another mark of modernity. By 1994 there were more than 500,000 female soldiers serving in regular and irregular armed forces (Smith 1997: 64), but women still typically made up less than 10 percent of state militaries as a whole, with many militaries still excluding them altogether. There were some increases, however, in those countries with the highest percentages in the mid-1990s. By 2005, the US went from 12 to 15 percent; Canada, from 12 to 16.3 percent; and New Zealand, from 14 to 15 percent, with others holding relatively steady, such as Australia at 13 percent and Russia at 11 percent. Israel, Latvia, and South Africa had the highest percentages of women in the military, at 37, 23, and 22 percent, respectively (Enloe 2007: 70; Seager 2009: 103). By 2010, New Zealand and Australia increased to 16.5 and 15.7 percent, respectively, but Canada was down to 14.5 percent (Mathers 2013), indicating that upward progress is not only slow, but also can be reversed. Canadian data reveal that as of 2014, 14.8 percent of the total of the Canadian Armed Forces, including regular and primary reserve forces, were women, which is a slight uptick from 2010 (Government of Canada 2014). But, as of 2015, both the New Zealand and Australian militaries showed a drop to 15 percent and 15.3 percent, respectively, from 2010 figures (Gillies 2015; Defence People Group, Department of Defence, Australia 2015: 11). The Russian military's female representation has dropped significantly in recent years. In 2013, under 4 percent of the Russia military was made up of women, which further dropped in 2015 to under 2 percent (McDermott 2013; European Country of Origin Information Network 2015). In Austria in 2014, only 1.8 percent of its military was composed of women (Koeszegi, Zedlacher, and Hudribusch 2014: 227). Israel's military in 2015 remained one-third women (Lomsky-Feder and Sasson-Levy 2015: 178) and as of 2017, the Latvian armed forces were composed of 17 percent women (NATO 2017). Twenty-five percent of South Africa's military forces were women as of 2015 (Cape Chameleon 2016). Perhaps the most visible all-female fighting unit is within the Peshmerga, a Kurdish force that fights against the Islamic State of Iraq and Syria (ISIS) both as state military troops under the Kurdistan Regional Government of Iraq and as a militia within the Syrian Democratic Forces.

As of 2017, women remained at 15 percent of active-duty military personnel in the US. The greatest number of US military women personnel serve in the Air Force (19 percent) while the branch with the lowest female presence is the Marines (8 percent), with US women at 18 percent of the Navy and 14 percent of the Army (Parker, Cilluffo, and Stepler 2017). Notably, female military active-duty personnel are more racially and ethnically diverse than their male counterparts, as, for example, 31 percent of service women but only 16 percent of service men were African American in 2011 (Patten and Parker 2011; Eager 2014). In the same year, Latinas constituted 19.6 percent of Marine enlistments and Asian and Pacific Islander women constituted 20 percent of Navy enlistments (Enloe 2014: 152).

The vast majority of countries disallow or substantially limit women in combat, although, significantly, the US ended its policy of combat exclusion in 2013, opening up as many as 200,000 more positions for women in the US military. In addition to the still relatively low rates of female participation in state militaries worldwide that speak to the continuing masculinization of military jobs, Enloe (2007) reminds us that increases in women's soldiering must be analyzed very carefully. On the surface, they may appear to be the product of "'postsexist' enlightenment" and modernity, but underneath there are different stories (Enloe 2007). The unprecedented South African case represents the results of a postapartheid debate (that included feminists) about the need to create more democratic armed forces in terms of both race and gender, but the Israeli case reveals a more cynical approach that relies on conscripting Israeli women to make them complicit in the occupation of Palestine while portraying Israeli female solders as sexual appendages to and assigning them more domestic duties in the army to keep them in their place (Enloe 2007: 73, 75).

Also contributing to women's relatively low participation in most state militaries is the fact that many countries still ban LGBT people from their armed forces.[1] Although by 2017 most global North and some global South states had lifted bans on the military service of lesbian, gay, and bisexual people, only 19 countries, exclusively in the global North, had fully lifted such bans for trans people, and the US Trump administration is in the midst of reversing the trans ban lifted by the Obama administration in 2016. Other forms of discrimination against women in the military continue to operate. Despite the fact that women have "routinely been assigned to combat operations" (Enloe 2007: 66) in the US wars in Afghanistan and Iraq in which by 2015 over 280,000 US women had served (Military.com 2015; DAV 2015: 2), formal combat exclusions, only recently lifted, have disabled most women from claiming the combat experience that has often served as a prerequisite or a test of leadership skills for those seeking high political office. Moreover, when we consider that as of 2016, worldwide military spending reached $1.69 trillion, with the US accounting for 36.2 percent of that, followed distantly by China at 12.7 percent and Russia at 4.1 percent,[2] the considerable resources devoted to war-making end up in overwhelmingly male (and mostly Western) hands. These huge political and material consequences for women of men dominating the means of destruction are sustained by keeping women's numbers down in militaries and by creating elaborate prohibitions on and punishments of women who do get into militaries.

Although women enter militaries for many of the same reasons as men (including out of patriotism or nationalism), in the US they report most often that it is for education, jobs, and career training (Eisenstein 2007: 21). However, because militaries are first and foremost about maintaining masculine (typically along with racial majority and class) privilege, women must enter them on certain terms—those that conform to "gender differentiation" (Eisenstein 2007: 6) while at the same time adopting masculinist militarist values. While the film version of *GI Jane* (1997) had her become a "man" to fit into the culture of an elite commando unit and thereby end the sexual harassment she was subjected to by her comrades-in-arms,[3] the more typical reality for women soldiers is they are expected to remain "women" and put up and shut up about sexual harassment and assault, which goes on in "epidemic" proportions, despite revelations about it over the past three decades that supposedly were being addressed by military hierarchies.

From the 1991 Navy Tailhook Convention and the 1996 US Army Proving Ground scandals to the 2012 Lackland Air Base case and the 2017 Marine photo scandal (see Box 4.1 for this

Box 4.1 Gender Violence in the Military: US Marine Photo Scandal

It came to light in 2017 that almost all male Marines in the US armed forces were sharing for several years amongst themselves on their closed group Facebook, Instagram, and Tumblr accounts nude photographs of female Marines that were obtained illicitly. Female Marine complaints were met with no action and even derision, leading some to resign. As one female veteran put it, "this diminished me. It took away everything. My voice didn't matter because my nudes were out there." As a female member of the Army observed, "in the Marine Corps it's a brotherhood that doesn't have room for women" (quoted in Gibbons-Neff 2017).

latest scandal), evidence continues to pile up that sexual harassment and assault are rife within all US military branches. Similar scandals have rocked Canadian, Australian, and Israeli armed forces, to name just a few. Just prior to the release of the 2013 Department of Defense (DOD) report on military sexual assault within the ranks (DOD 2013), which found that reported sexual assaults had increased from 3,192 in 2011 to 3,374 in 2012 and an estimated 26,000 assaults occur each year (an average of 70 per day), the Academy Award-nominated documentary *The Invisible War* (2012) was aired. It detailed the stories of multiple female and male survivors of sexual assault in the military from the 1970s on, the punishments they received for reporting their rapes, and the damage done to their mental health and their careers not just by their rapists, but also at the hands of the military chain of command and its anemic and victim-blaming approaches to dealing with the rampant problem. The film, building on the organizing work of the Service Women's Action Network, had already triggered congressional hearings to upbraid the military for its poor response and for structural perversities that forced victims to report their rapes to their superior officers, even when these were their rapists or friends of their rapists, and allowed superior officers to overturn rape convictions adjudicated in military courts. The DOD's 2013 report, coupled with allegations that at least two officers charged with overseeing sexual assault response and prevention had committed sexual assault and domestic violence, redoubled the efforts of congresswomen to introduce bills to take sexual assault and harassment reporting and adjudication out of the hands of the chain of command. The latest report on military sexual assault within the US military found that reported sexual assaults had decreased from 20,300 sexual assaults in 2014 to 14,900 in 2016, which averages out to about 41 assaults per day (DOD 2017: 9).

While more men have come forward to report sexual abuse (perpetrated almost exclusively by heterosexual men), women constitute the vast majority of those who report sexual harassment and assault (Enloe 2014: 154–155), leading to only 160 convictions that resulted in court-martial in 2012. In 2015, 6,083 reported sexual assaults led to 543 court-martials. Of these court-martials, 254 cases resulted in charges related to sexual assault—only a 4 percent conviction rate (Tilghman 2016). Thus, while military officialdom primarily in the West now tracks sexual crimes and has even recognized Military Sexual Trauma (MST) as a debilitating outcome of them, it is typically only after some highly visible incident or event that more serious responses are demanded. Heretofore, keeping the lid on sexual assault in the military has typically been driven by the fear of undermining male soldier morale (and recruiting) by reducing the sexual privileges that heterosexual male soldiers expect to go along with the job.

At the same time, women have been discouraged from reporting such incidents because they are rarely acted on except to punish those who do report (and who are also threatened with retaliation, including death, by perpetrators for reporting), but also in the name of protecting (male) military morale to which they are expected to kowtow. Revelations about the extent of gender violence have catapulted concerns about the cost of this to military readiness, which is what largely drives attempts to address it. What is not discussed is how an institution that is organized for "sanctioned" masculinist violence can eradicate newly "unsanctioned" masculinist violence. Gender violence in the military mirrors the experiences of civilian women in other male-dominated occupations, but there are deadlier twists in the case of the military, which is a far more captive and dangerous environment for military women (and feminized men), who are at more risk from their own militaries than from foreign ones, even as female casualties have mounted on the battlefield.

Feminists who question whether it is possible to democratize the military tend also to question democratizing moves by the military insofar as an increased presence of women serves to legitimize the institution by giving it a façade of egalitarianism. When women accept the "warrior mystique," they soften the image of the military as an agent of coercion/destruction and help promote the image of the military as a democratic institution, an "equal opportunity employer" like any other, without reference to its essential purpose. In this sense, they serve as what Zillah Eisenstein (2007) refers to as "sexual" or "gender decoys" (and in the case of women of color, "race" as well as gender decoys). Such decoys "camouflage" and distract attention from any actual evaluation of the efficacy of militaries and the consequences of militarist values. If the symbol of modernity is the equal participation of women in acts of torture, such as those perpetrated at the Abu Ghraib prison in Iraq by US women soldiers, then gender equality based on women conforming to masculinist and racist norms becomes not a significant source for reducing structural and direct violence but rather a basis for furthering it.

Women's Political Violence

Despite the seemingly more commonplace event of seeing women in militaries, the image of them as actual killers and purveyors of other forms of direct violence, rather than simply "support" personnel who happen to carry weapons, still remains unsettling under the gendered division of violence. It is particularly unsettling when that violence is "proscribed violence," or violence that violates laws within and between states, including torture, genocide, and terrorism. As Laura Sjoberg and Caron Gentry (2007) argue, women who commit such political violence are reduced to mothers, monsters, or whores (or all three) to explain their behaviors because they are not accorded rational political motivations for their crimes. The association of aberrant violence with aberrant womanhood has a long pedigree. As Kelly Oliver points out, motherhood is constructed as Janus-faced in patriarchal culture—at one and the same time the source of life-giving and the source of death (through the power of withholding nourishment from infants and the symbol of mother earth to which the dead return) (2007: 21). Female sexuality is also constructed as intoxicating, beguiling, and more treacherous than anything men can deploy, and women's bodies themselves are seen as sources of concealment and dangerous fluids (Oliver 2007: 31, 38). Thus, it is a fine line in these imaginings between women's natural passivity and womanhood gone mad if not properly restrained. This supposed dual nature of women is used not only to justify their control but also to explain their behavior. But as Oliver also chronicles, this mythology has been "rationally" deployed in calculated ways to make women's bodies weapons in the "war on terror."

Detainees at Guantánamo Bay were smeared with (fake) menstrual blood by US interrogators, and all-female teams of interrogators practiced "sexual lechery" on the most "troublesome" inmates to break them (Oliver 2007: 28–29).

Thus, in an age of terror, women are constituted as the most ruthless and terrorizing when unleashed. This then accounts for the particular horror many found in the real-world images of US women soldiers sexually terrorizing inmates at Abu Ghraib because it evoked deep patriarchal (and heteronormative) fears (Peterson 2007; Puar 2007). These acts were also dismaying to those feminists who held out some faith in women as being more peaceful and potentially tempering of military excesses. But in the uproar over the (un)naturalness of women torturers, attention was deflected from what we now know was state-sponsored torture and terrorism, not just the work of a few bad girls and boys.

As Sjoberg and Gentry (2007, 2011) and Gentry and Sjoberg (2015) have chronicled, women have long engaged in state and (both left- and right-wing) insurgency terrorism, most often in logistical support roles, but also as perpetrators of direct violence. However, it is in the twenty-first century that women have become highly visible as torturers, suicide bombers, hijackers, kidnappers, and genocidaires. During much of the twentieth century, some women, primarily in the West, gained some notoriety for their involvement (including playing leadership roles) in the Ku Klux Klan and the Weather Underground in the US, the Baader-Meinhoff gang in Germany, the Red Brigades in Italy, the Irish Republican Army in Northern Ireland, and the like. The focus of Western counter-terrorist policymakers today is trained on the rise in non-Western (primarily Islamic) women's terrorist acts, particularly in the form of suicide bombings (or martyrdom operations as they are referred to in the Middle East), 26 percent of which had been attributed to women by 2007 (Brown 2011: 194). In 2016, women were involved in 16.4 percent of the suicide bombings that took place that year (INSS 2017: 1, 3). Seeing this rise as evidence of the increasing uncontrollability of insurgents and a measure of their desperation, security policymakers construct women, especially in the Islamic world, as particularly dangerous security threats (Sjoberg, Cooke, and Neal 2011: 5). That al-Qaeda began recruiting women to conduct suicide bombings as a strategic move and a way to swell its ranks with both women and men has heightened the state security lens through which women in the Islamic world are now being scrutinized, demonized, and pathologized (Brown 2011). Rather than seeing women who commit insurgent terrorist violence as willing actors responding to political crises and resisting, as a matter of nationalist and/or religious duty, the insecurities they experience, the securitized (and Orientalist) lens on female suicide bombers, whether they be members of the Tamil Tigers in Sri Lanka, the Chechen rebels in Russia, Hamas in Palestine, or al-Qaeda in Iraq, portrays them as vengeful mothers, brainwashed dupes of Islam, or monsters. Such a lens deflects attention away from the political claims of their movements and the role state terrorism has played in producing insurgent movements.

State terrorists include such genocidaires as Biljana Plavšić of Serbia and Pauline Nyiramasuhuko of Rwanda, both of whom have been tried by the International Criminal Tribunals for Yugoslavia and Rwanda, respectively, for their roles in fomenting genocide and genocidal rape in those countries in the 1990s. To attempt to excuse their actions, they fell back on gender stereotypes, constructing themselves as avenging or protective mothers of the nation, while being portrayed as madwomen by others (Sjoberg and Gentry 2007: 152, 155, 165, 167; see also Gentry and Sjoberg 2015). Such stereotypes denied that both were highly educated, highly placed political women who used their political power to perpetrate political genocide, not victims of maternalism gone awry. As long as the latter is foregrounded, then genocide as a political act of which anyone is capable given the means, ideologies, and contexts is backgrounded. Similarly, as long as women are constructed only as victims, the brutal treatment of them will be invited in times of war and "peace."

In short, violence can be "resexed," in Eisenstein's (2007) words, as long as it does not disturb the power of gender to valorize violence, militarism, and war. Moreover, femininity can be militarized without threatening male privilege and can even bolster it as long as women play "idealized militarized femininity" roles as "capable" but "sanitized" and supportive "Just Warriors" who retain the "innocence" and "vulnerability" of "Beautiful Souls" (Sjoberg and Gentry 2007: 86).

Men, Militaries, and Gender Violence

In societies where masculinity is associated with power-over and violence, men are under constant pressure to prove their manhood by being tough, adversarial, and aggressive. There are, of course, a variety of forms of male aggression that have been deemed unacceptable or illegitimate within civil societies (such as murder, assault, gang warfare, and, at least in terms of the laws of some countries, wife battering and child abuse). However, in one highly legitimated and organized institution within most societies, men not only can but also—to be successful—must prove their masculinity through violence: the military.

State militaries serve many functions. According to world politics wisdom of the (neo) realist variety, militaries serve to protect the borders of states and the citizens within them from outside aggression, inevitable given the anarchic interstate system, which is based on power politics, not the rule of law. In this view, militaries are deemed necessary for the maintenance of national security, either as deterrents to would-be aggressors or as effective fighting machines capable of vanquishing actual aggressors.

More critical world politics perspectives see militaries serving other less laudable functions, such as protecting repressive state elites from rebellion by their own people. This is often described as maintaining the internal security of states at the expense of non-elite citizens. Also, militaries are implicated in maintaining permanent war economies arising from the infamous "military-industrial complex," which organizes a state's economy around producing weapons rather than civilian goods. Under such conditions, the military can become one of the few sites for "employment," not only for the poor and least educated who turn to soldiering or working in weapons plants but also for large numbers of middle class voters engaged in, for example, research and development activities. More recently, there have been references to the "security-industrial complex" that has arisen since 9/11 in which private industries are organized around producing and purveying intelligence, surveillance, and control systems as extensions of the state and even providing private armies for the state, such as the infamous Blackwater (now known as Academi) operation in Iraq. Such private military and security companies (PMSCs) have increasingly become a subject of feminist inquiry (Eichler 2015), which has found that they are hypermasculinized and far more racially organized and heteronormalized as compared with regular armies, as well as more costly not just in economic terms but also with respect to more indiscriminate and colonizing violence for which they are also unaccountable. It is also no accident in neoliberal times that the "prison-industrial complex," in which inmates are used as captive slave labor to produce goods for private industries and are surveilled and controlled at ever higher levels in increasingly private prisons and increasingly worldwide (Sudbury 2005), has emerged simultaneously with the security-industrial complex, which organizes not only the economy but also much of life around the dictates of security at the expense of human rights and welfare.

Despite now voluminous feminist research on the subject, many critical global politics observers still fail to address or analyze the role that militaries play in producing and reproducing masculinity. As Enloe argues, militaries need men to act as "men"—that is, to be willing to kill and die on behalf of the state (or rivals to it) to prove their "manhood" (1983: 212). This remains the linchpin for sustaining vast coercive apparatuses and practices.

Militarized Masculinity

As a social construct, masculinity is not a given but rather is made. Moreover, as pointed out in Chapter 1, there are multiple masculinities, most typically divided up between hegemonic masculinity (associated with elite, Western, upper-class, race-privileged, and heterosexual men) and subordinate masculinities (associated with racial minority or global South, lower-class, and sexual minority men). But the nature of hegemonic masculinity also shifts over time as well as across cultures. According to Charlotte Hooper, there have been at least four forms of Western hegemonic masculinity historically: the "Greek citizen-warrior," the "patriarchal Judeo-Christian model," the "honor-patronage" form, and the "Protestant, bourgeois-rationalist" man (2001: 64). She hypothesizes that in the 1990s a new "globalization" man was emerging, particularly in the Anglo-American context. These differing formations, although emerging over time, never cancel each other out. Rather, each morphs from the last so that each model retains elements of previous ones adapted to maintain hegemony in the face of changing socioeconomic, geopolitical, and even technological contexts (Hooper 2001: 65). Thus, although the homosocial martial qualities of the Greek citizen-warrior and the military heroism and risk-taking adventurism bound up in the European aristocratic ideal of the honor-patronage system are downplayed in the more modern bourgeois-rational man—who is all about the "reason and self-control or self-denial" needed to command capitalism rather than armies—aggression and power-over remain common threads (Hooper 2001: 65). They are simply rechanneled for new arenas of power. The captains of industry and the titans of finance who followed in the age of globalization speak in martial terms, wield economic and technological weapons, and aspire to ruthless takeovers. Such men no longer need hard bodies and physical strength to play out their martial identities, but they carry on the ideal of militarized masculinity nonetheless.

Even though actual military service as the ultimate test of manhood has been somewhat displaced as hegemonic masculinity came to be expressed in other forums, for most men without the highest class privilege and in patriarchal culture more generally, it retains pride of place as the most masculine activity. It also enjoyed somewhat of a renaissance in the post-9/11 period with the heavy reenactment of the security myth that has re- and hyper-valorized male military protection and rescue. As the titans of finance faltered in the face of the economic crisis of their own making, globalization man gave way to some extent to "security man." We are now witnessing some *uber*-security men on the world stage in the form of new (and older) authoritarian leaders. Some are military generals in charge of states; others, like Trump, were never soldiers, but lionize and rely on military generals as their source of authority and legitimacy.

As we saw previously, modern militaries actively preserve the association between masculinity and militaries by limiting the participation of women and effeminate or feminized (gay, trans) men. But they also actively construct militarized masculinity through the making of soldiers. As Sandra Whitworth chronicles, this involves a whole range of grueling, humiliating, and degrading techniques, starting in boot camp, to break down men's (and a smaller number of women's) sense of individuality and inhibitions about violence and then to build up conformity, "toughness, obedience, discipline, patriotism, lack of squeamishness; avoidance of certain emotions such as fear, sadness, uncertainty, guilt, remorse and grief, and heterosexual competency" (2008: 114). To make a militarized man means "killing the woman" in him (Whitworth 2008: 114), but as Aaron Belkin (2012) argues, it more accurately entails being forced to live out the contradictions, in a world based on hierarchical gender dichotomies, of being simultaneously masculinized and demasculinized. As he puts it, "The U.S. military has compelled the troops to embody masculinity and femininity" by requiring them to dwell in the "filth" of combat training and combat while kowtowing to the military's obsession with "cleanliness" (e.g., being hygienic and free of sexual disease contamination); to be both "impenetrable" as a predominantly heterosexual male fighting force protecting the homeland and "penetrable" in a military culture rife with routinized heterosexual-male-on-heterosexual-male rape; to be both "dominant" over those invaded and "subordinate" to the chain of command; and to uphold "civilization" as a "noble institution" through "barbarism" against those deemed uncivilized (Belkin 2012: 173).

Thus, alongside and underneath the norms and façade of militarized masculinity (or hypermasculinity) lie deeply feminizing processes in an institution based on relations of domination and subordination. Such relations not only are normalized by the institution, but also structure a military masculinity that requires servicemen in particular to embody both domination and subordination while disavowing feminine weaknesses. Internalizing these contradictions makes militarized men particularly susceptible to obedience to a military that demands they conform to this schizoid structure of military masculinity, but it also ensures that they rarely report the sexual assault and the post-traumatic stress disorder (PTSD) that are pandemic in the military. Previously referred to as shell shock during the world wars, the more clinical diagnosis of PTSD was applied during the Vietnam War, and it was later found that 30 percent of male Vietnam veterans suffered from it (Whitworth 2008: 115). The particularly high rates of it for soldiers coming out of Iraq and Afghanistan, partially as a result of continuous redeployments, endanger the mystique of the warrior brotherhood and its invincibility. Thus, male soldiers are discouraged from reporting their symptoms and censor themselves for fear of seeming weak and unmanly. Indeed, US soldiers with PTSD, numbering approximately 300,000 in 2009 (Alvarez and Eckholm 2009: A1), are still disallowed from receiving the Purple Heart in honor of their sacrifice, further pushing sufferers in the closet. Left untreated, the symptoms of "anxiety, fear of death, anger, depression, nightmares" and "hypervigilance" from reliving battlefield memories can also result in "unemployment, alcoholism, and even suicide," as well as divorce, domestic violence, and even murder (Whitworth 2008: 116).

Contemporary military efforts to play down the vulnerability of the male psyche are matched by current military efforts to compensate for the vulnerability of the male body. Armoring military men is not new, but Cristina Masters (2008) argues that the modifications and extensions of the male body have reached new heights, creating a "cyborg soldier" who will never die and will be willing to kill without remorse. The extreme technologicalization of postmodern warfare, symbolized by the Obama administration's reliance on drone warfare, but more recently by the dropping of the "Mother of All Bombs" on Syria by the Trump administration, seeks to circumvent the comparatively weaker male body, inserting it within machineries of command and control both in and highly distant from the battlefield that are "stronger, faster, more agile, and have much more staying power" (Masters 2008: 95). This displacement of militarized masculinity onto machineries enables such masculinity ideologically to survive the maimings and deaths of flesh-and-blood male bodies, assuring that militarized conflict will not be slowed down by the failings of male bodies and that the maiming and killing of "other" flesh-and-blood bodies will not be seen as other than "blips on radar screens, infrared images, precision-guided targets and numbers and codes on computer screens" (Masters 2008: 99). Thus, militaries are able to retain the mystique of militarized masculinity by disembodying it, even as they still rely on male bodies to represent them and do much of their work.

Of course, the reality is that male warriors still die and are maimed psychologically and physically in great numbers because they make up the vast majority of the world's fighters—"the militant many" (Elshtain 1987). According to Joshua Goldstein, the twentieth century, possibly the "bloodiest relative to population" on record, produced approximately 110 million war dead from both direct and indirect violence (such as "war-induced famines and epidemics") (2011: 36–37). Combatants made up two-thirds of those killed by direct violence, while civilians made up two-thirds of those killed by indirect and direct violence. Direct violence is most often perpetrated by males on other males, but the "collateral damage" is much greater for non-combatants, although who among non-combatants suffer most depends on the conflict and the nature of it at any given time. Estimates of civilian deaths from violence in the Iraq War between 2003 and 2017 range from 171,137 to 190,891 with 268,000 total fatalities including combatants, and it appears that the great majority of civilians killed in that war have been men performing police and neighborhood and private security work.[4] In the case of the war in Afghanistan, civilian deaths (estimated at more than 31,000 since 2001, with 41,000 civilians injured since 2001)[5] have also been much greater than US and coalition forces fatalities (3,528 between 2001 and 2016, albeit with an additional 17,674 US combatants wounded from 2001 to 2012[6]). Early numbers for 2017 reveal a 5 percent increase in civilian casualties compared to the same period in 2016, and the number of female civilians killed and wounded increased by 24 percent.[7] These costs of war do not count the millions of refugees and internally displaced persons (IDPs) and the amount of food, shelter, and health insecurities produced or worsened by these two twenty-first-century conflicts, with the Iraq conflict resulting in the creation of ISIS that has killed at least 1,400 people and enslaved thousands more, mostly women and children of the Yazidi community in Syria, while the coalition against ISIS has killed an estimated 5,961 civilians as of November 2017, particularly as a result of far more massive and indiscriminate aerial bombing by the US and Russia.[8] Thus, male combatants pay a heavy price in terms of their lives, their psyches, their bodies, and even their humanity; however, civilians of all genders bear the largest brunt of past and contemporary armed conflicts, which goes well beyond dying in them.

Gender Violence

"Gender violence" typically refers to acts of domestic and sexual violence directed at maintaining gender hierarchies and punishing femininities. It most often means male violence against women, ranging from battering and burning to sexual harassment, assault, mutilation, slavery, trafficking, and torture as well as forced pregnancy and sterilization. However, men also visit gender violence on other men, and women, too, can commit gender violence against other women and men. Women's gender violence occurs less frequently, and because it often involves fewer weapons, it often produces less physical harm; however, armed women and women who have the power to use men as proxies to perform their gender violence can exact considerable harm. Gender violence can also refer to violence visited upon LGBTQ people targeted for their sexuality and gender. Although notoriously underreported in national and UN statistics, gender violence is acknowledged by the UN as epidemic throughout much of the world and across cultures, ethnicities, and classes. It is a regular feature of civilian life in heteronormative patriarchal societies, but it is especially rife in military settings. As we have seen, military women suffer gender violence most frequently at the hands of their male comrades, and this is the largest cause of PTSD and/or MST suffered by women soldiers (Whitworth 2008: 120). Military wives and girlfriends experience domestic violence at the hands of their male partners at three to five times the rate that women in civilian relationships do, and men "who have been in combat are four times more likely to be physically abusive" (Eisenstein 2007: 24). In the US, rates of domestic and sexual abuse in military families particularly escalated since 9/11 (Eisenstein 2007: 24).

Even though widespread gender violence by "friendly" forces against their own is unsanctioned in theory, militaries actually institutionalize gender violence against "allied" and "enemy" women. According to Enloe, there are

> three "types" of institutionalized militarized rape: "recreational rape"—the assumption that soldiers need constant access to sexual outlets; "national security rape"—when police forces and armies use rape to bolster the state's control over a population; and systematic mass rape as an instrument of open warfare.
>
> (quoted in Seager 1997: 116)

Although recreational rape is a feature of most state militaries, it is particularly associated with the US military, in part because the US maintains the largest number of foreign military bases. This aspect of the US military gained worldwide attention in September 1995 when two marines and a navy seaman gang-raped a 12-year-old Japanese girl in Okinawa (Seager 1997: 116). The storm of protest and anti–US military feelings on the part of the Japanese that this case evoked have not stopped military bases from also being deeply implicated in the business of prostitution.

Many military men have come to expect sexual servicing not as a perk but as a right and even a necessity during their stints overseas. Given that recreational rape can unleash protest against a foreign military presence (as in the Okinawan case), providing military men access to legitimate sex (with prostitutes) has been a policy of the US government. As part of Status of Forces Agreements (SOFAs) between the US government and its allies that codify the conditions under which US forces can be stationed in a host territory (Enloe 2000: 92), there are R&R agreements that detail the conditions for permitting and controlling the sexual servicing of the US military (Enloe 1993: 154). Perhaps the most notorious site was Subic Bay Naval Base in the Philippines. In the late 1980s, Filipino feminist organizations reported that as a result of high unemployment and extreme poverty, more than 20,000 Filipino women and about 10,000 Filipino children regularly acted as prostitutes for US servicemen at Subic Bay (Enloe 1989: 66). This situation contributed not only to the spread of HIV/AIDS but also to racial tensions and nationalist fervor: Filipinas/os denounced militarized prostitution as a symbol of their compromised sovereignty. The Subic Bay base was closed in 1991 when the Philippine government revoked its lease, but it has recently reopened, given close relations between Trump and authoritarian Philippines leader Rodrigo Duterte, to counter China's activities in the South China Sea. Thus, we are already seeing an uptick in the nexus between military bases and prostitution and other forms of sex work there (Enloe 2014: 167–168) as well as elsewhere.

Katharine Moon's study of the SOFAs between the US and South Korea since the Korean War finds that the numerous "camptowns" that grew up around US troops stationed there, particularly between the 1950s and 1970s, constituted a "GI's Heaven" where "20,000 registered prostitutes were available to 'service' approximately 62,000 US soldiers by the late 1960's" for as little as $2 for a half-hour sexual encounter (1997: 30). In the face of rising venereal disease, HIV/AIDS, and racial tensions born of Korean women's disinclination to service military men of color, US and Korean military officials engaged in elaborate measures to "clean up" the camptowns. These efforts were not designed to protect sex workers or to change the postwar economy that left so many primarily rural women, as well as men and children, scrambling to provide "entertainment" for GIs, but rather to make them safer for GIs to continue to be sexually serviced with less fear of disease and racial discrimination. As Moon argues, in this way the US–South Korean alliance was preserved on the backs of women literally on their backs.[9] Although nuclear war-mongering between US and North Korean leaders has subsided for now in the wake of the 2018 Singapore summit (where human rights were not even raised), this is no guarantee US troops will be withdrawn from South Korea or that this alliance dynamic will not continue on the Korean peninsula or on or near US bases elsewhere. The Gulf wars in the Middle East required a different approach to alliance building. In cultural and religious deference to such hosts as Saudi Arabia, the US issued a "no-prostitution-allowed" policy, but there is evidence that soldiers returning home or redeployed stop along the way for sexual servicing in other ports of call, particularly in Southeast Asia (Enloe 2000: 72). Moreover, there is no evidence that prostitution or no-prostitution agreements reduce rape.

"Genocidal rape" refers to a systematic program of raping women and girls (and forcing captured "enemy" men and boys to rape each other) to humiliate (feminize) the enemy and to dilute it as a (biological) nation through the impregnation of the enemy's women (Hague 1997: 56). It gained worldwide attention when reports surfaced that during the war in Bosnia-Herzegovina that began in 1992, up to 60,000 women (most of them Bosnian) had been raped by 1993, largely by Serb forces (Bunch and Reilly 1994: 36). The massacres and countermassacres engaged in by the Tutsi and Hutu ethnic groups that began in Burundi in 1993 and in Rwanda in 1994 left well over 1 million people dead, and estimates put the number of women raped in the Rwandan conflict as high as 500,000 (Leatherman 2011: 41). The Sierra Leone civil war (1991–2001) subjected 64,000 female IDPs to rape, and the war that has been staged in all or parts of the Democratic Republic of Congo (DRC) between 1998 and 2013 has been associated with high degrees of brutal gang rapes of women by combatants at the war's height in the mid-2000s and especially in the eastern Congo since (Leatherman 2011: 2, 118–119, 128–129). Some call the war in the DRC Africa's "world war" because it began as a spillover from the Rwandan conflict and escalated as armies and militias within the DRC and from neighboring countries scrambled to profit from illicit trade in the DRC's mineral resources, with the complicity of Western TNCs.

Although rape has been a feature of all wars, its current visibility and more targeted and mass nature are attributed to the changing nature of war in the post-Cold War era. There has been a startling decline in wars and war deaths, with "90 percent fewer people each year" killed in armed conflicts in the twenty-first century than were killed "in the average conflict in the 1950s" (Leatherman 2011: 23). The reasons for this decline are multiple: more intrastate than interstate warfare, greater reliance on smaller armies and small arms, more "geographically limited war zones," more "precision" bombing and other "technological" warfare, improved public health services, and a greater amount and efficacy of humanitarian aid (Leatherman 2011: 22–23). Reductions in the resort to war and to some scourges of war are also associated with "spreading norms about peace and human rights," which are also seen as related to increasing numbers of NGOs and women in politics (Goldstein 2011: 15).

But as Janie Leatherman argues (2011: 34), what particularly characterizes the so-called "new wars" in the post-Cold War period, in which rape has been most visibly used as a significant and calculated tactic of war, are "runaway norms," or the fomenting (often by elites for political and economic gain) of hate of the "other" that is so extreme and boundless that it precipitates and prolongs a cascade of social harms. What particularly sets up runaway norms and are signals that a conflict is being generated include nationalist discourses that polarize gender and ethnic identities, demonize sexual minorities, and extol hypermasculinity (Leatherman 2011: 80–83). Runaway norms in recent (and some notable past) armed conflicts have fostered the widening of who commits rape (men, women, and children) and the specific targeting of who is raped (females or males, children or elderly) for particular strategic purposes, which frequently breaks peacetime taboos as to who is rapeable, as well as increasing the ferocity of sexual violence (including gang rapes and sexual torture and mutilations). Runaway norms also justify the veritable imprisonment by military commanders and combatants of women and children primarily through "forced" incest, marriage, prostitution "or survival sex," trafficking, and child soldiering. Finally, these norms ensure that there is no "safe" or "neutral" space for civilians, whether inhabitants, aid workers, or peacekeepers, to live, work, or attempt to mediate conflict, a condition that is made even worse by the fact that aid workers and peacekeepers have also been implicated in perpetrating gender violence against local women (Leatherman 2011: 42–61, 104–107). Thus, while war has decreased in its frequency and lethality, it has become more thoroughgoing in the brutality exacted on and through civilians and civil society, leaving deep wounds and continued gender violence well after the conflict is officially ended. Although sexual assaults have been defined as crimes of war since the 1940s, it was not until recently that rape has been prosecuted as a crime of genocide and against humanity (Oosterveld 2005). However, as further addressed in this chapter, this has had little effect on rape as a continuing tool of war or on destabilizing gendered divisions of violence.

Although gender violence is most associated with direct violence, it involves considerable structural violence. The sheer costs of military spending ensure that money is not available for meeting the human needs for which women are most responsible and that they are most denied. Despite dramatic post-Cold War declines in interstate warfare and even a precipitous drop in worldwide nuclear arsenals (down to 14,900 as of 2017), as Goldstein observes, state officials responsible for military budgets have not gotten this memo (2011: 19). Worldwide military spending reached Cold War levels again in the first decade of the new millennium, and there was only a miniscule reduction in this in 2012, driven not by the new realities of war but by budget austerity measures in the wake of the 2008 economic crisis, and had moved up again by 2016.[10] As of 2015, although global health spending outpaced global military spending as a percentage of global GDP, it will take 46–54 percent of global military spending to fully achieve the SDGs.[11] In 2014, The Women's International League for Peace and Freedom (WILPF) provided examples of what one year of global military would alternatively buy to advance social welfare (see Box 4.2). Tellingly as well, the largest arms dealers in the world are the US, Russia, China, Germany, and France (all permanent members of the UN Security Council), which sell primarily to the global South, including countries they have officially deemed human rights violators.

Given that in 2005, it was estimated that females made up 70 percent of the world's approximately 1.3 billion people living in absolute poverty (making less than $2 per day), two-thirds of the world's 800 million illiterates, and the majority of the world's refugees, HIV/AIDS sufferers, land-mine casualties, and sex trafficking, rape, and domestic violence victims (NCRW 2006), military largesse translates into massive structural as well as direct

Box 4.2 Costs to Human Security and Gender Equality of World Military Spending

According to the Women's International League for Peace and Freedom (WILPF 2014: 13), in 2014, "one year's worth of the world's military spending" would equal:

- "Over 650 years of the UN's regular budget"
- "Over 2500 years of the annual expenditure on international disarmament and non-proliferation organizations"
- "Over 6300 years of the budget for UN Women"

gender violence, enormously affecting women in the global South. Worldwide women's movements and NGOs have long made the connection between war and militarization and the compromising of women's security. Their efforts to bring this to world attention started during the UN Decade for Women, when women first held their own tribunals for crimes against women, followed by their promotion of women's human rights at the World Conference on Human Rights in Vienna in 1993 and the codification of the connection between armed conflict and gender violence as a violation of women's human rights at the 1995 Fourth World Conference on Women in Beijing (Joachim 2007). Amnesty International and Human Rights Watch also began monitoring and reporting on gender violence in the 1990s, ever since making it a major focus of their human rights campaigns (Joachim 2007: 128), and the genocidal rape in Bosnia and Rwanda also catapulted gender violence and its relationship to armed conflict onto the UN agenda. As explored in the following section, although UN action on this has been unprecedented, it has been weak at best, largely upholding gendered divisions of violence, gender violence, and especially the power of gender to privilege militarization and neocolonial or (neo)imperial relations.

Gendered Peacemaking, Peacekeeping, and Peace-building

Although part of a longer and wider struggle for women's security from militarized violence, the NGO Working Group on Women and International Peace and Security, consisting of the century-old WILPF, the Women's Caucus for Gender Justice, Amnesty International, International Alert, the Women's Commission for Refugee Women and Children, and the Hague Appeal for Peace in collaboration with UNIFEM, is credited with the final push to have the UN Security Council pass Resolution 1325 in 2000 (Cohn 2008: 187). Although non-binding, 1325 "calls on" the UN and member countries to do the following: protect women from gender-based violence (GBV) in war zones and include women (and gender perspectives) in peace negotiations, support their peacemaking initiatives in addition to providing gender-sensitive training to peacekeepers, and engage in gender mainstreaming through UN monitoring of and reporting on the gender dimensions of conflict and conflict resolution, including the impact of armed conflict on women and girls and the roles of women in peacemaking. As noted in Chapter 1, this is part of the larger UN Women, Peace, and Security (WPS) agenda, which promotes the implementation of such resolutions, including the development of national action plans on women, peace, and security.[12] Within the context of this, TFNs have also been successful in having GBV included in the 2013 Arms Trade Treaty that obligates ratifying countries to ensure that the small arms they export are not used to conduct widespread GBV (Enloe 2014: 27).

However, the effects of 1325 have been muted at best. Widespread rapes in the DRC conflict as well as in the Darfur genocide in Sudan and increased reports of rape by peacekeeping forces were featured in subsequent UN secretary-general studies and reports on women, peace, and security that were mandated by 1325. This acknowledgment of worsening gender violence in war led to the passage of additional UN Security Council resolutions that codify sexual violence as a matter of peace and security, call for the development and strengthening of measures to address sexual violence and to have more women present in peace operations and negotiations, mandate tracking of the implementation of 1325 and documenting of "credibly suspected" perpetrators of sexual violence in armed conflicts, and make HIV/AIDS resulting from sexual violence in armed conflicts a focus in peacekeeping and peacebuilding processes (DeLargy 2013).

These resolutions, which have been the first to address women and, most notably, women as security actors rather than only as victims in the history of the Security Council (Enloe 2007: 129), were preceded by the formation of international criminal tribunals for former Yugoslavia (ICTY) and Rwanda (ICTR) in 1993 and 1994, respectively. Rape was first prosecuted by a World War II military tribunal that found several Japanese commanders responsible for systematic rapes in Nanking, and the 1946 Fourth Geneva Convention and 1974 UN Declaration on the Protection of Women and Children in Emergency and Armed Conflict speak amorphously to protecting women from war violence (Oosterveld 2005: 68–69). However, the ICTY and ICTR were the first tribunals to begin developing international case law and precedents that spell out a wide range of gender violence (including gender violence perpetrated against men) that is prosecutable as a crime of war and a tool of genocide (Oosterveld 2005: 79).[13] By 1998, these were codified in the Rome Statute of the ICC, which recognizes multiple forms of gender violence in armed conflict as crimes against humanity and war crimes, and requires gender-sensitive judges and court proceedings that do not retraumatize victims (Oosterveld 2005: 67).

These are significant gender gains in the struggle against gendered insecurities, but they remain problematic on a number of scores. With respect to 1325 and its successors, there has been great resistance to including women in peace negotiations on the part of the male establishments of warring parties, international donors, and conflict resolution specialists, and the few who are included are typically proxies for those male establishments, having no political base of women to whom they are accountable, and/or having been left out of "real" backroom negotiations (DeLargy 2013). Moreover, in 1325 and related resolutions since, gender violence is reduced to sexual violence against women and only in the context of armed conflicts, ignoring that it is just as rife before and even worse after conflicts (True 2012: 137). There is no mention in these resolutions of a central need to address hegemonic/militarized masculinity or of the critical relationship between sexual violence and the global economic interests that have driven armed conflicts, ranging from the trade in illicit blood diamonds as in Sierra Leone and minerals as in the DRC to the licit small arms trade (Leatherman 2011: 164). Similarly unaddressed are the gendered economic harms that arise from the neoliberal economic restructuring that is often imposed after conflicts, including far greater resources given by international donors, and reflected in postconflict national budgets, to security apparatuses (including the disarmament, demobilization, and reintegration of combatants—or DDR programs) as opposed to basic needs, much less gender equality, which makes it very difficult for resource-poor women to perform peacebuilding in their societies (True 2012: 146–147, 151). Moreover, under the gendered division of violence that assumes women are peaceful, DDR programs have also failed to pay attention to female combatants and their special problems with reintegration into still patriarchal societies (Leatherman 2011: 169).

Perhaps most problematic for disrupting the gendered division of violence is that gender and especially sexual violence is repeatedly reduced to violence against women in the WPS agenda, upholding the "sex essentialism" that renders the idea that women can be perpetrators, including rapists, unimaginable (Sjoberg 2016) and misrepresenting much wartime rape as organized, and thus controllable by international policy and punishments, rather than seeing it as part of the disorganization of war itself which is not placed under indictment (Baaz and Stern 2013). Indeed, as sexual violence and contraction of HIV/AIDS in war have become securitized, the agenda is simply to "protect women" from these in wartime (not in peacetime), increasing the power of already powerful states to punish others while regulating rather than actually addressing the inequalities and injustices that enable these violences (Jansson 2017). Ultimately, the WPS agenda reproduces very narrow constructions of gender and gender violence that do not disturb and, in fact, reinforce the international order that is productive of gender harms (Shepherd 2008).

The maintenance of that order can be seen with respect to the question of holding perpetrators accountable for sexual violence, which is now part of the successor resolutions to 1325. Although women now constitute the majority of judges on the ICC, those states that are not signatories to the Rome Statute, such as the US, are exempt from having their officials and troops prosecuted by the ICC; much individual military peacekeeper gender violence cannot be proven to rise to the level of crimes against humanity in non-genocidal contexts; SOFAs typically keep peacekeepers as well as militaries immune to prosecution in the host country, and they are rarely, if ever, tried in their home countries; and civilians and private contractors serving as military or peacekeeping extensions are also immune (Bedont 2005). Finally, there is no international jurisdiction for gender violence perpetrated against a soldier's own comrades-in-arms.

Thus, beneath the failures of these formal mechanisms lie a range of insidious processes that the following discussion of peacekeeping connects. Peacekeeping remains a male bastion, with women constituting about 4 percent of the military experts, troops, and police who carry out peacekeeping missions (Cohn and Jacobson 2013), a figure that has barely changed by 2017. As feminist IR experts have pointed out (Enloe 1993; Whitworth 2004), donning a "blue beret" sets up contradictions for the military men who become peacekeepers. Military training that inculcates militarized masculinity neither prepares peacekeeping troops for the humanitarian work they are expected to perform nor encourages them to embrace the light weapons they carry or the force restraint they must observe. Peacekeeping can also breed male resentment for "missing the 'main' show—conflict and warfare" (Whitworth 2004: 150), but it also ensures that peacekeepers (from both the global North and the global South) expect the same perks as other military men, as they "run brothels, assault local women, and kill local citizens" (Whitworth 2004: 152).

On the other side of the coin, as Whitworth (2004) argues based on her study of Canadian peacekeeping operations, the UN's new interest in "adding women and stirring" simply grafts on (essentialist) gender analysis, which assumes women will just ease and assist the already predetermined business of peacekeeping and peace negotiations by bringing information on women and "women's issues" into these activities. This predetermined business disregards any considerations of militarized masculinity as a major source of prolonged conflict or such sources of structural violence as neocolonial economic and political relationships and neoliberal economic restructuring that may lie at the heart of the conflict (Whitworth 2004: 133, 137). Instead, this business focuses on "when the fighting broke out" and how to control, if not cease, it (Whitworth 2004: 133). Thus, rather than causing a rethinking of peacekeeping and peace negotiations, "analyses of women and of gender thus become part of the 'programmatic solutions' that form the UN repertoire of responding to conflict and insecurity around the world, and, in this way, confirm the appropriateness of the repertoire" (Whitworth 2004: 137). In this sense, like gender equality that is subsumed under neoliberal governmentality, gender perspectives on international peace and security are subsumed under a kind of security governmentality. Nine out of 11 peace agreements by 2005 had involved some focus on including women and providing for their security (mostly with respect to sexual violence), although that dropped to six out of nine agreements by 2010 (Ellerby 2017: 36–37). But the tenuous and minimalist nature of treating women as add-ons to an overall approach to simply managing conflicts underscores Whitworth's conclusion that the issue is not so much adding more women to peacekeeping and peacemaking operations as it is questioning the sole reliance on militaries to do the job of peacekeeping and, by extension, on military leaders and civilian defense elites to do the job of peacemaking (2004: 183).

Even more problematic, Whitworth (2004) points out that peacekeeping itself is a colonial practice. Given that 14 of the 30 UN peacekeeping operations launched between 1988 and 2005 were in Africa (Hudson 2005), with almost all the rest in the South as well, contemporary peacekeeping

> comes from an understanding of the places in which those conflicts occur, "conflict-prone third world countries," which are defined by what they lack: the institutions, the liberalism, the rationality, and the order of Western states. Peacekeeping, as part of the contemporary "*mission civilatrice*," is the means by which that "lack" can be addressed, bringing meaning and order where there are none. Peacekeeping is, in short, part of the "subject constituting project" of the colonial encounter.
>
> (Whitworth 2004: 185)

Beyond the irony that the weapons the North sells to the South enable and increase brutal conflict there, the colonizing dimensions of peacekeeping not only invite greater militarization of peacekeeping and the conflicts it seeks to quell, but also undermine the peacebuilding efforts of "local" women (and their male allies), who are ignored or discounted and under-resourced.

(De)Militarizing Feminism

Given that all "*genders lose in war*, although they lose in somewhat different ways" (Goldstein 2001: 402), we still confront the problem of dealing with the recurring linkages identifying masculinity with aggression and war and femininity with passivity and peace that shore up militarization. Judith Hicks Stiehm (1989) argues that achieving gender parity in the US armed forces might ultimately force an acknowledgment that war is not "manly" and that women can protect themselves. In this view, women's equal participation might destabilize the ways in which the gendered division of violence and the gender inequality upon which it rests contribute to militarization. Intriguing on this score is that US female veterans of the Iraq and Afghanistan wars have expressed far more skepticism about the value of those wars than male veterans (Eager 2014: 32–33). However, given the historical patterns, gender parity seems an unlikely development in any state military. Moreover, as the jobs of militaries and even peacekeeping forces are increasingly privatized into the hands of essentially paid mercenary forces like Academi (formerly Blackwater), such contracting ensures that the "real" business of war will be kept largely in male hands and remain "manly," regardless of some "resexing" of state militaries.

Other feminists have pointed out that, although comparatively few women are or will be soldiers on the battlefront, many more serve the military on the home front, working (typically at the lowest levels) for defense and related industries. It could also be argued that this labor contributes more to life-taking than do individual male and female soldiers on the battlefront. At the same time, as we have seen, women's political violence has become more visible as women gain more political power and enter the ranks of militaries and "terrorist" groups, even though their violence is typically not represented as political violence. And images and realities of military men's vulnerability are becoming harder to hide and contain, even though there continue to be herculean efforts to do so.

Still other feminists point out that in times of violent conflict, gender dichotomies are not only rigidified but also can lose their rigidity. In contrast to the post-9/11 response in the US that brought a particularly virulent restaging of gender (and race) binaries and asymmetries, Simona Sharoni (1998) finds that in cases such as "the troubles" in Northern Ireland and the Israeli–Palestinian conflict, women under British and Israeli occupation became significant political actors as patriarchal taboos were lifted in the midst of conflict. This has also occurred in a range of especially Latin American guerrilla or armed national liberation movements against repressive authoritarian governments in which women have been involved in large numbers as politicized and often explicitly feminist actors and combatants (Kampwirth 2002). At the same time, some men, such as imprisoned Irish Republican Army (IRA) members, have developed new understandings of their own vulnerabilities as a result of their prison experiences. As Sharoni (1998) recounts, captured IRA members incarcerated in British prisons learned to protest their treatment in prison out of vulnerability. For example, in resistance to being marked as criminals rather than as political prisoners, they refused to wear prison-issue clothing for more than four years, choosing to be naked instead and using only blankets to cover themselves. This is the opposite of and in opposition to the armored man. They also gained new appreciation of feminist perspectives on conflict and peace as a result of working with feminist educators and supporters on the outside who backed their protests. By coming to recognize the interconnections among gender, sexuality, race, class, nationality, and international violence, they thereby learned to eschew militarized masculinity on the understanding that it gets in the way of broad and inclusive struggles for justice and peace that are more non-violent than violent.

This example brings up an important distinction: imperialist violence versus resistance to it, whether non-violent or violent. Since 9/11, feminist debates have shifted to grapple with the militarization of feminism (particularly Western, but especially US feminism) when it was appropriated by the George W. Bush administration. In Ann Russo's (2006) analysis of the US Feminist Majority Foundation's (FMF) campaign to stop "gender apartheid" in Afghanistan, she argues that beyond the well-known claim by the Bush administration that the war against Afghanistan was at least partially about liberating Afghan women from the male oppressors of the Taliban, thus using feminist rhetoric as a stimulus for war, the FMF also actively enabled, supported, and partook in this rhetoric at the expense of Afghan women and women's movements. Although the FMF's pre-9/11 campaign against gender violence could be seen as "counterhegemonic," this campaign ended up colluding with the "project of US imperialism and retaliatory violence as a method of maintaining US power" (Russo 2006: 558). The reasons for this, according to Russo (2006), include the FMF's desire to be taken seriously on the foreign policy stage by pointing to the success of its impact on the Bush administration; its ahistorical reading of the causes of gender violence in Afghanistan, including the Soviet invasion of it and the subsequent US arming of the Taliban; its myopic focus on lifting the burka and on "freeing" that nation's women, which led the FMF to support the war without consideration of the greater costs that war would visit on Afghan women; and its participation in colonialist and Orientalist thinking. As pointed out earlier, Orientalism assumes Western superiority and constructs the West as the source of rescue and salvation for the rest, which has justified over the centuries invasions and colonizations that have caused the havoc from which "others" must be saved. The FMF's alliance with the US State Department in support of the Afghanistan War caused a split between the FMF and the Revolutionary Association of the Women of Afghanistan (RAWA), which rejected the invasion and the post-invasion installation of more gender violence-producing patriarchs in the form of the Northern Alliance, a development that the association had warned would be the result of the invasion (Russo 2006: 574). Western, particularly US, LGBTQ activists have also been implicated in shoring up bellicose US foreign policy when they have protested "state homophobia" in selective parts of the global South, such as Iran, thereby providing further ammunition for invasion talk when it suits US policymakers (Nayak and Selbin 2010: 80).

These kinds of problematic actions by especially Western social movements are bound up in the development of the "Responsibility to Protect" (R2P) doctrine promulgated in 2001 and adopted in the form of a resolution by the UN General Assembly in 2005. Although often seen as a human security measure that justifies militarized humanitarian intervention, some feminists have been particularly critical of it as a variation on the time-worn 'protection racket,' reestablishing 'dominant narratives that are gendered and racialized "which position the international community as the heroic, white male necessary to protect the vulnerable, inferior, feminized 'Other'—the state it must rescue" (quoted in Detraz 2012: 144).

Feminists and queers who share such a critique have resisted the "war on terror," sometimes justified under R2P principles, have pointed to how extensive racialized, gendered, and sexualized violence within savior states, and "imperial feminism" and imperial "global gay" or homonoromative politics (see, for example, Richter-Montpetit 2014; Agathangelou 2013; Puar 2007), the latter of which imposes Western approaches to gay liberation on other cultures in ways that make it difficult for sexual minorities in them to engage in their own struggles while also demonizing global South countries for their homophobia (Alexander 2005), militate against transnational solidarity to resist war and militarism. Imperial feminisms are not new as they have been present in a range of historical colonizing projects based on white(ned) men saving white women from racialized men (see, for example, McClintock 1995). However, contemporary feminist and global gay imperialisms help to construct, buy into, and represent the imperial, racist, heteronormative, and homonormative project of white(ned) women/Western gays saving "brown women [and brown sexual minorities] from brown men" and brown homophobes (Spivak 1988: 297), and thus further contribute to continued imperialist militarism.

As we shall see in the next chapter, the combination of security regimes or globalized militarization with global capitalism allows greater exploitation and oppression. This is not only because globalized militarization causes greater desperation and, thus, more and more at-risk or captive and thus cheapened and quiescent labor—as well as a way for private industry to reap enormous profits from war industries—but also because the "war on terror" and global capitalism have been constructed as *the* way to "democracy" and, therefore, are not to be questioned.[14] This is sometimes referred to as the logic of "Empire" (Hardt and Negri 2000) or the "neoliberal imperium" (Agathangelou and Ling 2004). In recent times, with the rise of new authoritarians, the neoliberal veneer of justifying military action and intervention in the name of humanitarianism, democracy, and saving women is wearing off, replaced by more naked appeals to xenophobia and especially Islamophobia. While there is still a subtext that keeping out or attacking (including extra-legally) racialized men as the sources of rape, crime, and violence constitutes a "pro-woman" agenda—one that is protective of white,

Western femininity and, thus, gaining some female adherents to this non- and even anti-feminist ideology—feminists transnationally are resisting such an agenda, as we shall see in the final chapter of this text.

Disarming Security

As indicated at the outset of this chapter, security is always elusive and partial. This does not undercut the argument for the need to confront the crisis of insecurity, which is born of the pursuit of absolute security. The desire for absolute security is the product of hardened masculinist identities that imagine themselves and the world as a series of armed camps set up to preserve their respective autonomies. Whether security can be completely detached from this imagining is an open question, but security has come to mean far more than that (Sutton, Morgen, and Novkov 2008), and it can be pursued without compromising the security of "others" by resisting "othering" itself and recognizing that processes that compromise the security of others compromise the security of a reimagined "self" in solidarity with others.

The newfound attention of "security" IGOs to the compromising of women's security through armed conflict is, on the one hand, welcome, but, on the other hand, has reproduced gender ideologies that construct women as "natural" victims and peace proponents. This sets up women to carry the burden of peacemaking and peacebuilding while lacking the material resources and political representation and sway to do so. It also deflects attention from the continued and overwhelming prerogatives of elites, states, and markets to make war and unjust peace. Even the new prosecutions of gender violence in war can have non-humanitarian effects, including providing additional "fuel for nationalist fervor" and thereby resulting in reprisals against women who testify and the sustaining of conflict (Giles and Hyndman 2004: 13). As we have seen, peacekeeping is also more of a colonizing practice than a peaceful one, and refugees and IDPs are far from safe from combatants as well as peacekeepers and aid workers. Thus, humanitarian efforts are increasingly being exposed by feminists as part of the "security myth."

Although there are many good reasons to disconnect peace from women (as well as war from men), there remains some value in Gayatri Spivak's concept of strategic essentialism to resist war and other forms of violence. The notion that women, especially as mothers, are more peaceful has been thoroughly problematized, but the fact remains that women continue to mobilize against war based, in part, on this very notion. Once into such struggles, they may shift their political identities and recognize that homogenizing notions of womanhood or motherhood are not enough for, and may stand in the way of, transcending or working through political differences and economic and social inequalities. But however women become politicized to resist war together, in doing so they "reject the prevalent relationship to the state (and sometimes with their spouses and partners) and redefine it" (Kaufman and Williams 2007: 30). Thus, identity "myths" can be useful for peace and justice mobilizations as long as they are seen as provisional and political, not foundational or natural.

Notes

1 See "The Hague Centre for Strategic Studies LGBT Military Index" at www.projects.hcss.nl/monitor/88/ for an interactive map that ranks 100 countries with respect to their policies on LGBT people serving in the armed forces.

2 See the Stockholm International Peace Research Institute's (SIPRI) interactive map on world military spending in 2016 at www.visuals.sipri.org/.

3 All films cited in this text are referenced in the Web and Video Resources in the accompanying e-resource to this text (or at the end of the text, p. 000), which also includes many more film and video resources.

4 See "Iraq Body Count" at www.iraqbodycount.org/database, www.iraqbodycount.org/ and www.iraqbodycount.org/analysis/reference/announcements/5/.
5 See "Watson Institute Costs of War" at www.watson.brown.edu/costsofwar/costs/human/civilians/afghan.
6 See "ICasualties" at www.icasualties.org.
7 See "United Nations Assistance Mission in Afghanistan First Quarter 2017 Civilian Casualty Data" at www.unama.unmissions.org/sites/default/files/27_april_2017_-_unama_first_quarter_2017_civilian_casualty_data_english.pdf.
8 See "AIRWARS" at www.airwars.org.
9 Recently, former sex workers in South Korea have sought an apology and compensation from their government for its role in serving as "one big pimp" for the American military, likening their case to that of the "comfort women" who were pressed into serving as prostitutes for the Japanese military during World War II and who also sought (and received in 2015) an apology and some compensation from the Japanese government (Sang-Hun 2009).
10 See "Military expenditure" at www.sipri.org/research/armament-and-disarmament/arms-transfers-and-military-spending/military-expenditure.
11 See "The opportunity cost of world military spending" at www.sipri.org/commentary/blog/2016/opportunity-cost-world-military-spending.
12 The UN Security Council subsequently adopted seven additional resolutions on women, peace, and security: 1820 (2008), 1888 (2009), 1889 (2009), 1960 (2010), 2106 (2013), 2122 (2013), and 2242 (2015). Taken together, the eight resolutions represent a critical framework for improving the situation of women in conflict-affected countries. See www.unwomen.org/en/about-us/guiding-documents.
13 See Henry (2011) for accounts of these tribunals.
14 See Grewal for an analysis of how security has become the dominant mode of governmentality, using race and gender to "produce figures of risk" who must be disciplined and must adopt self-discipline in order not to threaten the "'security,' happiness and freedom" of those who determine who is "risk-producing" and "at risk" (Grewal 2005: 202).

Chapter 4

Questions for Discussion

1 What are the problems with conventional notions of security and processes of securitization?
2 How do gender(ed) divisions of violence operate to associate women with peace and men with war, and how are these assumptions contradicted in "real" life across the world?
3 What are the relationships between gender and international violence within militaries and civilian societies, how are they being addressed (or not) by IGOs and in international law, and why are these measures insufficient and/or problematic for reducing these violences?
4 Why is there such resistance to "adding women" to both military and peace structures, and how are such structures, beyond their minimalist inclusion of women, reproductive of the crisis of insecurity for the majority of the world's people?

Activities for Further Research

1 Go to www.pbs.org/wnet/women-war-and-peace/ to watch a range of US Public Broadcasting System documentaries in the "Women, War, and Peace" series and be introduced to a range of accompanying materials on this subject. How do different women in different conflict contexts experience war and what different and common factors bring them into struggles for peace? How might you further research such cases?
2 Go to www.youtube.com/watch?v=LEAYxr8Xo7I to watch the US Institute of Peace introductory video on the "Men, Peace, and Security: Agents of Change" initiative arising from a symposium in 2013 co-sponsored by, among others, Women in International

Security. Why has such an initiative taken longer to develop than the Women, Peace, and Security agenda? Could this initiative translate into international policymaking? Could this challenge militarized masculinity among not only non-elite, but also elite men? Consider also the effects of not recognizing men's civilian vulnerabilities in war in the video, "Gender, Civilian Security, and the Paradox of War Norms" by Charli Carpenter at www.youtube.com/watch?v=zyh_noIpITs.

3 Do some more research on women in peacebuilding by visiting the (Boston) Consortium on Gender, Security, and Human Rights Web site (www.genderandsecurity.org) and the PeaceWomen Web site (www.peacewomen.org), which have a number of rich resources. After you review some of this material, what do you see as the potentials of and problems with including women in peacemaking and peacebuilding projects? Does it matter which women are included and by whom? Do you think including more women in post-conflict processes can help to prevent further armed conflict, or must other things also happen, and what might those be?

5 Gender and Global Political Economy

How are women and men positioned and repositioned in and by global economic processes and with what effects? What do gendered divisions of labor and resources tell us about how work and the natural world are defined, valued, and distributed? How does the power of gender affect who has access to and control over economic and environmental resources? How has neoliberal globalization undermined social reproduction and environmental protection by producing, on the one hand, apolitical, market-based responses that leave structural inequalities intact and, on the other hand, ethnonationalist and anti-environmentalist responses that exacerbate them?

This chapter looks at the relationship between gendered inequalities and global political economy (GPE).[1] It puts globalization, a process introduced in previous chapters but elaborated on here and which is associated with the rise and spread of *neoliberal global capitalism*, at the center of this examination. It argues that globalization in its many manifestations and the economic processes that preceded it are gendering and gendered in ways that reflect both continuity and change, both sustaining inequalities and injustices.

As we have seen, the ideology of neoliberalism has organized global governance and aspects of global security around market principles, reducing governance to the exercise of elite technical expertise and security to the mere management of violent conflict. This has resulted in the "adding women" approach in both instances, either to appear more modern or democratic or to protect female "victims" from a few "excesses" of war. Such approaches have not fundamentally disturbed the gender(ed) divisions of power and violence and thus have done little to stem crises of representation and insecurity. By failing to deeply address the former, the latter are expanding in present times of political backlash and resurgent national security approaches that are highly masculinist, ethnonationalist, heteronormative, and transphobic in character in some (and some particularly powerful) quarters. This chapter continues the analysis of the problematics of "adding women," in this case into extant GPE power structures, arguing that the economic *repositioning of* (some) *women* and (some) *men* is not disrupting the *power of gender*, which undermines broader economic justice by breeding the economic and ecological *crisis of sustainability*.

On the one hand, according to the latest UN Progress of the World's Women Report (UN Women 2015), more women worldwide are seeking and gaining employment, thus becoming income earners and presumably benefiting from the enhanced self-esteem and economic empowerment that formal work affords. On the other hand, the feminization of employment has done little to alter expectations regarding gender divisions of labor or valorizations of masculinized work over women's work, or to enable women in the aggregate to significantly increase their control over economic decision-making or environmental resource use. Although gender mainstreaming now features in the World Bank's and other international agencies' economic development policies, the objective is to integrate women into markets rather than to promote social justice by altering hierarchical gender relations. The power of gender here operates to reproduce divisions of labor and responsibility in social reproduction and formal production that favor short-term neoliberal objectives and sustain commitments to competition and growth—but at the price of long-term crises of social reproduction and environmental sustainability.

With reference to owning economic resources and wielding economic authority, the positioning of men and women, despite "adding" more women to the workforce and in economic policymaking, suggests more continuity than change. Gender stereotypes persist in assigning men the primary responsibility for generating income in households worldwide, and men in aggregate still hold higher-paying and more secure jobs than do most women (UN Women 2015: 46). Women in aggregate also perform more household labor than most men, 2.5 times as much as of 2016 (UN Women 2015: 46), and thus are most associated with (unpaid or low paid) carework (of their own and other families as well as communities). This carework of women is extended to making them most responsible for coping with the impact of economic and environmental harms on households and communities with fewer economic resources to do so. Moreover, women themselves are treated as ever-elastic resources and their reproductive bodies are particularly subject to the effects of environmental pollution and are most subjected to controls designed to deny or limit women's reproductive choices. The continuing assumptions that men are independent producers of both goods and culture and women are dependent reproducers mired in nature constructs these manifestations of *gender divisions of labor and resources*.

With respect to *gendered divisions of labor and resources*, men—specifically those who are economically, ethnically, racially, and geopolitically privileged—continue to control power-wielding and decision-making authority in economic development planning, corporate investment strategies, and IFIs which favor economic profits and growth over human and planetary welfare. However, men subordinated by class, race, sexuality, non-normative gender, and/or (neo)colonization face already bad or deteriorating economic status and conditions created by economic elites, which can result in self-destruction, further subordinating and controlling the bodies of non-elite women, particularly those in their lives, to try to reclaim some sense of masculine authority, and/or blaming other non-elite groups, such as (typically racialized) "outsiders" for their plight. Economically subordinated men and women may also be forced to choose between jobs and protecting the environment, a false choice presented to them by elites and one that subjects especially race- and class-subordinated women and men to the greatest effects of environmental destruction, including the extraction of natural resources from and the dumping of toxic waste in poor countries and neighborhoods and especially indigenous lands.

Thus, interrelated gender divisions of labor and resources include production–reproduction, independent–dependent, paid–unpaid work, culture–nature, and market–care, while interrelated gendered divisions of labor and resources include subject–object, advanced–primitive, skilled–unskilled, users–resources, and exploitation–stewardship (see Table 5.1). The power of gender keeps these in place through masculinist, racist, classist, and heteronormative assumptions and objectives in economic and geopolitical thinking and practice, despite some recent economic attention to women. This is most visible when we observe how policymaking remains largely top-down, formulaic, and over-reliant on growth and quantifiable indicators, often at the expense of being focused on provisioning, human well-being, and social and environmental sustainability, contributing generally to the crisis of sustainability.

Still, globalization is disrupting familiar gender patterns and repositioning women and men by altering assumptions, roles, identities, and livelihoods worldwide. These disruptions

Table 5.1 Gender/ed Divisions of Labor and Resources Productive of the Crisis of Sustainability

	Masculinized	*Feminized*
Gender (Male–Female Dynamics)	Productive	Reproductive
	Paid work	Unpaid work
	Providers	Dependents
	Market	Care
	Culture	Nature
Gendered (Intersectional Dynamics)	Subject	Object
	Advanced	Primitive
	Skilled	Unskilled
	Finance	Consumption
	Users	Resources
	Exploitation	Stewardship

are especially visible in relation to economics, in part because gender is so key to unequal divisions of labor and their valorizations, and in part because new technologies are so profoundly altering what is produced, how, where, and by whom worldwide. Some changes are small and incremental, whereas others challenge our deepest assumptions (male breadwinner roles) and most established institutions (patriarchal families where male heads of household are the primary "providers"). The effects of these repositionings and disruptions are complex and defy easy generalizations. As more women enter the paid workforce, this both empowers some women and complicates expectations of hegemonic masculinity for most men. The geographical unevenness of employment opportunities spurs internal and external migrations that alter "traditional" household formations, and diasporas reconfigure ethnic/racialized identifications and alignments. Also spurred are greater designs on and demands for natural resources and expansion of land use for both production and waste disposal. These processes are prompting masculinist, ethnonationalist, and anti-environmentalist responses that are worsening the crisis of sustainability. Such responses are also the result of neoliberal economic approaches, ranging from top-down approaches to poverty abatement, primarily in the global South, such as the SDGs, to imposed or self-imposed austerity measures directed at reducing public funding and privatizing public goods and spaces, including the environment upon which human life depends, to deal with perpetual financial crises created by privileging private capital expansion, mostly at the very top. As this chapter argues, a focus on gender and the GPE, which draws upon F(I or G)PE scholarship, reveals starkly how the power of gender constitutes not only a gender division of labor and resources that exploits women (and feminized "others"), but also a gendered, polarized valorization of skills, work, and bodies under gendered economic and resource presumptions that serve to "naturalize" the exploitation of most of the earth's population and the planet itself.

To make this case, the following provides a history of the gendering and gendered processes of colonization, capitalist development, and global capitalism, referred to most often as globalization. Included in this are examples of some feminist critiques of these processes and interventions made by GPE governance actors to mostly "add women" to existing economic structures. This is followed by discussions of feminist analyses of women, gender, and the power of gender in relation to globalization (including financialization and climate change as its latest manifestations). The chapter concludes with a discussion of resisting dominant GPE priorities and structures which meld with dominant global governance and security ones to produce the triadic crises of representation, insecurity, and sustainability as a lead into the final chapter which focuses on feminist, queer, and trans resistances to global politics-as-usual.

Gendering and Gendered Development Processes

Prior to modern state-making, colonization, and industrial capitalism, rigid dichotomies were less familiar because all able-bodied family and community members were expected to contribute. Work was therefore a more communal activity, and divisions between public and private spheres, paid and unpaid labor, were not yet institutionalized. Although specific tasks might be gender coded, the particular coding varied greatly over time and across cultures, and activities in general were valued as necessary and complementary contributions to sustaining families and households. Processes of colonization and industrialization were key to constituting more rigid, less equal, and thus less complementary conceptions of how labor should be divided between and among sexes, classes, and nations.

Colonization and Industrialization

This Western gendered division of labor was imposed on many cultures in the Americas, Asia, and Africa beginning in the fifteenth century (Federici 2004). In many instances, the economic status and well-being of women in diverse cultures were diminished by the patriarchal and political ideologies imposed by colonizers. For example, farming in many African countries was almost exclusively women's work, and men were responsible for clearing fields, hunting, and engaging in warfare. Western colonization undermined communal land use and women's land rights. In addition, the rise of Western science transformed peoples' notions of nature and instituted a worldview that saw nature strictly as a resource for Eurocentric, "man-made" projects, thus discrediting belief systems associated with "primitive" cultures in which nature was revered as a manifestation of feminine divinity. Early Western science, coupled with Christian ideology, still thought of nature as feminine, but rather than powerful and goddess-like, nature in this view was a passive resource from which European men could take anything they needed or wanted without care for the effects of their interventions. This attitude paved the way for rapacious land-use patterns and technologies (Merchant 1980). On the flip side, the concomitant racialization of nature as brute and savage during the colonial period has justified efforts to tame it for (white) "man's" purposes ever since (Federici 2004).

Because Western colonizers assumed land should be "owned" and men should be the "heads of households" and, hence, the primary earners, they transferred land rights to men (away from women under communal systems) and ensured that men (rather than women) received agricultural training and technological supports as well as access to cash and credit. Giving some men titles to small plots of land not expropriated by Europeans for plantation agriculture or other uses, and turning men as well as women into farm laborers—either as slaves or minimally paid workers—did not mean empowerment (enhanced capacity) for most colonized men. It favored men's positioning relative to women's, but not relative to those who gained from European colonization. As Gita Sen and Caren Grown observe, "The colonial period created and accentuated inequalities both 'among' nations, and between classes and genders (also castes, ethnic communities, races, etc.) 'within' nations" (1987: 24).

These gendered effects of the imposition of Western "modernity" were extended with the rise of "industrial capitalism" from the late eighteenth century on (Mies 1986). Industrialization drove a significant wedge between the home and the workplace, which were more or less melded in agricultural economies. As caste divisions (aristocrats versus peasants/indentured servants versus slaves) slowly and unevenly (and still not completely) shifted to class divisions (upper versus middle versus lower class) in the industrializing West, certain women (those in upper and rising middle classes and of European descent) were to be confined to the home to provide a "safe haven" for male industrialists. European-born and immigrant poor and working-class women (and children) of European descent were a part of the Western industrial workforce in some (especially textile) industries, constituting preferred "cheap" and "controllable" labor in the form of factory and piecework performed at home for a time. However, male labor increasingly became preferred (in part as a result of social reforms to relieve women and children from the most exploitative factory labor as well as the rise of male-led unions), and the ideal of the heteronormative family supported by a male wage earner became a norm (if not a reality) even for the working classes. Women of African descent, even after slavery was legally abolished throughout the West, remained in the fields or as maids for white(ned) women in the rising middle classes who were expected to remain at home. In the still colonized or newly "independent" parts of the global South still subject to neocolonial relations with their former colonizers, resource extraction to fuel the industrial revolution occurred on the backs of men and women, although it was men who were brought more into wage labor (in the mines and increasingly mechanized fields owned by former colonizers), while women were left to engage in subsistence farming on what land remained to poor families, too often held under men's names as sole owners.

Development as Modernization

Western development strategies launched in the mid-twentieth century to "modernize" (essentially industrialize) the "Third World" (to allow the expansion of Western manufacturing, to create new markets for Western-manufactured goods, and to gain allies in the global South during the Cold War) exacerbated this pattern of leaving women out of landowning, wage labor, and support from Western development agencies. Western aid, loans, and technical assistance favored landowning men as recipients of assistance, thus disregarding women's vital role in food production and in many cases worsening the conditions of female farmers, which led to malnutrition for families dependent on subsistence crops. Moreover, large-scale, highly mechanized farming to produce crops for export undermined the female farming systems central to the maintenance of food self-sufficiency in many countries of the South.

It was this pattern that feminists studying development first identified and responded to by agitating for women in development (WID) programs within development agencies. WID scholarship initially sought more effective *inclusion* of women in the practices and presumed benefits of development. This orientation was important and productive for revealing inequalities of positioning among women and men. Cumulative research suggested, however, that simply "adding women" did not address significant problems: the devaluation of feminized labor, the structural privileging of men and masculinity, or the increasing pressure on women to work a triple shift (in familial, informal, and formal activities) to ensure family survival during economic crises. In response, feminists increasingly asked how the power of gender was shaping underlying assumptions, expectations, and even rules of the game. For many researchers, the liberal, modernist inclinations of WID approaches were gradually displaced by the more constructivist, critical starting points of gender and development (GAD) orientations (Rai 2002). GAD scholars problematized the meaning and desirability of development (especially as modernization) imposed by Western development experts and agencies, interrogated the definition of work and productive activity generally and how to "count" that activity, and exposed the masculinism of men's reluctance to "help" in the household even as women were in or entering the labor force. These scholars also challenged some Western liberal constructions of feminism that imagined women's economic independence as necessarily freeing; investigated intersections of sexualization, racialization, and neocolonialism that enabled hyperexploitation of labor; and criticized narratives of victimization that particularly denied agency to poor and racialized women (Griffin 2016). However, development agencies were (and continue to be) more amenable to WID and GAD strategies as they moved to a new focus on "development with a human face" that foregrounded fighting poverty and "including" those most marginalized under modernization approaches to economic development.

Since then, the greater focus on food insecurity represented by the first MDGs and later the SDGs has brought more focus to women's roles in food production. However, despite the introduction of more gender-sensitive tools for use by development planners and workers and the initial primary focus of the MDGs on income and food insecurity, according to UN Women (2011: 104), the numbers of undernourished people went up from 827 million in the early 1990s to 906 million in 2010. Had women really been provided equal access to agricultural inputs such as seeds and tools, it is estimated that hunger would have gone down by 150 million as women still constitute the majority of farmers in sub-Saharan Africa and South Asia, where extreme poverty is concentrated, and a significant number of farmers in the global South generally (UN Women 2011: 105). But there are much wider problems that account for the increase in food insecurity, and these have to do with the power of gender to devalue the lives and health of the poor, of which women and children make up the majority.

For example, most food is grown not for local or even national consumption but for the now global network of food circulation, which is problematic in terms of local health and larger environmental concerns. Crops have also been diverted from providing food to being used as alternative fuel sources, primarily in the West. Moreover, the steady decline of value attributed to agricultural and other (non-oil) primary commodities is devastating for individuals and countries that depend on the sale of primary goods for their economic well-being. Individuals and countries find themselves without sufficient cash for purchasing food and other goods to meet even basic human needs. Top-down and arguably masculinist responses feature accelerating food production through large-scale mechanization, widespread use of chemical fertilizers, and even genetic modification of seeds, plants, and livestock. This strengthens corporate control over food production, further distancing local farmers, particularly women farmers, from the means to adequately and safely feed their families, communities, and nations. Several decades ago, Sen and Grown (1987) called this the "food-fuel-water crises." Women's displacement from the land by large-scale agricultural development for export has contributed to high levels of famine, particularly in Africa. But there are additional consequences of this displacement, contributing not only to continued hunger but also to deforestation and desertification. Women are the main food producers and processors in most of the rural areas of the global South, and they must have access to clean water and firewood for fuel. As their land is lost to corporate farms and as water sources are polluted by agricultural runoff from fertilizers and pesticides or suspended by large-scale dam projects or privatization efforts, rural women and children are forced to travel farther and farther in search of clean water, spending as much as 40 billion hours per year on this pursuit in Africa alone (UNIFEM 2008: 130).

Similarly, as forests are cut down for large-scale agricultural, industrial, tourist, or even residential enterprises, women must go farther afield to look for the firewood needed to cook and to boil water, making it safe to drink. This has exposed them even more to "firestick" rapes in such places as the DRC and the Darfur region of Sudan. When water and fuel sources are being depleted, not only does food become scarce, but also the basis for ecologically sound agricultural practices is eroded. First, female subsistence farmers are forced to cultivate small plots of land repeatedly rather than engage in crop rotation. Monoculture depletes vital soil nutrients and can eventually even lead to small-scale desertification. Large-scale desertification is the result of the overuse of crop lands by corporate farming practices, including not rotating crops, overwatering and salinating the soil, and/or growing crops using methods that destroy fragile topsoil.

Second, when the soil is too depleted to produce crops, rural populations are reduced to consuming the seeds for future crops, destroying their capability to produce their own food. Another alternative is to seek food, as well as fuel and water, farther away from their homes. This pushes rural peoples into marginal and, therefore, sensitive ecosystems, even conservation areas and parks. Different interests motivate poor rural peoples, who have few alternatives for survival in the short term, and ecologists, who take the longer view toward saving the environment but who do not work on remedies for the unequal distribution of land and resources that forces poor people to seek food, fuel, and water in protected areas.

This unequal distribution of land and resources arises not just from class status but also from gender divisions in a world in which women own much less land than men.[2] The Western assumption that women are not farmers has led both to the loss of women's land rights and to the failure to provide technological assistance to women who work the land. As we have learned from the unforeseen consequences of high-technology experiments such as the green revolution, not all technology is good or appropriate for every socioeconomic and environmental context. Development mistakes—mistakes for the large number of people impoverished by them—might have been avoided if women farmers in the global South, who are central to subsistence food production and thus mindful of conserving the land, had been consulted about how best to use the land and what technologies are most appropriate (Rodda 1991).

Most women agricultural workers are not formally educated in modern, Western agricultural techniques. However, they work closely with and on the land and have developed significant informal knowledge about ecosystems and appropriate land-use patterns. As farmers, women often know which plants have the most nutritional value and what forms of cultivation lead to the least soil erosion and water consumption. As traditional healers, women often know which plants have medicinal value and what practices sustain the biodiversity of an ecosystem to ensure that such healing vegetation is preserved. As fuel gatherers, women know they are dependent on forests to provide renewable sources of firewood.[3] International and national development planners and agencies that ignore women's knowledge and introduce inappropriate technologies can do much more harm than good. And there is every indication that land and water are becoming increasingly privatized and corporatized—processes addressed next—which are undermining access to these sources of basic needs for poor and working-class women and men in rural and urban areas (Barthwal-Datta and Basu 2015).

Neoliberal Development

As noted earlier, (non-security-related) development has always been greatly underfunded by almost all donor nations relative to their GDPs, and so, as the discussion next on neoliberal globalization indicates, development became more "marketized" since the 1980s as countries in the global South were expected by IFIs to open their economies to global market forces to improve the lives of their citizens. Whereas WID and GAD approaches tended to focus on small income-generating development projects for poor women, the globalization of global South economies brought great numbers of poor women into light industrial work for export, particularly in export-processing zones (EPZs)—a development referred to as the "feminization of labor." Similar to early industrialization patterns in the West, poor, young, and unmarried women without children were designated as a source of "cheap" and "docile" labor. Even though such light industrial work gave women more income than they could have made in agricultural labor as that sector continued to decline, superexploitative and highly dangerous labor practices (including unregulated exposure to toxic chemicals used in workplaces and dumped in workers' neighborhoods) have been documented by feminists and protested by women workers since the onset of this marketized "development" strategy (Fernandez-Kelly 1983; Fuentes and Ehrenreich 1983). The 2013 physical collapse of a Bangladesh textile plant, which serviced major US clothing retailers, killed hundreds of women workers (see Box 5.1), underscoring how poor the conditions remain for female factory workers, particularly in the global South. Although poor women continue to be the preferred labor force in textile/clothing industries, their employment has declined more recently in other industries overall and/or relative to men's. When production shifts either to other countries in the relentless corporate search for cheaper labor or toward more automation, women lose their jobs. Relatedly, as men's income sources have declined under globalization, they have become more amenable to taking "feminized" (poorly paid, unregulated, non-unionized) jobs. Moreover, women's unemployment in all sectors increased substantially after the 2008 economic crisis, and of those who still have wages, too many have little say in how they are spent (UN Women 2011: 105). Thus, there is nothing secure or necessarily uplifting or poverty abating about this marketized strategy for development.

In the new millennium and on the faulty assumption that increasing women's wage work alone, especially given how little poor and working-class women in the formal economy actually earn, would address poverty in the global South, development agencies began to look at poor men as the problem. Deciding that poor men were keeping poor women in heteropatriarchal households from their income-generating potential by failing to assist with domestic responsibilities in the home, perpetrating domestic violence against women who attempt to work outside the home, and controlling and wasting the money that women do earn, the World Bank in particular began to pursue a development policy that would encourage men "to care better" in order to release women "to work more" for incomes (Bedford 2009: 22). Even though there is much evidence of such heteropatriarchal constraints on poor women and, in fact, on women across the socioeconomic spectrum in the global South and North, such a policy targets and demonizes poor, racialized men in the global South rather than holding more structural factors in the GPE responsible, such as maldistributions of

Box 5.1 Disposable Bangladeshi Women Workers in the Global Garment Industry

Rana Plaza in Dhaka, Bangladesh, was the nine-story building that collapsed from the fire that started in Tazreen Fashions that it housed and where 70 percent of the workers were women making, on average, 37 dollars per month sewing clothes for the likes of "Walmart, Disney, and Gap" (Enloe 2014: 252). Despite claims that the global garment industry, heavily concentrated in Bangladesh, observed basic standards for workers, a former child worker in the industry and head of the Bangladesh Center for Worker Solidarity noted, "In this factory there was a pile of fabrics and yarn stored on the ground floor that caught fire. Workers couldn't evacuate through the stairs. What does this say about compliance?" (quoted in Enloe 2014: 255–256).

wealth and power among nations, socioeconomic classes, and races that have their roots in heteropatriarchal (neo)colonizing and modernizing practices. This policy also constitutes a form of social engineering engaged in by IFIs that Kate Bedford (2009) identifies as a global-level attempt to govern intimate relations for the purpose of aligning private life with the needs of the global economy, rather than aligning economies to enable the social provisioning necessary for more equitable and just, as well as less violent, familial (and other) relations. What such a policy also ignores is that some poor women are either single or sexual minorities who do not live in heteropatriarchal households (Lind 2010). The heteronormative lens of development ensures that female-headed and lesbian-headed households are either marginalized or unseen and, therefore, significantly excluded from development assistance.

Neoliberal development has also ensured that environmental issues are subsumed to the interests of capital, constituting a colonization of nature itself while also naturalizing inequalities. As Nandita Ghosh puts it,

> Promoting market values above all else also reduces complex human relationships with nature to ego-driven, need-based interactions. Nature is also perceived as universal and encompassing of all human society. Here too it is externalized and can be used to justify the "natural" ethnic, sexual, and class oppressions that are always gendered. Both ideologies obfuscate the contributions of human labor to the process by which nature is externalized, produced, and consumed.
>
> (2007: 446)

This "marketization of nature" also pits "diverse cultures and ecosystems against the privatization and enclosure" of the global resource "commons" (Ghosh 2007: 446).

What has also occurred in the new millennium is a "financialization of development" (Roy 2010: 31), which is discussed in the following focus on the gendering and gendered nature of neoliberal globalization. Suffice it to say here, and in light of the foregoing, that despite greater attention to women and gender relations, contemporary development approaches have done little to alter the gendered divisions of labor or stem poverty, and have instead reinforced a range of power relations in the GPE that are associated with the power of gender.

Gendering and Gendered Neoliberal Globalization

Since approximately the 1970s, globalization has been driven primarily by neoliberal economic policies favored by geopolitical elites (mostly men), especially economists trained in the global North and acting as policymakers in IFIs, such as the IMF, the World Bank, and the WTO. Advocates of neoliberalism—also known as supply-side economics, the Washington Consensus, or market fundamentalism—draw on neoclassical economic theory to argue that markets function most efficiently and productively, and generate the greatest overall prosperity, when they are unfettered by government regulation. As noted in Chapter 1, many advocates also claim that unconstrained markets "naturally" foster liberty, democracy, and more peaceful societies. From these assumptions, neoliberal advocates promote a combination of restructuring policies aimed at achieving "freedom" from state-imposed restrictions and opening national borders to create a "world" economy.

The code word of neoliberal capitalism is *liberalization*: ensuring a free-market economy by removing governmental interference in and impediments to the "free" flow of money, goods, services, and capital (financial assets). Policy reforms are variously aimed at eliminating such restrictions (while continuing to constrain the movement of workers). *Deregulation* refers to relaxing or removing existing state controls, for example, on wages, prices, and foreign exchange rates, and reducing state regulatory functions, for example, in regard to protecting workers' rights and the environment. *Privatization* refers to replacing the "inefficiencies" of public ownership and control by reducing state ownership and management of enterprises (often those providing public goods and services, such as electricity, transportation, security) in favor of the private sector. Complementing these supply-side reforms are fiscal and monetary *stabilization policies* to reduce government spending, deficits, and aggregate demand; these involve fewer public-sector jobs and a decrease in state expenditures on social programs (welfare, education, health). *Specialization* in economic activities is promoted—based on the assumption of comparative advantage—and export-oriented policies are favored in pursuit of economic development and growth.

Informalization of Labor

In order to be more competitive by cutting costs (especially of labor), firms and nations take measures to render their operations more flexible. *Flexibilization* in general refers to shifts in production processes: to more spatially dispersed networks and decentralized control (the global assembly line, subcontracting); to increasingly casualized (non-permanent, part-time) and informalized (unregulated, non-contractual) jobs; to small-batch, "just-in-time" (short-term rather than long-term) production planning; and to avoidance or prohibition of organized labor. At the core of flexibilization are efforts to deregulate production processes and labor markets—hence, increasing freedom for management—ostensibly to eliminate inefficient rigidities imposed by regulation and to ensure that the "freedom of the market" is unconstrained. Here the discourse of neoliberalism invokes flexibility as essential for competitive success and as an inherently positive practice and orientation. In contrast, critics argue that flexibilization erodes hard-won workers' rights and constitutes a retreat from the progressive agenda of achieving what the International Labour Organization (ILO) characterizes as "decent work" for all workers.

Cutting back on the workforce is most visible as loss of employment for significant numbers of workers, especially those holding what were previously regarded as full-time, permanent, protected, or secure positions. But a more apt generalization refers not simply to unemployment per se but also to the polarization of available employment, with increasing opportunities for those who "fit" the demands of postindustrial or informational capitalism. At the top end are valorized (masculinized and primarily elite male) workers sought for their technical, informational, and knowledge-based skills. At the bottom are those in demand as semi- or unskilled workers: they are valuable to employers and to the accumulation of global capital but are devalorized by their location in feminized jobs. In fact, flexibilization constitutes *feminization* of employment, understood simultaneously as a material, embodied transformation of labor markets (increasing proportion of women, deteriorating work conditions for men), a conceptual characterization of deteriorated and devalorized labor conditions (less desirable, meaningful, safe, or secure), and a reconfiguration of worker identities (feminized managers, female breadwinners). As the proliferation of lower-end jobs requires fewer skills and flexibilization becomes the norm, employers seek workers who are perceived to be undemanding (unorganized), docile but reliable, available for part-time and temporary work, and willing to accept low wages. Migrant workers, especially undocumented ones, are particularly positioned to have to accept such precarious employment, but gender stereotypes depict women more generally as most suitable for these jobs, and gender inequalities render women especially desperate for access to income. In short, as more jobs are casual, irregular, flexible, and precarious (read: feminized), more women—and feminized men—are doing them.

Although neoliberal policies have the effect of decreasing *formal*—especially permanent, secure, decent—employment, they spur phenomenal growth in *informal*—unregulated, unprotected, and insecure—economic activities. Until recently, conventional accounts paid little attention to informal activities, which were trivialized as remnants of "incomplete modernization" associated with "traditional" (read: non-European) societies. But economists are increasingly aware that informal activities are inextricable from and indeed make possible the "productive" economy, in part because they are based on flexibilization: the outsourcing and subcontracting processes of flexibilization shift production toward less formal, regularized, and regulated work conditions; the erosion of labor power accompanying flexibilization exacerbates the decline in family income, which "pushes" more people into informal work; and flexibilization reduces tax revenues, which exacerbates the decline in welfare provisioning and spurs informal work to compensate in part for this loss.

Women especially rely on informal activities as a survival strategy to ensure social reproduction. They are overrepresented in informal activities worldwide (for example, constituting 63 percent of workers in family businesses with no direct pay), the informal economy is the primary source of earnings for women in most global South countries (where 75 percent of the workforce is in informal occupations), women are the majority of part-time informal workers in rich countries (constituting two-thirds of those working involuntarily in temporary employment in OECD countries), and the gender gap that persists globally (with women making, on average, 24 percent less than men) is even wider in the informal than in the formal economy (with self-employed women making almost half of what self-employed men make in some countries) (UN Women 2015: 96, 104, 106).

Homework, domestic work, and sex work are "old" forms of informal labor most associated with women, but they have become growing features of and major enterprises in the new, postindustrial global economy, becoming almost emblematic of it. Under neoliberal globalization, poor and working-class women from the global South (and some poorer areas of the global North) are now migrating beyond borders as much as men are for economic survival, very often to perform traditionally "feminine" and "feminized" jobs—homework (or industrial production done in the home typically involving piecework, such as sewing garments), domestic work (including housekeeping and child care), nursing (including home care of the elderly), and sex work (either coerced or voluntary)—in the global North (and some wealthy areas of the global South). In some countries, such as the Philippines, women are encouraged and assisted to migrate as "guest workers" to perform "care" labor as a matter of state development policy because the remittances they send home from the comparatively higher wages they can make abroad help to sustain families and communities at home, effectively subsidizing the national economy. Remittances sent home by (im)migrant laborers worldwide reached an estimated $305 billion in 2008, and although declining the following year to $290 billion in the wake of the financial crisis, they still dwarf "official development aid and private capital flows" (Bach 2011: 133). But, as further discussed in this chapter, there are high costs to (im)migrant women and their families for propping up developing economies and cheaply servicing developed ones.[4] Moreover, many migrant women, like many migrant men, are increasingly forced to migrate as undocumented workers as states in the global North have tightened borders and immigration requirements in the wake of 9/11 and with the rise of far-right anti-immigration regimes in the global North. This heightens the exploitation of migrant workers and puts them at far greater risk from punitive actions by the host state, including arrest, indefinite detention, deportation, and family separation, but also denial of access to health (including reproductive health) care, education, domestic violence programs, and a whole range of other social services.[5]

Homework is not a residual form of production, but is in fact integral to industrialization and current restructuring processes: it exposes the blurred boundaries between unpaid housework, paid informal work, and formal waged labor. Global growth in homeworking is attributable to several factors: corporate desires to cut labor and overhead costs by outsourcing production tasks (e.g., sewing, light assembly work) that can be performed by subcontracted laborers in their homes anywhere in the world, large pools of migrant and immigrant workers who are drawn into homework because of racist and sexist discrimination and restrictive immigration laws that prevent them from working in the formal sector, and increasing pressures on women to generate income in support of household survival. These same factors are also associated with the reappearance of sweatshops in the North as well as the South, where (immigrant) women and children toil at sewing machines, typically under unsafe and "hidden" conditions, to produce designer clothing and niche market commodities as part of just-in-time production (Enloe 2014). Women especially are sought for homework, even among more "middle-class" service workers in the so-called "gig economy," because they are considered available and reliable, and their below-subsistence earnings are justified as merely "supplemental" income. Employers may also promote homework as a means of gaining more control over labor by decentralizing and thus undercutting traditional sites of unionization and the development of solidarity among workers (Benería 2003).

Subcontracting to (female) homeworkers can reap the additional benefit of controlling workers through masculinist ideologies and practices. Like informal activities more generally, homework is very poorly paid, and this is justified by characterizing homework as an extension of (unpaid) housework or as merely supplementary income. The increasing reliance of the formal economy on the informal economy to produce goods and services under poor working conditions and at extremely low pay rates begins to explain why it is that at a time when women are entering the formal workforce in record numbers, the global phenomenon of the feminization of poverty is increasing.

In addition to homework, another burgeoning transnational economy of a "domestic" nature is the "maid-trade" (Ehrenreich and Hochschild 2002a; Benería 2003; True 2012; Enloe 2014), in which gender is not only pervasive but also clearly racialized. Domestic work is called that because it presumably occurs in a private location—"behind closed doors"—typically a family household or the "temporary home" afforded by commercial accommodations when people are on the move. In addition to the unpaid domestic work of most women in their own homes, class-privileged women and families often seek domestic workers to maintain their homes and care for their children. This transference of domestic labor may be due to employment by the "woman of the house" that precludes her doing it or to sufficient resources that she need not do it herself. In a less familial but still domestic sense, tourist hotels, conference facilities, training and research institutions, and global cities depend on a large number of maids, cooks, and cleaning workers, as well as other service providers.

Domestic work is a rapidly growing global business involving vast networks of people and agencies that facilitate transnational flows, such as moneylenders, airlines, hotels, translation services, training institutions, and banks. It is important to note that payments for domestic work, especially caregiving work related to a health provision, constitute an important source of foreign remittances for countries of origin and reduce labor costs in receiver countries. In spite of providing socially necessary labor, domestic workers typically reap few benefits and face multiple hardships—especially women who migrate for these jobs. Gender stereotypes associate cleaning and caretaking as women's work; domestic work is understood to be unskilled, and it attracts women who need paid work, have little (valued) training, may require housing accommodation, and/or seek work where citizenship status is not monitored. Not surprisingly, domestic workers in private households are often immigrant women. As non-citizens, and even non-native speakers, they are particularly vulnerable to employer intimidation and abuse occurring in spaces that are understood to be separate from the public gaze and state regulation. Domestic workers who "live in" are especially subject to a variety of exploitative practices: they work long hours and may even be considered "on call" 24 hours a day, they are typically paid very poorly and may have few resources or time for venturing beyond the household, their activities and personal behavior are closely scrutinized, and their live-in status makes them especially vulnerable to sexual exploitation or to being construed as "promiscuous or exotic" due to racialized stereotypes (Pettman 1996: 192).

Wives and mothers who pay other (often racialized and migrant) women to do "their" domestic work avoid disrupting gendered divisions of labor within the household, but at the expense of exacerbating class (and often racial and national) divisions among women. Even though the hiring of domestic workers ostensibly "frees" women who employ such workers from household chores, it also effectively relieves pressure on men to do their share of caring labor and relieves pressure on states to provide child care and support social reproduction. These dynamics are further complicated by the fact that many—perhaps most—domestic workers are themselves married women with children, many of whom face the stark choice of either living with their children in poverty or earning desperately needed money by living away from them (Ehrenreich and Hochschild 2002b: 2; Barber 2011). Who hires and who serves may reflect colonial histories (black maids of white madams in South Africa) or newer hierarchies of international debt and employment opportunities (Filipino maids in Saudi Arabia). But in all cases it appears that cultural and racial stereotyping occurs in terms of preferred—"suitable" or "trusted"—domestic workers. As Bridget Anderson observes, "Racist stereotypes intersect with issues of citizenship, and result in a racist hierarchy which uses skin color, religion, and nationality to construct some women as being more suitable for domestic work than others" (Anderson 2000: 2).

The 2011 ILO Convention 189 on Domestic Workers is the first such convention to extend labor rights to domestic workers (see Box 5.2). This came about through decades of organizing by the International Domestic Workers Network (IDWN) in concert with the International Union of Food, Agricultural, Hotel, Restaurant, Catering, Tobacco, and Allied Workers'

Box 5.2 Rights and Protections for Domestic and Other Informal Workers

The **ILO Domestic Workers Convention** requires states that adopt it to legislatively ensure that domestic workers are accorded "normal hours of work with regular periods of rest, overtime compensation, annual paid leave, minimum wages, a safe and healthy working environment and social security benefits" (UN Women 2015: 106). In addition to the transnational organizing to gain this convention of domestic workers through the IDWN, which recognized in its statements that the poor treatment of domestic workers was due to gender "power relationships" (Enloe 2014: 338), female homeworkers and self-employed workers have also organized and led hunger strikes through, for example, the Self-Employed Women's Association in India, which gained the Street Vendors Act in 2014 that accords vendors the right to work in safe and sanitary conditions without fear of harassment (UN Women 2015: 107).

Associations (IUF) and the transnational Women in Informal Employment: Globalizing and Organizing advocacy group (Enloe 2014: 336–337). However, as of 2016, only 17 countries had ratified this convention that obligates them to changing national laws to extend and enforce these rights.

Sex work exists worldwide. It appears, however, to be increasing as economic conditions deteriorate, the Internet affords novel and elusive activities, and geopolitical developments alter migration flows. Who buys and who sells may vary, but similar to domestic work, in all cases it appears that cultural and racial stereotyping occurs in terms of preferred—desirable, exotic, submissive—sex workers. Barbara Ehrenreich and Arlie Hochschild offer this explanation:

> Immigrant women may seem desirable sexual partners for the same reason that First World employers believe them to be especially gifted as caregivers: they are thought to embody the traditional feminine qualities of nurturance, docility, and eagerness to please. Some men feel nostalgic for these qualities, which they associate with a bygone way of life. Even as many wage-earning Western women assimilate to the competitive culture of "male" work and ask respect for making it in a man's world, some men seek in the "exotic Orient" or "hot-blooded tropics" a woman from the imagined past.
>
> (2002b: 9–10)

Like the commodification of caring and domestic labor, sex for purchase is controversial, and analyzing sex work is particularly problematic for feminists. On the one hand, due to hetero-patriarchal identities, ideologies, and practices, it is *female* bodies[6] that are most objectified, manipulated, violated, and physically harmed. This makes the sex industry—including advertising, pornography, videos, prostitution, and trafficking—a particular concern to critics of women's subordination. On the other hand, sex is a profoundly personal and intimate realm of human activity, which cautions against simplistic and moralizing pronouncements regarding appropriate, desirable, or despicable sexual conduct. Moreover, (typically conservative) sexual mores and moralizing judgments feed directly into pathologizing and criminalizing non-normative sexual behaviors, whether for profit or not, stigmatizing and even imprisoning not only sex workers but also, for example, LGBTQ persons (Kempadoo 2005). So whereas the violence entailed in coercing sexual activities or trafficking people for such purposes must be condemned, evaluating the array of sexual activities a person might voluntarily engage in—commercially or otherwise—is problematic.

Of further concern is how sensationalized sex trafficking has become when it, in fact, constitutes only a part of the much larger problem of human trafficking for all kinds of coerced labor. Although few countries have ratified UN conventions for protecting the rights of migrants (True 2012: 58), such as the 1990 International Convention on the Protection of the Rights of all Migrant Workers and Members of Their Families, at least 100 have signed onto the 2000 UN Protocol to Prevent, Suppress, and Punish the Trafficking in Persons. Partially accounting for this has been the concerted efforts of "abolitionist" or "prohibitionist" feminists and some strange bedfellows—religious conservatives particularly associated with the US Christian Right—working in global arenas to end "sex slavery" (Kempadoo 2005). Although this protocol signaled international recognition of sex trafficking, it and the national legislations it has spawned against sex trafficking are more motivated by "securing" states against unwanted migrants, including criminal and criminalized elements associated with the sex trade. Moreover, because the focus is on punishment, it is a "securitizing" approach to anti-sex trafficking that fails to address the economic pushes and pulls of all trafficking in persons and does little to assist those trafficked, whose agency is denied and who are frequently revictimized by punitive state actions (Kamrani and Gentile 2013). This approach also militates against the decriminalization or legalization of sex work that is advocated by "prosex" or "sex-positive" feminists and that has been found to be a necessary step for enabling sex workers to articulate their own needs (including through labor unions they form) and generally improving their working conditions (Goodyear and Weitzer 2011).

The "moral panic" that has privileged sex trafficking over other forms of human trafficking as a matter of international and national concern also operates to either demonize "prostitutes" (more so than their pimps and procurers) or to reduce them to helpless victims in need of neocolonial "rescue" by more enlightened Western or Western-supported actors. These points are cogently made by Laura Maria Agustín (2007) in her study of migrant sex workers and the European social workers and activists dedicated to "helping them." In particular, she exposes the self-importance of middle-class women (normalized by Eurocentric imperialism), their presumption of moral clarity and cultural superiority, and their denial of voice and agency to non-European women while claiming to aid them through rescue. The neocolonial basis of rescue missions becomes even more visible when we consider the actions of Western-based evangelical NGOs, which storm brothels in the global South to "free" girls, who typically return to brothels because underlying ideologies and socioeconomic structures remain untouched.

Structural Adjustment and Global Restructuring

The most widely known and ongoing neoliberal policy developed early on in the globalization process has been the imposition by the IMF of structural adjustment programs (SAPs) in many developing countries in the wake of a series of debt crises produced by Northern financial markets in the 1980s. Unfortunately, these programs have eroded whatever gains were made earlier in getting public and private development lending agencies to recognize the importance of women's work and gender issues to successful economic development. Until recently, most critiques of neoliberal restructuring focused on the effects of SAPs in the South, where the costs have been starkly visible (Joekes and Weston 1995; Rai 2002; Eisenstein 2009). Many of these countries seek foreign currency loans to finance continued or new debt obligations, and to secure such loans, they must accept a variety of neoliberal conditions imposed by World Bank structural adjustment or IMF stabilization programs. Yassine Fall provides a succinct description:

> Structural adjustment policies are meant to sustain and reinforce conditions that will invite foreign investors to exploit either the labor or natural resources of a country to produce foreign currency for balance of payments purposes and to repay national debt. They encourage the use of a country's resources for export development rather than for domestic development (again to produce foreign currency to repay debt). They encourage the privatization of services, which reduces the autonomy of local governments and often generates massive unemployment. They encourage cuts in health, education, and social welfare budgets for the purpose of reducing deficits, leaving people, especially women and children who are already impoverished and disadvantaged, in desperate and life-threatening situations.
>
> (2001: 71)[7]

Because of their initial interest in women and development, feminists have generated the most extensive research on the effects of SAPs. Although there are important differences among countries subject to restructuring, cumulative studies reveal patterns: the enormous social costs of adjustment, increases in income inequality, tendencies toward social polarization that aggravate conflicts, shifts in control over resources, and the "existence of class, gender and ethnic biases in the adjustment process" (Benería 1995: 1844).

Neoliberal globalization has been operating to produce similar patterns in "developed" economies, particularly since the end of the Cold War. Former Soviet bloc countries instituted, also under pressure from Western governments and lending agencies, "shock therapy" programs designed by Western economists to quickly turn socialist economies into capitalist ones. These programs drastically cut and/or privatized government services while also privatizing production to increase productivity, exports, and foreign direct investment. In these countries, working-class women have been disproportionately bearing the costs and economic inequalities are expanding, as unemployment grows and socialized benefits, welfare supports, and medical services that were formerly available are no longer assured. Western countries, to greater and lesser degrees, have also been steadily self-imposing the privatization and diminution of public services, particularly under neoconservative governments and now far-right ones (Marchand and Runyan 2011). Since the 2008 economic crisis, this "austerity" approach has widened and accelerated, particularly in Europe and the US, but also throughout the West and under a range of political regimes (Hozić and True 2016). The establishment of the Eurozone, which created a common currency for most members of the EU, meant that the subsequent debt crises, again produced by Northern financial markets, hitting a number of southern European countries endangered the Eurozone itself. So as a condition of bailouts provided by the European Central Bank as well as the IMF and European Commission and brokered by the richest members of the EU, these countries have also had to undergo SAP-like restructuring to the detriment of their peoples (including their middle classes) and their democracies. The US bailed out banks and large corporations that were "too big to fail" during the financial crisis, but while they are now running record profits and Wall Street is booming, ordinary people continue to suffer. As a result of a weak stimulus program coupled with largely stymied regulations of financial capital and little relief for home owners facing home foreclosures arising from the mortgage crisis, which was among the factors that precipitated the financial crisis, large swaths of working- and middle-class people have been facing high unemployment and underemployment and stagnant or reduced wages. This has led them to default on their (mostly unadjusted) mortgage loans for houses worth less after the crisis, thereby losing a great deal of their assets.

The production of a huge cadre of the working poor is associated with the "Walmartization" of the US economy, or the business model of retail giant Walmart, taken up and globalized by Amazon and many others, including high-tech firms such as Apple. This model relies on global supply chains of cheap labor and goods, which drive down wages, unions, and employee benefits in the deindustrialized North and superexploit workers in the South. The working poor in the North become reliant on the cheap goods produced in the South (especially China) for Walmart and others. To make up, if possible, for poverty-level wages and for a lack of health, retirement, and other social welfare benefits withheld by these huge and obscenely profitable conglomerates, these workers must supplement their incomes with a host of government programs, such as food stamps. Cuts in these programs translate into even greater food, housing, and health insecurities. Such now truly "global" restructuring is most visibly gendered when we look at its effects on welfare provisioning, which is key to social reproduction. In large part due to feminist interventions, economic policy analysts and critics now recognize that, while the effects of restructuring have been most severe in the global South, there are parallel racialized gender and class effects in the North, where cutbacks in public welfare also have their greatest impact on feminized populations: women and the (working) poor, but particularly (working) poor women.[8]

Just as neoliberal global restructuring (or globalization) has produced the crisis of social reproduction, it has also produced ecological crises, while undermining responses to them. Shock therapy capitalism has been accompanied by what Naomi Klein (2007) refers to as "disaster capitalism." As "natural" disasters, ranging from the 2004 Southeast Asian tsunami and the 2005 Hurricane Katrina to the unprecedented 2017 hurricanes and earthquakes that destroyed parts of the Caribbean and Mexico, have become more frequent and intense due to "man-made" climate change, the range of social and technological safety nets that would have better protected people and their environments when such disasters struck has been structurally undermined by a free-market ideology that transferred resources from public services and works to private corporate hands. Such "natural" disasters, rather than serving as wake-up calls to shift resources back into serving public needs and environmental protection, have actually accelerated private accumulation through privately contracted disaster "relief" and development geared for gentrification that pushes poor people out of their neighborhoods or leaves their neighborhoods (or whole nations, such as in the ongoing case of Puerto Rico) still in ruin. This has deepened human immiseration and worsened environmental vulnerability. As also discussed more in this chapter, the effects of climate change have been most borne by the poor, the racialized, and the indigenous in the global South and North, but especially women within these contexts. Thus, neoliberal globalization is deeply implicated in the social reproduction and ecological crises that combine to produce the crisis of sustainability. Exacerbating this further, however, are several other forms of gendering and gendered financial capitalism that have emerged as neoliberal global restructuring has worn on. These are addressed next.

Gendering and Gendered Financialization

Neoliberal policies have been altering not only production processes and the value of "work," but also financial arrangements and the value of "money." In brief, and necessarily oversimplified, deregulation enabled tremendous expansion of cross-border capital flows—of bonds, loans, currencies, equities, and so on. This afforded new opportunities to create profits ("wealth"), not through the real economy of production, commodities, consumption, and trade, but through trade in capital (financial) assets—in effect, making money from money that is the hallmark of "financial capitalism." What matters is that these processes of wealth creation are based less on exchanges in the "real" economy of goods and services than on *perceptions*—primarily in the minds of male traders and financial investors—of expected revenues and potential risks. Although the bubble of inflated perceptions generates mind-boggling wealth for some for a while, when it bursts, it has devastating effects on the many.

When financial matters assume priority, status and decision-making power within businesses, governments, and IGOs shift to those who "manage money" and "know" how to invest. Access to credit becomes decisive for individuals and states and is deeply structured by familiar hierarchies: women, the poor, and those who are un- and underemployed face much greater obstacles when credit is sought. Financial markets thus have pervasive effects, and when they are free of governmental regulation, these effects are primarily to enhance concentrations of wealth among elites.

Financial Crises

Examining the generation of financial crises and their effects reveals the power of gender in operation. First, women and gender-sensitive analyses are absent—or at best marginalized—in the decision-making processes and analytical assessments of the financial order. Women are underrepresented in the institutions of global finance, a model of elite agency and (instrumental) economic "efficiency" is deemed common sense, and the masculinism of financial players and their practices is presumed. Second, these exclusions and blinders filter what elite analysts are able—or willing—to "see," especially the dangers of short-term greed and the arrogance of power. They particularly obscure the gendered costs of financial crises.[9] The costs of the 2008 GFC and the austerities that followed have entailed "the loss of homes, unpayable debt, public sector job losses, and cuts to services," which "have substantially increased the risk of violence for women, but especially for single mothers and refugee and ethnic minority women, while diminishing the resources for police, community, and welfare services" to address gender and other forms of violence (Hozić and True 2016: 9). LGBTQ people also face greater violence with less recourse to public protection services, while being blamed, as are (im)migrants, for social disorder actually caused by the economic disorder of the GFC (Smith 2016). The costs of the GFC have also included a pronounced increase in male suicide in the global North and South (Hozić and True 2016: 9).

The disorders created by the GFC did produce, however, some, albeit brief, attention to gender inequality at the level of the world's financial elite. Immediately following the crash, a host of behavioral economists, media commentators, and even the World Economic Forum began to ask, what "if Lehman Brothers had been Lehman Sisters"? (Prügl 2016: 21). While there is no question that finance capital is a decidedly male domain and there is some evidence that the far fewer female traders are more risk-averse, the newfound attention to the dearth of women at the top of the financial world became just a replaying of old gender stereotypes, evoking "familiar associations of woman with succor, householding, and mending, supporting man, a doer who had erred" (Prügl 2016: 32). The idea that more women in finance would "save" financial capital from male excesses, while problematic, was also short-lived as, by 2009, the majority of those laid off in the financial sector were women, who were also poorly represented in the ultimately weak, and now endangered (particularly in the Anglo-American context), regulatory sector, set up to minimally protect Main Street from Wall Street and Fleet Street after the crash (Prügl 2016: 38–39).

The power of gender has operated here to obscure the deeper reforms required. Among these from feminist perspectives would include requiring gender equality across all economic sectors, taxing all financial transactions to restore and expand public infrastructures and services, and supporting women's and other social justice movements working for resource redistribution (Roberts 2016: 72). But at an even deeper level is the questioning of capitalism itself, which is productive of perpetual economic crises. This is forestalled by resorts to "gender-washing," or the covering over of complex systems of injustice by claiming to be supportive of gender equity while not actually practicing it.[10] This not only deflects attention away from power structures invested in sustaining multiple inequalities, but also perpetuates the "quick fix" of "adding women," stereotyped of late as the solution to economic ills afflicting not only the rich, but also the poor as a result of financial crises.

Financialization of Development

While the GFC focused brief attention on getting more women at the top of financial markets and decision-making to avert financial crises, women at the bottom of the world economy have been the focus of microfinance, which has been embraced by development agencies as the way to abate poverty. As part of the financialization of development or finance capital for the "bottom billion" (Roy 2010), microfinance or microcredit projects disburse small loans to a group of borrowers who collectively share responsibility for repayment. Access to the credit (US$50–200) rotates among members, who use it to jump-start or advance entrepreneurial activities, the success of which enables increased earnings, repayment of the loan, and further reinvestment and accumulation in an upward and out-of-poverty spiral. This strategy especially targets poor rural women precisely because their lack of any conventional collateral excludes them from access to credit, without which they have no hope of jump-starting a small business, of achieving their entrepreneurial potential, and of breaking out of the cycle of poverty. Women are also targeted because they are presumed to be better at forging social networks and sustaining the trust necessary for group success, and because their presumed fear of letting the group down will ensure they make an optimal effort toward repayment (Bergeron 2003: 166–167). Finally, women are targeted because of the expectation, and considerable evidence, that they are more likely than men are to use resources in support of family well-being (health, school fees).

Although there is growing evidence that this strategy is not reducing poverty and/or empowering women, it remains widely endorsed as a tool for alleviating poverty that is now being extended to poor men (Roy 2010). Some feminists initially saw microcredit projects as useful for directing attention to poor rural women who face limited options and who may be able to realize entrepreneurial benefits from access to these loans. By widening their focus to include issues of social status and the world's poorest women, development agencies draw attention to women as clients of development and provide openings for addressing related gender issues and mobilizing resources (Keck and Sikkink 1998). And in contrast to conventional narratives of devalorization, enthusiasts for microcredit promote positive representations of women's capacities and "traditional" community values. These shifts provide new opportunities because they target women as agents and beneficiaries, but these opportunities are proving to have considerable undersides.

A growing number of feminist critics of microcredit initiatives (Goetz and Gupta 1996; Poster and Salime 2002; Bergeron 2003; Roy 2010; Hossein 2016) have identified several problematic assumptions on which they rest. Such initiatives presume that the "solution" for ending poverty is to integrate the poor into commercial market activity by ensuring access to financial credit—what Gayatri Spivak characterizes as "credit-baiting without infrastructural reform" (Spivak 1999: 418); that poor people can be quickly and easily "rescued" by making small amounts of money available to them; and that poor people have the entrepreneurial skills and wider social system supports necessary for sustainable enterprises, including favorable market conditions and uncorrupt lending contexts. The premise here is that incorporation into circuits of capital enables successful competition and, hence, prosperity; in other words, capitalism can fix the (poverty) problem that capitalism produces—hence, this approach has been dubbed "poverty capitalism." These initiatives additionally presume that women can simply take on additional work responsibilities, will have the support of family and community members to do so and to prosper, and will be able to control how the money is invested and the profits used. The premise is that institutionalized gender, class, and race inequalities can be overlooked or easily transformed.

Critics raise other issues as well. A focus on microfinance avoids asking larger questions regarding the structural causes of poverty and its reproduction through neoliberal policies, the "quick fix" of microcredit projects shifts support from longer-term and more socially oriented programs addressing the complexity of effective social change, and the foregrounding of quantifiable success indicators (repayment rates) deflects attention from the quality of women's participation and whether and in what ways empowerment actually occurs. We see the power of gender operating in several ways: the framing of development strategies through a "paternalistic colonial lens" (Bergeron 2003:168), the reproduction of gender stereotypes and unchanged distributions of household labor, and simplistic expectations regarding domestic, gender, and class relations in community settings. In these senses, microcredit initiatives exemplify both the promise and flawed delivery of "women-oriented" policies problematized throughout this text: they are a too-simplistic answer to complex problems. The popularization of microcredit, however, obscures this. Microcredit enthusiasts, who market it as an empowering solution for women's poverty in the South to consuming publics in the West through such images as a poor woman "photographed with both 'primitive' abacus and 'modern' calculator" that turn her into a "magical object," enable the financialization of development to carry on largely unquestioned "in her name" (Roy 2010: 71).

Financialized Philanthropy and Consumption

The financialization of development has in some sense democratized development, increasingly drawing ordinary consumers in the developed world into financially supporting campaigns for such things as micro-credit, fair trade, and HIV/AIDS treatment initiatives sponsored by NGOs and corporations that frequently employ Western celebrities (Bono, Gwyneth Paltrow, Madonna, and so on) to encourage giving. This trend has been variously referred to as "celebrity-driven development," "philanthrocapitalism," or "brand aid" (Rowley 2011; Richey and Ponte 2011; King 2013) and often consists of campaigns that exhort consumers to buy products made available to them that supposedly "save" the lives of poor people, particularly women, in the global South who are to benefit from (some of) the proceeds from the products bought. Although more "ethical consumption" that foregrounds the needs of poor women and engages consumers in caring about them and doing something for them can be seen as a positive development, too often these campaigns obscure the poor working conditions of those who produce the items for sale, endear consumers to the very corporations involved in large-scale labor exploitation in the developing and developed worlds, play on stereotypical images of either victimized or beautified poor women generically from the global South (and especially the African continent) to open purse strings, and, in some cases, give little of the proceeds to combating the problems they claim they seek to solve (Rowley 2011). Just as problematically, these initiatives turn shopping into a moral act, feeding into the faulty assumption that this is all that is necessary to alleviate the pain of faraway vulnerable bodies of color, while increasing the profits of the corporations implicated in sustaining those vulnerabilities. Thus, this trend constitutes only a new twist on the sordid relationship between global capitalism and consumerism detailed below.

Market processes involve the production of goods and services, the circulation of cash or credit for purchasing them, and the creation of consumer desires that shape what we purchase. A great deal of attention and resources goes into producing a pervasive market *culture* that encourages consumption by inculcating consumer *subjectivities*—that is, orienting people to always desire and thus consume "more" and, more recently, to imagine that their endless consuming will "do good." The power of gender operates through marketing, advertising, and deepening the commodification of social life and relations. The politics of advertising—who decides what we "want"—is explicitly about using cultural codes to manipulate consciousness and create ever-changing tastes and fashions (McCracken 2014). Stereotypes of gender, ethnicity/race, sexuality, and age are used strategically and prominently in advertising to project selective images of bodies, cultures, sexualities, and lifestyles as the "most desired" and "most desirable" or the most "helpable," as in the case of marketing for ethical consumption. Celebrity-studded arts and entertainment are also big business on a global scale, where selling sex, sensationalism, stereotypes of "good" and "bad" cultures, and now "brand aid" is a lucrative strategy. At the same time, the more corporatized popular music and videos become, the more violent and sexually violent they become. Women's bodies continue to be objectified, whether as hypersexual commodities available to consumers or as asexual victims in need of saving by consumers.

In recent years, "sustainability" has become a new global buzzword in IGO and NGO circles and has entered popular discourse. But it too has also been taken up by the market, seeing more profits to be made by creating a niche market for "green" production and products. Like "brand aid," the "ecobranding" of products and corporations as "green" too often devolves into "green-washing," which both taps into and creates consumer desires for more ethical consumption but sells only somewhat modified versions of still polluting, wasteful, and labor-exploiting commodities (Parr 2009). And like brand aid, ecobranding and green-washing manufacture an essentially depoliticized response to the crisis of sustainability.

Although affluent consumption is the privilege of only a small elite, it shapes the desires, choices, and valorization of those without affluence. Pervasive advertising and global media encourage even the poorest to desire consumer goods as an expression of self-worth. Northern desires for cheap goods as well as luxury items—clothes, cars, electronics, flowers, furs, diamonds, gasoline—determine Southern patterns of production, including poorly paid workers, hazardous work conditions, and environmentally unsound practices. Even political activities shift to market-based expressions: identity-based groups become particular targets of marketing and use consumption as an identity "marker," and political action is increasingly consumer-based as people "vote" through what they do and do not buy, just as they are now expected to "save" feminized "others" by their mere purchases. But we might ask: Whose needs, desires, and interests are served by consumerism? Whose bodies and environments are devalorized—rendered disposable—in pursuit of consumerism and the neoliberal commitment to growth (rather than redistribution) that fuels it?

Gendering and Gendered Climate Change and Resource Destruction

The devalorization of the environment upon which industrial capitalism and more recent neoliberal globalization rest has led to a wide array of resource shortages and maldistributions, ecological degradations, and "natural" disasters, the most serious of which in terms of global impact is the onset of climate change. Although there is a global scientific and, until recently, even a global political consensus that climate change is "man-made" by largely industrial pollutants and curbing it is part of the SDGs, this has not yet caused a fundamental rethinking of commitments to neoliberal globalization that might curb this ecological meltdown.

According to a range of US and global surveys in the new millennium, women and people of color are consistently more likely than white men to express more concern about environmental harms and believe that climate change is real and a serious problem. Why this is the case has most to do with women and people of color bearing the brunt of ecological breakdowns, while especially conservative white men, the most elite of whom have led the climate change denial campaign in recent decades, have economic interests in retaining a fossil-fuel and carbon-emitting economy (Nagel 2016: 166–173). Moreover, studies in some industrialized countries (such as Canada and Sweden) have found that men have far greater ecological footprints than women, emitting far more greenhouse gases as a result of "their employment, transportation use, and masculine lifestyles, including their 'risk-taking, aggressiveness, and violence'" (Nagel 2016: 98). And, of course, the most industrialized countries are the largest carbon emitters, with China, the US, Russia, India, and Japan leading the pack by 2011 (Nagel 2016: 205).

Such masculinist, conservative, wealthy, and powerful forces are arrayed against reigning in neoliberal commitments to ever expanding economic growth and resource exploitation at the expense of women, people of color, and the planet.

Gendered divisions of resources and the consequences of them heavily account for climate change and divergent responses to it. As noted earlier, masculinist and (neo)colonial ideologies that undermined communal land and women's land rights in colonized contexts, as well countenanced the rape of feminized (and racialized) nature, have a long pedigree. Industrialization and modernization greatly accelerated the abuse of lands and waters through large-scale agricultural and manufacturing production and their effluents, which also pushed small-scale and subsistence farmers (the majority of whom are women) into fragile ecosystems that they once protected. Neoliberal globalization has pushed these patterns to extremes, privatizing and corporatizing much of the world's natural resources, which has bred some of the most violent and sexually violent conflicts in Africa in the scramble for mineral wealth. The ensuing uptick in "natural" disasters associated with climate change in recent decades have also had highly gendered consequences. For example, it is estimated that three times more women than men died in the Southeast Asian tsunami in 2004, and a study of "natural" disasters between 1981 and 2002 (during which "natural" disasters began to climb exponentially) in 141 countries found that women died on the order of 14 times more than men during disasters (True 2012: 161, 164). Moreover, women are more likely to experience more sexual and domestic abuse in the wake of disasters as a result of displacements and insufficient shelter (Detraz 2015: 157). The major reasons for women's greater vulnerability in such disasters include the usual litany:

> [they] are generally poorer than men, they do not own land, they are less likely to have an education or access to health care, they are often less mobile due to cultural constraints, and they have less of a political voice in environmental planning and decision making.
> (True 2012: 161)

The loss of life and particularly women's disproportionate mortality in disasters are somewhat lessened in developed country contexts where infrastructures are more solid and disaster relief is more available (although poor disaster responses in the US, ranging from the succession of hurricanes to the Flint, Michigan water supply poisoning, are putting this in doubt, particularly when it comes to responding to poor, working-class, and racialized areas). Nevertheless, the majority of the world's women, most of whom inhabit the global South economically and racially, have particular stakes in confronting climate change.

Despite such documented evidence that (predominantly white) men contribute far more to climate change and women (predominantly of color) have greater interests in addressing it, women have been conspicuously underrepresented in official international policymaking circles on climate change. The adoption of the UN Framework Convention on Climate Change (UNFCCC) in 1992 in Rio de Janeiro was followed by the 1997 Kyoto Protocol that actually set emission-reduction targets for and regular reporting by signatory countries at Conference of the Parties (COP) meetings. Although feminist environmental NGOs were actively present at the Rio conference (and at subsequent ones), of the governmental representatives at the Kyoto conference, only 15 percent were women. The focus on climate change as a largely scientific and technical problem and the low representation of women in high-level governmental posts conspired to keep women's representation low. However, the combination of pressure from feminist NGOs (including GenderCC—Women for Climate Justice formed in 2008), the growing UN gender equality agenda, and the failure of the 2009 Copenhagen

Climate Conference led to the adoption of a UNFCCC gender and climate change agenda by 2012 at the COP18 (Nagel 2016: 199–202). The successful 2015 Paris Agreement (COP21), under the tutelage of UNFCCC Executive Secretary Christiana Figueres who was appointed after the failed Copenhagen Conference, further mandated reporting on progress in mainstreaming gender equality into National Adaptation Plans and related national policy documents on climate change.[11]

The Paris Agreement, which went into force in 2016 with 170 ratifications, aims to limit planetary temperature rise ideally to 1.5 degrees Celsius above pre-industrial levels, achieved by Northern countries reducing and Southern ones mitigating their greenhouse gases to reach this goal, requiring by 2020 monitored national plans and financing as well as Northern funding to support Southern mitigation to do so. While the Paris Agreement was a breakthrough and one which requires attention to gender equality in its implementation, there have also been ominous signs that national responses to climate change could follow typical patterns of gender and gendered injustice. Consider the following examples. To the degree that curbing population growth is targeted by countries to reduce climate change, women's reproductive bodies and rights, already highly circumscribed throughout much of the world (see Chart 5.1), will be targeted for greater control by states and development agencies (Detraz 2015: 156). Nuclear power is gaining some renewed prominence as a climate change solution. While claimed to be "clean," its production, including the mining of uranium, and radioactive waste it produces that lasts for eons is far from clean. And most significantly, 70 percent of the world's nuclear power and weapons mining, production, testing, and waste disposal occurs on indigenous lands—a process referred to as "nuclear colonialism," while women's bodies have been shown to be most susceptible to the harms of radiation (Runyan 2018). Nuclear power's capital-intensive nature and centralized control also sets it apart from truly renewable energy sources (Klein 2014: 57). And to the degree that climate change is viewed as a threat to the state, leading to the securitization of the environment entailed in environmental security approaches, militarized solutions, such as cordoning off climate refugees (Nagel 2016: 137), will take "environmental racism" to new heights, while the racialization of the environment as a dark force to be combatted through the military-science industrial complex will also increase.

	Africa (53)	*Asia (47)*	*LAC (33)*	*Europe (43)*	*Oceania (16)*
Save a Woman's Life	53	47	29	42	16
Woman's Physical Health	33	32	19	38	8
Woman's Mental Health	30	30	19	38	8
Rape or Incest	18	25	13	37	4
Fetal Impairment	20	27	9	38	3
Economic-social Reasons	4	19	6	36	2
On Request	3	17	3	32	1

Chart 5.1 Denying Full Reproductive Rights: Global Abortion Restrictions*

Source: Drawn from United Nations Department of Economic and Social Affairs (UN DESA). 2013. *World Abortion Policies 2013: Trends and Statistics*. New York: United Nations. Available at www.un.org/en/development/desa/population/publications/pdf/policy/WorldAbortionPolicies2013/WorldAbortionPolicies2013_WallChart.pdf (accessed December 19, 2017).

*African countries excluding South Sudan; European countries excluding Vatican; Canada and the US are not included in chart, but both legally allow abortions for all these reasons, although the US Supreme Court may outlaw abortions in the near future; Ireland legalized abortion on demand by referendum in 2018.

LAC: Latin America and Caribbean.

What is particularly problematic with respect to "adding" women to the global climate change agenda is that it conflicts with "adding women" to the GPE agenda. In typical neoliberal fashion, a "business case" is made for each by international policymakers, one claiming that women are sources of sustainable development and conservation and the other claiming that women are necessary for GDP growth, increased consumption, and financial savings and stability. On the one hand, constructing women as engines of growth could be used to actually limit gender equality in the workforce in the name of protecting the environment (Nagel 2016: 214). On the other hand, constructing women as environmental saviors disables a critique of state and corporate capitalist commitments to growth, logics of accumulation, and desires for financial expansion, which inevitably leave most women and feminized others with few resources to perform this. When these two business cases combine, very unhappy consequences for women can also result. For example, Joane Nagel points to a case in Bangladesh where a solar lighting project imagined to empower women by paying them to keep the system going in their homes at night actually sorely extended their already long workday and did not result in men assisting them with either their domestic work or with this added onerous task (2016: 231–232).

As problematic as "adding women" is to global climate change and GPE agendas, the very international agendas to lessen climate change and to make capitalist development more sustainable are in severe jeopardy with the rise of the far-right, particularly in the US. The announced departure of the US from the Paris Agreement under the Trump Administration is part of a much larger assault on progressive aspects of newer and hard-won global and national norms in support of human rights, democracy, conflict reduction, sustainable development, and environmental protection. But as Naomi Klein (2017) argues, this retreat from such norms (and the gender equality or women's empowerment norms that have come to be seen as critical to them) has not meant a departure from neoliberalism. Not only is Trump the embodiment of neoliberal corporate branding and finance capital (producing nothing while simply trading on a brand), but also is associated with extreme outsourcing for cheapened (made cheap by gender, race, and class power relations) labor and exploitative labor practices in his real estate deals and on his properties. He has surrounded himself with others in the top 1 percent, ranging from neoliberal Wall Street figures to oil executives (not to mention a number of military generals), who are dismantling public agencies (with the exception of defense), services, funding, and regulations at a dizzying speed (including scrubbing the very words "climate change" from government websites) while instituting, through the Republican Congress, massive tax cuts for the rich, which will ensure that deficits will disable restoring public spending. As Klein also documents, the Trump administration is full of beneficiaries of private prisons, private military contracts, private bank home foreclosures, and private disaster relief, making money on misery. And whatever trade deals are renegotiated are likely not to include even minimalist labor, environmental, or other protections.

Klein also argues that how the far-right came to power has everything to do with neoliberalism. She reminds us that the majority of Trump voters had incomes of $50,000 to $200,000, so were not among the poor or people of color most impacted by neoliberalism. Many of these (white) voters, however, felt they had lost economic ground (Klein 2017: 88) as the "real" economy was being hollowed out and labor, even at some higher ends, became more precarious by neoliberalism, including through the precipitous decline of organized labor (which is typically more progressive) it brought about. But at the same time, those most impacted by neoliberalism (such as Black people who lost 31 percent of their wealth compared to whites who lost 11 percent during and after the GFC, as well as low-income women, who constitute two-thirds of minimum-wage workers in the US) as well as those who critiqued neoliberalism (such as Bernie Sanders voters) voted in less numbers for a Democratic candidate that was also tied to neoliberalism, albeit a more inclusive version of it (Klein 2017: 93–99). As Klein observes,

> inclusion of the other within an inherently unjust system will not be powerful enough to defeat those [far-right] forces. . . . Instead the overarching task before us is not to rank our various issues—identity versus economics, race versus gender—and for one to vanquish all others in some sort of oppression cage match. It is to understand in our bones how these forms of oppression intersect and prop each other up, creating the complex scaffolding that allowed a kleptocratic thug to grab the world's most powerful job.
>
> (2017: 94)

Toward Resisting Neoliberalism

The picture of a gendering and gendered GPE that has been presented here reveals a polarization of value between masculinized elites and the global majority of feminized "others." This generalized analysis also exposed how the cultural code of feminization naturalizes the economic (material) devaluation of feminized work, whether that work is done by women or men who are culturally, racially, and/or economically marginalized and invites the degradation of the environment. Hence, this chapter has illuminated not only how women and men are positioned and being repositioned globally by gendered divisions to maximize exploitation, but also how the power of gender continues to operate in ways that deflect attention away from such exploitation by naturalizing or depoliticizing it. At the same time, this chapter has exposed how neoliberal globalization has exacerbated the disposability of resources and bodies, particularly those that are most gendered, racialized, and classed, ultimately threatening the planet itself.

The focus on the gendering and gendered processes of neoliberal globalization in this chapter has particularly revealed how the informalization of labor, the restructuring and financialization of economies, and marketized responses to climate change have driven neoliberal attention to "adding women" as a solution to the decline in public provisioning (upon which women most depend), the persistence of the feminization of poverty, the scourge of unsustainable development, the severity of financial crises, and the acceleration of environmental degradation. But these features of neoliberal globalization have also produced the political ground for the rise of an authoritarian version of neoliberalism, which strips away liberal norms and more blatantly seeks to undermine public institutions and provisioning, divide and conquer labor (especially along racial lines) for the enrichment of the elite, deregulate finance so as to make it more able to inflict harms and even less accountable for the harms its crises produce, and reject any notion of sustainability of peoples and the planet in favor of wholesale resource extraction and degradation. Thus, in spite of the severity of human exploitation that has led to widespread breakdowns in social reproduction and environmental degradation that has led to widespread ecological breakdowns, there is continued resistance by neoliberal international officialdom to address these harms beyond problematic inclusion into marketized approaches, while there are now outright refusals of far-right neoliberal national regimes to even recognize them as they are major sources of elite wealth accumulation. To actually stem them would require fundamental shifts in human relationships and in human relationships with the environment, which are precluded by the maintenance of the power of gender.

Vandana Shiva (2005) calls for such a shift in her concept of "Earth Democracy," which makes connections between the crises of representation, insecurity, and sustainability and tells us that the peoples of the world still have many capacities to bring about alternatives to neoliberalism.

> Earth Democracy allows us to overcome the artificial scarcity and manipulated and manufactured insecurities by seeing and experiencing connections. We begin to see the connections between corporations and corporate states, the connections between the economic wars and military wars, the connections between corporate profits and people's poverty, the connections between globalization and religious fundamentalism. We also start to discover the connections we have to the earth and one another. Exposing the connections of dominant powers enables us to evolve appropriate strategies to transform dead democracies into living democracies. Our ecological and social connectedness enables us to create living economies and living cultures, while building the solidarities which crack open the alliances of the powerful.
>
> (Shiva 2005: 185)

Resistance through building solidarity is the subject of the concluding chapter of this text. It explores thought and action that seeks to engender global justice in order to enable more meaningful responses to the interconnected crises of representation, insecurity, and sustainability.

Notes

1 Referring to global political economy (GPE) rather than to international political economy is preferable insofar as GPE draws our attention to increasingly *transnational* processes and requires *transdisciplinary* perspectives that pay attention to everyday life in the GPE rather than only the interactions of states and markets.
2 See "Killer factcheck: 'Women own 2% of land' = not true" at www.oxfamblogs.org/fp2p/killer-factcheck-women-own-2-of-land-not-true-what-do-we-really-know-about-women-and-land/.
3 In Mali, for example, certain trees are designated as "women" trees. This means they are reserved for firewood, which is typically harvested from dead branches, and thus the trees are not to be cut down (Rodda 1991: 75).
4 Sexual minority (im)migrants are often rendered invisible by migration and refugee studies, both feminist and non-feminist, and often face horrific treatment as they cross borders and in detention centers. See Luibhéid and Cantú (2005).
5 For more on gendered migration in the North American context, see Runyan et al. (2013). Although the US began the wholesale incarceration of undocumented immigrants, refugees, and asylum-seekers in 2018 under the Trump administration, Hungary passed a law in 2018, in defiance of the Council of Europe, that enables the imprisonment of even members of human rights organizations who assist refugees and asylum-seekers.
6 Sex workers are not only women (and girls) but also men (and boys) and trans people, and their customers include not only heterosexual-identified men but also gay-identified men (and some women, straight and lesbian). As M. Jacqui Alexander argues, some male and female sex workers in the Caribbean (and the global South generally) are constituted as markets for the white gay (including lesbian) tourist industry and are thus subservient to "white gay capital" (2005: 11). This is yet another example of how otherwise progressive actors, in this case those who struggle for sexual minority rights at home, engage in colonizing and imperializing practices abroad.
7 For more visceral and lived accounts of the impact of SAPs on peoples in the global South, particularly in the Caribbean and Africa, see the films *Life + Debt* (2001) and *Bamako* (2006).
8 The literature is long-standing and extensive. See, for example, Sen and Grown (1987), Vickers (1991), Bakker (1994), Einhorn and Yeo (1995), and Moghadam (1994), on transition economies of eastern and central Europe. For more recent literature on gender, structural adjustment, global restructuring, and austerity, see Eisenstein (2009), Marchand and Runyan (2011), and Hozić and True (2016). See also Smiley and West (2012) on old and new impoverishment in the US, particularly of women.

9 On gendering global finance and its crises, see Aslanbeigui and Summerfield (2000, 2001), Truong (2000), Floro and Dymski (2000), Van Staveren (2002), Peterson (2003), De Goede (2005), Marchand and Runyan (2011), and Hozić and True (2016).

10 In addition to gender-washing, there is also pink-washing in which corporate and state injustices are covered over by their claims to promote LGBTQ rights (Spade 2015).

11 Parties have focused on two goals under the dedicated gender and climate change agenda item: 1) improving gender balance and increasing the participation of women in all UNFCCC processes, including in delegations and in bodies constituted under the Convention and its Kyoto Protocol; and 2) increasing awareness and support for the development and effective implementation of gender-responsive climate policy at the regional, national, and local levels. See www.unfccc.int/gender_and_climate_change/items/9619.php.

Chapter 5

Questions for Discussion

1 How are colonialism, industrial capitalism, development as modernization, and neoliberal globalization all implicated in the production of gender and gendered divisions of labor and resources?

2 How have WID, then GAD, and now SDG strategies tried to correct for gender divisions of labor? But how are the informalization of labor, the financialization of development, and austerity programs negatively affecting social reproduction?

3 What is the relationship between the neoliberalization of the labor of women and other marginalized peoples and the neoliberalization of nature? How does this relationship result in the crisis of sustainability?

4 How is climate change gendered? How do we go beyond "adding women" to climate change amelioration programs to developing more caring and sustainable economic, political, and social relations?

Activities for Further Research

1 View the film "Who's Counting? Marilyn Waring on Sex, Lies and Global Economics" at www.youtube.com/watch?v=WS2nkr9q0VU. Consider how it connects the crises of representation, insecurity, and sustainability through a critique of what is accorded economic value through an intersectional feminist lens. What implications does this have for what we should be counting to reveal and reflect actual levels of human and planetary well-being?

2 Visit the Human Rights Watch Web page on domestic workers at www.hrw.org/topic/womens-rights/domestic-workers. Read some of the news items and stories on their conditions in different countries. What commonalities do you find in terms of the treatment of domestic workers across a range of host countries and worker resistances to these conditions? How are these conditions related not only to a relative lack of informal labor and migrant labor protections but also to gendered assumptions about care work and the women (and girls) who do it? Do you think the relatively recent International Labour Organization convention for domestic workers protection will matter? Why or why not?

3 Consult the "Delivering on the Paris Agreement: Combatting Climate Change while Protecting Rights" report at www.ciel.org/wp-content/uploads/2017/05/Delivering-On-Paris-Web.pdf, co-sponsored by such organizations as the Women's Environmental and Development Organization (at www.wedo.org). How does it highlight protecting the rights of women, indigenous peoples, and workers in relation to efforts to ameliorate climate change? Why is this critical?

6 Engendering Global Justice

How have diverse women resisted the gendered divisions of power, violence, labor, and resources? What new social movements have developed as a result of and in response to global restructuring? What are their problems and potentials in terms of disrupting power relations from the intimate to the global? How does feminist, queer, and trans IR and transnational feminist scholarship center resistances to global politics-as-usual by decentering the power of gender? Why is it necessary to go beyond "adding women" to challenge the crises of representation, insecurity, and sustainability?

As we have seen in this survey of gendering and gendered processes in current global politics and the contemporary feminist and other critical IR inquiry that has brought these to light, the *power of gender* continues to foster dichotomizing, stratifying, "othering," and depoliticizing in thought and action. These moves produce and maintain *crises of representation, insecurity, and sustainability*, despite some *repositionings of some women and men* on the world stage. Repositionings, such as those moves that give some women greater access to the means of destruction and more men less access to the means of production, are more the result of the deepening and widening of militarization and neoliberal globalization than of justice-inspired gender equality commitments and policies. Thus, *gendered divisions of power, violence, labor, and resources* are not seriously disturbed by some "resexing" of actors, especially when those actors are still expected to play dutiful or acquiescent roles in support of power-over, militarization, and economic and resource exploitations associated with neoliberalism (or neoliberal capitalism), neocolonialism, and neoimperialism. In fact, in the face of neoliberal strategies of inclusion at the international level (mostly by "adding" women, but sometimes extending this approach to other marginalized groups, albeit not intersectionally), we are now seeing significant retreats from inclusion in some national contexts as a result of worsening economic disruptions and conditions for ever larger numbers of people. Far-right elite channeling of economic anxiety into race-baiting, immigrant-bashing, pro-militarism and incarceration, and anti-women's and LGBTQ rights discourses and policies has also enabled a doubling-down on neoliberal economic policies of deregulation, privatization, flexibilization, and resource extraction to benefit the wealthy. Such moves, along with departures from international norms and agreements that have just begun to address global crises and their gender(ed) dimensions, albeit in very limited and problematic ways, are exacerbating those crises.

However, there are plentiful alternative responses to global crises that resist both superficial international policies of inclusion and the anti-equality politics of masculinist ethnonationalisms. Although emanating from a variety of movements across the globe of every shape and size that engage in offline and/or online activism, such responses in aggregate have been referred to as comprising the *global justice movement* (GJM) (della Porta 2007;

Eschle and Maiguashca 2010). This "movement of movements" makes interconnections between inter-national, class, race, gender, and sexual inequalities as well as environmental degradation, and attributes their sustenance to neoliberalism in its many guises. However, as we shall see in this chapter, just as feminists had to struggle to gain some serious attention to gender in international policymaking circles, they have had to struggle to integrate feminist and particularly feminist intersectional perspectives into the GJM, expanding and reorienting what constitutes global justice.

Perhaps the most visible example of an intersectional feminist GJM action was the global Women's March (see Photo 6.1), held on January 17, 2017, just after Trump's inaugural. According to the Women's March website,[1] 673 large and small marches involving almost five million people occurred on every continent in support of the unity principles of ending violence (sexual, domestic, racial, police, and carceral) and advancing reproductive rights, LGBTQIA (including intersex and asexual) rights, workers' (including im/migrant and undocumented) rights, civil rights (across all identity categories), disability rights (with a special focus on disabled women), immigrant rights (regardless of status or country of origin), and environmental justice (including protection of public lands and life-giving resources from corporate exploitation). This manifesto for unifying social justice causes spread across the world through websites, Facebook, and Twitter (for example, #womensmarch and #womensmarchglobal), animating marches and now encouraging young social justice activists to run for political office.

In the spirit of that march, this concluding chapter explores feminist-oriented agency directed to resisting gender(ed) divisions and the power of gender, mindful that the question is not one of agency alone, but rather whose agency and for what. Although it offers more examples of feminist and allied social justice movements, it does so in the context of providing an examination of the range of thinking and findings about resistance practices and formations arising out of feminist IR and transnational feminist inquiry. It ends with a review of what this text has argued and how that contributes to what it would mean to engender global

Photo 6.1 2017 Women's March in Cincinnati, USA

Author's photo of Women's March in Cincinnati, Ohio, on January 21, 2017.

justice in more thoroughgoing ways to simultaneously address the crises of representation, insecurity, and sustainability.

Transnational Feminist Politics for Global Justice

Women and Social Movements

Even as some women gain greater access to formal political power, it is more often the case that critical masses of female political actors who more radically challenge gender dichotomies are found outside of formal power structures. Because they typically organize outside of state apparatuses, these actors tend to be invisible through the state-centric lens on global politics that prevailed until recently. Now that market forces, in the form of private firms and IFIs, are challenging and complicating traditional state prerogatives in global politics, IR has begun to direct attention to what is frequently referred to as "civil society." Neoliberals and neoconservatives tend to conceptualize civil society in terms of the private sector, defined as corporate and individualist interests that are in tension with and seek to maintain autonomy from the state. Critical perspectives tend to view civil society in terms of social movements that resist both state domination and capitalist market exploitation (Macdonald 1994). This latter definition of civil society is making women more visible as actors in world politics. However, only feminist perspectives highlight the central roles that women play in social movement activism.

Women have long been found in large numbers in social movements for peace, human rights, economic justice, and environmental protection as members of both mixed organizations (which include men and women) and separate organizations (which are women-centered in terms of leadership, focus, and membership and thus are referred to as "women's movements"). Until recently, the activities of such social movements have been concentrated below the level of the state and confined within state boundaries. However, as economic, environmental, and social issues increasingly cut across state boundaries due to globalization forces, and as IGOs have become more significant sites for global policymaking and more open to NGO claimants and partnerships, women's movements, but particularly the NGOs that claim to represent such movements, are becoming more transnational in focus, organization, and impact. These processes are raising the profiles of women's movements in global politics. In this sense, they are part of what is being termed *global civil society*, which is seen as either a countervailing balance to or as an intervention against state and corporate power (Stienstra 1999: 262).

Women in their social movement roles as non-state and transnational actors shift attention from "fitting women into" traditional IR frameworks and toward an understanding that accommodates and empowers women's struggles against the hierarchical consequences of practicing global politics-as-usual. More often, women's activism not only resists oppressive state and market forces but also often seeks to transform civil society. Indeed, their emphasis on the transformation of civil society is what makes women's movements somewhat distinctive among social movements. Feminists tend to go beyond many critical formulations of civil society by arguing that civil society is not that autonomous from the state and the market, nor does it always resist the negative effects of these forces. All ideals and social movements have potential for variously regressive as well as progressive consequences. Just as there are progressive aspects to civil society, there are also regressive dimensions insofar as civil society reproduces oppressive structures (such as the heteronormative patriarchal family) and ideologies (such as sexism, racism, ableism, and homophobia) inculcated by a range of forces, from the state and the market to religion, the media, education, and the family. If these oppressive dimensions of civil society are not confronted and changed, it is unlikely that progressive, inclusive, and democratic social movements of the type the GJM ideally represents or global civil society more generally will flourish or that the negative effects of states and markets (reflecting problematic aspects of civil society) will be thoroughly challenged.

Indeed, the recent rise of the far-right in Western contexts underscores how elements of civil society have been made more susceptible to typically deceptive anti-equality and anti-environmental messaging by political, religious, and media elites that deflect attention from deeper structural and ideological forces in the global political economy that privilege such elites at the expense of the world's vast majority and militate against a critique that sees interconnections among the inequalities and injustices produced by these forces. Women, both marginalized and elite, can be no less susceptible to (and can participate in) such messaging when it is framed as in their interests, such as "protecting" them from racialized men and (enemy) nations and/or preserving their chastity, femininity, or motherhood by withholding reproductive rights and the rights of sexual, gender, and ethnic minorities, the poor, and/or the racialized. Thus, women can actively promote sustaining gender and gendered divisions, which speaks to the power of gender to naturalize, normalize, and even make desirable hierarchical and dichotomous thinking and relations. Paradoxically, women who participate in or lead right-wing movements around the world that are against women's and other human rights and are even openly misogynist can find this politically empowering on an individual level (Blee and Deutsch 2012). And as we have seen, women, elite and non-elite and on the left and on the right, engage in political violence on behalf and against the state, including genocide and even sexual violence. In cases of the arguably greater numbers of women active in feminist and other social movements associated with the GJM, which is the focus of this chapter, their very participation as political actors and leaders in such movements can be liberating, but such movements, when narrowly construed or non-intersectional, can perpetuate at the same time they challenge gendered dichotomies. This caution is especially warranted when there is insufficient attention given to the transformation of civil society in the context of struggles to change states and markets.

Transnational Feminist Networks in Global Politics

As exemplified throughout this text, women's movements, and especially feminist NGOs that have emerged ubiquitously in the era of global governance, began to more concertedly direct their attention towards making change at the international level through the UN, particularly since the UN Decade for Women. In the face of sclerotic or hostile actions by states with respect to women's rights, older and newer TFNs organized to "leapfrog" the state by taking their cases to the international arena where they have had considerable successes over the past four decades. The successive production of a host of UN-sponsored gender equality (or again, more accurately, women's empowerment) norms, conventions, platforms, resolutions, goals, and programs, as well as the development of institutional structures to implement them in that short time, have been unprecedented. The TFN strategy of resorting to international actors to pressure state actors to agree to and comply with gender equality, human rights, human security, and environmental protection norms has been described as producing a "boomerang effect" (Irvine 2013: 21; Keck and Sikkink 1998). While there is considerable evidence that most states are agreeing to some norms and complying in varying degrees with them, particularly to appear modern and/or democratic and in the face of the wide range of global quantitative indicators now used to rank the performance of states in these areas, it is also the case that TFNs have experienced significant pushback at the international level to dilute and/or undermine such norms and agreements to observe them. As the pace of UN conferences producing plans of action on social and environmental issues in which TFNs played key roles accelerated in the 1990s, the global religious right also began mobilizing to counter those advances, emerging as a force at the 1994 Cairo UN Conference on Population (at which reproductive rights norms were forged) and the 1995 Beijing World Conference on Women (Buss and Herman 2004: 44). Claiming to protect "family values," religious right lobbyists at the international level, from the Vatican and evangelical Christians to Islamists and conservative Jews, have particularly taken aim at reproductive and LGBTQ rights. The global religious right also challenges the very idea of international norms and structures, even as, ironically, it participates in UN forums as examples of "the very international civil society it opposes" in an attempt to especially subvert feminist-informed social justice values forged within it (Buss and Herman 2004: 136).

As the religious right has globalized through its presence at the UN and efforts to sustain or develop new anti-reproductive and LGBTQ rights laws in the global South and North (as well as laying foundations for the rise of far-right governments in the West), TFNs and other GJM movements have become more wary of international-level policymaking venues where seemingly settled norms and conventions on equality and the environment could be set back. But they have also learned that getting international conventions and resolutions in place is only the beginning of the struggle. In her case study of the implementation of UN Security Council Resolution (UNSCR) 1325 in the post-conflict Balkans, Jill Irvine (2013) finds that women had to develop their own grassroots and regional organizations to pressure UN actors overseeing peacemaking, peacekeeping, and peacebuilding processes to abide by the requirements to include women in all these phases as required by 1325 and successor Security Council resolutions. She refers to this process as the "double boomerang effect" in which pressure must be exerted from below on the UN itself to make it more accountable to women as opposed to states in practice (Irvine 2013: 33). But even though the formation and mobilization of these local and cross-border movements did force some compliance with 1325, Irvine also found that increasing women's presence in peace processes did little to instantiate more thoroughgoing approaches to human security that would have addressed how to reduce the militarization of civil society in the Balkans and women's poverty in the region, resulting, in part, from neoliberal development policies pursued post-conflict (Irvine 2013: 34).

Similarly, Carol Cohn (2008) reports that women's organizations in Kosovo and Afghanistan have translated 1325 into multiple languages used in their home countries and turning UN-speak into understandable and useful language for grassroots women. Such practices have also been occurring in the DRC, El Salvador, Iraq, Liberia, and Rwanda, in part because of connections made in transnational workshops focused on implementing 1325 (Cohn 2008: 190–191). Were it not for DRC women's lobbying of the UN peacekeeping mission there, there would not be even the one gender adviser finally put into place (Cohn 2008: 190).

The double boomerang effect was also observable in 2007 when more than 150 Iraqi women's organizations signed a letter, sent to the US Speaker of the House and the UN secretary-general, charging that the post-invasion constitutional process in Iraq was neither inclusive nor observant of CEDAW, 1325, or Security Council resolutions on Iraq specifically. Not only were secular women largely excluded from the drafting process of the Iraq constitution, but also personal status law was being subsumed under Islamic law with the help of Islamic women legislators who were the only beneficiaries of the recently introduced women's quota of 25 percent in the Iraqi parliament (Al-Ali and Pratt 2009: 135–137). This letter fell on deaf ears, but it exposed the hypocrisy of US unilateralism and its claims on behalf of democracy and gender equality, and spoke to the widespread mobilizations of Iraqi women against war and US occupation and war. The Iraq war morphed into the war in Syria and the masses of refugees produced by it, three-quarters of which are women and children, yet women continue to be excluded from peace talks in that war (Davis 2013).[2] Continued dialogue and mobilization around 1325 are exposing its multiple problematics. These include the idea of protecting only women and only in war while leaving the prerogatives of war and the war system in place, making few connections between men and masculinities and war and thus doing little to address changing masculinities or men's participation in war, and leaving intact the idea that women are "more naturally" peaceful rather than widening responsibilities for all, elites and global civil society alike, to end war. As Cohn observes:

> While I do not think one can begin to understand war without gender; while I understand gender, war, nationalism, ethnicity, religion, capitalist forms of production, and consumption (how long should I make this list?) as mutually constitutive, I fear that "Women-as-peacemakers" places too much of war on gender. And in so doing, actually leaves the dominant political and epistemological frameworks untouched.
>
> I fear it is the easy way out. That it obscures all the parts of the war system, including, perhaps paradoxically, the working of gender regimes themselves.
>
> (2008: 202)

Feminists have also been using international conventions and resolutions to pressure their own state governments to observe them. As Susanne Zwingel (2005, 2016) points out, there have been numerous efforts by local, national, and transnational women's movements to bring CEDAW "home"—that is, to have it implemented at the domestic level by state authorities. In the vast majority of states in which CEDAW has been ratified—with the most notable exception of the US—feminists have had to organize long and hard to get their states to adopt the legal provisions required by CEDAW, even after lobbying long and hard for the ratification of it. Zwingel argues that the degree to which CEDAW can be brought home is dependent upon

> first, the degree to which political institutions enable the representation of women's interests within public policy formations; second, the existence of transnational governmental or non-governmental activism that supports the appropriation and implementation of international norms; and third, the level of cultural affinity with the Convention.
>
> (2005: 408)

In the case of Finland, which was alone among the Nordic states in not having a gender equality law when it ratified CEDAW, femocrats in the Council for Equality, a national women's policy agency, played upon the Finnish government's relative openness to women's interests and representation and its self-identity as space for socioeconomic equality to shame it into creating gender equality legislation by marshaling evidence from their femocrat contacts in other countries and at the global level that Finland was an outlier, particularly in the Nordic context (Zwingel 2005: 409). Chile first complied with CEDAW by creating a women's policy agency, SERNAM (Servicio Nacional de la Mujer). But in the relative absence of women in formal political positions at the national level and the presence of prevailing ideologies of "gender complementarity," which justify keeping women in their places rather than ensuring equality, SERNAM forged relationships with women's local NGOs and networks to bring some aspects of reproductive health onto the legislative agenda, including sex education and sterilization (Zwingel 2005: 410). As Zwingel notes, these local NGOs and networks advocated the more radical agenda of reproductive rights, including abortion, which SERNAM did not promote, but invocations of CEDAW by both SERNAM and networks of local movements pushed the right wing back to some degree, which included enabling the legalization of divorce (2005: 410–411). CEDAW has also spawned the development of transnational NGOs dedicated to disseminating information on CEDAW to women's groups at all levels and monitoring its implementation. Organizations such as the International Women's Rights Action Watch (IWRAW) in the US and sister organizations like the IWRAW Asia Pacific located in Malaysia are part of a "transnational community of gender experts" (Zwingel 2005: 413). However, networks of local groups and NGOs that work with these organizations and are not part of national or international elites benefit from and use the intersectional interpretation of CEDAW that IWRAW offices provide by connecting gender, race, and class discrimination and, in turn, make such CEDAW interpretations relevant and responsive to "the particular shape of gender hierarchies in their own contexts" (Zwingel 2005: 412–413). Thus, the otherwise dead law of CEDAW is made live and is constantly reinterpreted to further radicalize its meanings and implementation from diverse women's perspectives at all levels of organizing. Even in the US, feminist activists, frustrated by their government's repeated resistance to ratifying CEDAW across multiple administrations, have launched their own campaign, Cities for CEDAW, to urge city governments to observe the spirit of CEDAW by eliminating gender discrimination in their operations.[3] A number of US cities have also declared their intention to observe the Paris Agreement on climate change amelioration despite the announced US withdrawal from it, but it remains to be seen if this will include the gender and climate change dimensions of that agreement, which will require feminist efforts on the local level.

Thus, there are a plethora of ways in which feminist activists, operating not only at the international level, but also at national and local levels through transnational networks and local grassroots organizing, are significantly engaging with and influencing formal global politics. Continuing analyses of organizing around and contestations of global governance instruments for gender equality (Caglar, Prügl, and Zwingel 2012; Zwingel 2016; Basu 2017) show further headway in terms of making these work better for more women, except when it comes to challenging the war system itself, including efforts to demilitarize civil society, and financial institutions and their neoliberal policies. The unwillingness of international, national, and local institutions to address these deeper sources of direct and structural violence is what has mobilized the larger GJM to go beyond organizing in and around formal sites of power and policymaking in order to imagine and practice alternative social, economic, and political relations to produce a more just civil society from the local to the global. However, as addressed in the next section, the integration of feminist and particularly intersectional feminist perspectives into the work and manifestos of the GJM, as they are represented in World Social Forums that have taken place since 2001, has entailed significant struggle by feminist activists. At the same time, among feminists globally, there have been significant tensions as to how to bring about global social justice.

The Global Justice Movement and Transnational Feminisms

This GJM is most associated with large-scale demonstrations outside various meetings of IFIs and economic elites held in various parts of the world, as well as the huge World Social Forums, which have been held since 2001 in South America, Asia, Africa, and the Middle East, and most recently (2016) in Canada (the first time one was held in the global North, although regional forums have also taken place, for example, in Europe).[4] Variously referred to as the anti-globalization, new *internationale*, world's peoples, and most recently the GJM, it is constituted by congeries of local, national, and transnational social movements from around the world whose representatives gather periodically at World Social Forums to dialogue with each other, bear witness to, and contest economic globalization and militarized violence. Conceived as a leaderless, memberless, non-organizational model that stresses horizontal coalition-building, resists vertical control, and is open to all groups and individuals who wish to build a different world, the movement's main focus, as described in the World Forum Charter of Principles put forward at the first World Social Forum in Porte Alegre, Brazil, in 2001, is as follows:

> The World Social Forum is opposed to all totalitarian and reductionist views of economy, development and history and to the use of violence as a means of social control by the State. It upholds respect for Human Rights, the practices of real democracy, participatory democracy, peaceful relations, in equality and solidarity, among people, ethnicities, genders, and peoples, and condemns all forms of domination and all subjection of one person by another.
>
> (Sen and Waterman 2009: 70)

Although these principles suggest feminist influence at the outset, Catherine Eschle and Bice Maiguashca (2005, 2010) have found in their study of World Social Forums that feminists had to struggle to be substantially represented in forum-organizing bodies and plenaries, have separate organizing spaces within forums, reduce sexism and sexist practices among forum participants, and gain recognition of the relationships between patriarchy, exploitative neoliberal globalization, and militarism within civil society and global civil society. Eschle has pointed out that these struggles were necessary, despite large participation by women in forums and a long history of feminist activism on the Left, because of the more orthodox Marxism of predominantly male forum organizers who could see the struggle only as a class-based one and thereby promoted that limited ideology through their behind-the-scenes leadership of what is supposed to be a leaderless movement (Eschle 2005: 23–24). Cynthia Cockburn (2012) has documented similar problems in mixed peace movements dominated by exclusively class-based and male-centric thinking, requiring feminists to struggle to inject a gender analysis essential to the project of anti-militarism. Nevertheless, the increasing numbers and diversity of feminist organizations around the world participating in the GJM and its forums are forging some shared "ethical goals" for gender justice within and necessary for achieving global justice goals, including economic equality, democracy, respect for the environment, bodily integrity, and peace (Eschle and Maiguashca 2010: 114–122).[5]

Still, the development of greater solidarity among feminists in the GJM has not been without tension. As Johanna Brenner notes, just as some men in Marxist and labor movements attempted to marginalize feminist perspectives and issues such as reproductive rights in critiques of globalization generated at World Social Forums, women in some community-based movements—particularly those that are faith-based or receive funding from the Catholic church—have been silent on reproductive rights and the rights of sexual minorities even as they have advanced other feminist arguments at these forums, such as calling for attention to domestic violence as bound up in globalization (Brenner 2009: 34–36). But beyond frictions with respect to issue areas, there are more fundamental concerns raised about power differentials among feminists working for global justice.

As indicated by the above example of silences on reproductive and LGBT rights, and exemplified in the problematics of the FMF campaign against gender apartheid in Afghanistan discussed in Chapter 4, there are major ongoing debates in feminist thought and movements, particularly those that are transnational in character, about how to resist either regressive or imperial tendencies in order to build more equal and just solidarities to better confront crises of representation, insecurity, and sustainability. At core, intersectional feminisms seek to enhance a "politics of recognition" in which the diverse voices and perspectives of subjugated women and men, or, more accurately, multiple sexes and genders, are represented equitably, and they seek to amplify a "politics of redistribution," which challenges the classist, sexist, racist, and heterosexist ways in which the material world is divided up (Fraser 1997). A politics of recognition is most central to ameliorating the crisis of representation but also key to challenging the crisis of insecurity, and a politics of redistribution is most central to countering the crisis of sustainability but also key to reducing the crisis of insecurity and enhancing a politics of recognition.

At various times, however, there have been tensions between a politics of recognition and a politics of redistribution because one has backgrounded the other. For example, early Marxist feminism was critiqued for focusing on only gendered class relations and material redistributions to solve these inequities without recognition of the need for a greater democratization of struggles to identify and resist not only gendered class exploitation, but also other oppressions based on race, sexuality, and nation that intertwined with, variegated, and intensified class stratification. Later, various forms of cultural and ethnic feminisms were critiqued for a relative inattention to class analysis and a politics of material redistribution as they tended to pursue a kind of politics of recognition known as identity politics. Identity politics, while useful to foreground (and thus represent) the experiences and perspectives of a particular subjugated identity group (such as women, Asian women, Latinas, Chicanas, lesbians, and so on), also tended, on the one hand, to essentialize and homogenize such identity groups and, on the other hand, to so fragment identity into smaller and smaller groupings (young-disabled-lesbian-Chicanas) that no common cause could be seen among these groupings of infinite variety. The fragmentation of identity, however, served to draw attention to "hybrid" or "diasporic" identities that resist the forces of essentialism and homogenization and cut across identity groups (Anzaldúa 1999), and thus enable the development of coalition politics. Identity fragmentation (to the point of deconstructing all identities to expose them as always provisional and subject to change) also constitutes a poststructural feminist strategy (as well as a "queering" strategy) to denaturalize and thus destabilize identities, making them unavailable to be mobilized for the purposes of power and control or to be targets of power and control. Although, for a time, the developments of a politics of recognition overshadowed thinking about a politics of redistribution, today many contemporary feminist theorists and activists are emphasizing both to counter the rise of neoliberal globalization and governmentality and their security apparatuses. Developing and exercising both these politics entail anti-imperialist, anti-racist, anti-global capitalist, anti-heteronormative, anti-homonormative, and anti-transphobic inquiry and political commitments.

Such inquiry and political commitments have been hampered by the ways that some feminist inquiry, both Western and non-Western, is conducted and informs social movements. Chandra Mohanty (2003) identifies practices that militate against anti-imperialist feminist thought and action. What she calls the "feminist-as-tourist" model arises from "brief forays into non-Euro-American cultures" in which "particular cultural sexist practices are addressed" through a Western "gaze" (2003: 239). This universalization of gender through a Eurocentric lens both subsumes more complex explanations for oppression under an overarching and ahistorical notion of gender and singles out for critique only certain forms of gender oppression associated with stigmatized local cultural "backwardness" as opposed to "modern" international political and economic forces. This yields social movements that can more easily become supporters and agents of imperial violence in the name of rescue missions. Social movement politics in this mode also tends to conceive of women as experiencing gender oppression in similar ways rather than as differently inflected by race, class, sexuality, and nationality. This cultivates "too-easy" assumptions that women share the same experiences and interests and thus constitute a global "sisterhood" (Grewal and Kaplan 2001: 19). Solidarity is then seen as flowing "naturally" from shared experiences and interests rather than as something that needs to be developed through political dialogue and action. As a result, more-privileged women end up speaking for less-privileged ones under the assumption that women's perspectives are interchangeable and even more insidiously, under the assumption that Western women, in particular, are more "liberated" than others and thus should lead—rather than listen—and forge "the" path for "other" sisters.

These perspectives and practices deny the realities on the ground. Consider, for example, that through a more significant embrace of quotas, women in the global South are gaining greater access to positions of formal power than are women in some of the most "developed" states. At the same time, even the most privileged Western women are subject to (economically motivated) cultural beauty standards, and to achieve these often involves bodily harm (whether through cosmetic surgeries, anorexia, or toxic cosmetics). And these women are just as subject to domestic violence as women elsewhere. Yet progress narratives in the West promote the continuation of colonial mind-sets, which find their way into feminist theorizing and social movements that are based on the feminist-as-tourist model. This contributes to crises of representation by failing to practice a politics of recognition.

Mohanty's "feminist-as-explorer" model refers to "area studies" approaches (2003: 240–241), which, although more detailed, culturally sensitive, and historical in terms of examining women's lives in local, national, and/or regional contexts, still maintain a separation between the West and the non-West. In doing so, this model fails to see connections between global forces and national and local ones and the material conditions shared by the most subjugated women in both the South and North as a result of those global forces. Whether in cases of area studies performed by Western feminists or non-Western nationalist feminists, this model, in Mohanty's view, cultivates a kind of "cultural relativism" that erases any commonalities among women's struggles (2003: 240). This has the effect of confining social movements within state or regional borders and minimizing potential solidarities across those borders.

Catherine Eschle (2001) argues that these approaches set up a "universalist" versus "particularist" dichotomy from which polarizing debates ensue. The former is most implicated in imperialist tendencies and actions; the latter, although also mired historically in Western anthropological practices that legitimated imperial conquest, is alternatively implicated in nationalist, statist, and thus ultimately conservative frameworks (Eschle 2001: 201). Not only does a particularistic approach feed into maintaining an oppositional and static view of "western feminism as unified and necessarily imperialist," but also a notion that those from outside a particular state or region are "inauthentic" knowers and actors who cannot understand or share in struggles outside of the locales from which they come (Eschle 2001: 201–202). Moreover, a vision of feminism organized on the basis of distinct ethnic and cultural identities frequently relies on a pre-political notion of identity that delegitimizes contestation and dialogue within and across identities. It also marginalizes women who do not fit neatly into a predetermined category (Eschle 2001: 202). Such women who do not fit may be multi-ethnic, multi-national, or sexual and/or gender minorities; in this sense, just as a universalistic gender-based feminism undermines a politics of recognition, so, too, can a particularistic conception of ethnicity or culture-based feminism.

A related conundrum is the dichotomous construction of local versus global and the debates that ensue from this. Particularist advocates tend to privilege local or grassroots struggles as the most "authentic" and least contaminated by global power structures that co-opt and depoliticize social movements. Universalists tend to be most associated with global or international NGOs that lobby IGOs, garnering the majority of resources (although still relatively few compared with states, markets, and IGOs) for their larger-scale and more bureaucratic operations. International women's organizations are not new; they stretch back centuries in the form of women's peace movements, socialist women's *internationales*, and even missionary organizations that attended colonizing processes (Mackie 2001: 180–181). But the recent rise of feminist transnational NGOs has been met with a variety of concerns. First, there is the question of the relationship between the proliferation of contemporary NGOs and the rise of neoliberalism. As noted earlier, the "self-help" ideology of neoliberalism encourages private, voluntaristic, civil society operations to take up the slack—albeit with far fewer resources—for public welfare activities that states have been shedding. This reduces the accountability of states and markets, while also shifting services to unaccountable and relatively poorly resourced private bodies (as well as to under-resourced households). Second, to the degree that NGOs are funded by states, IGOs, and, most often, private corporate foundations, they become more beholden to these interests and their priorities (Dauvergne and LeBaron 2014). Third, the "NGO-ization" of social movements, a concept Sonia Alvarez (1999) first coined in relation to Latin American regional women's NGOs she observed springing up during and after the UN Decade for Women, privileges middle-class actors with access to more resources and entrée into corridors of power. At the same time, this NGO-ization can leave behind poorer, more grassroots women who do not have the economic, social, and physical mobility (including foreign, high-theoretical, and bureaucratic language skills) to travel to and be heard at international conferences and sites of power, such as state and global capitals, where lobbying occurs. Moreover, grassroots movement demands get packaged by NGOs into policy bits that are digestible by states and IGOs and the femocrats within them, thereby taking off their radical edge.[6] In all these senses, it has been argued that the "revolution will not be funded" (INCITE! Women of Color Against Violence 2007).

This local–global split has also been manifested in distinctions sometimes made between transnational feminism(s) and global (or governance) feminism. The former refers to a more postcolonial conception of transnational linkages among the many struggles of grassroots women of the global South more associated with the GJM, and the latter is tied to global (or cosmopolitan) feminist NGOs that are dominated by more resourced women from both the North and the South who have access to halls of power at the global level (Swarr and Nagar 2010). However, there have also been critiques of a fetishization of the local that is constructed as a more "innocent" space as if there were no power relations at the local level that silence some women over others and may result in parochial approaches that are unmindful of reproducing those power relations and their connections to larger and wider patterns and sources of abuse. Global feminism can also be charged with parochialism in representing only more privileged views or lenses. At the same time, there is worry that transnational feminism risks being reduced to "the romanticization of Third World activism in the global arena" and limits "transnational solidarity to Third World women workers across the First/Third World divide," thereby "becoming the 'other' to western white feminism" (Mendoza 2002: 309). In Breny Mendoza's view, this results from more attention given to cultural critique in much transnational feminist theorizing, which, although rightly directed to challenging ethnocentrism and confronting racism, heteronormativity, and gender normativity as well as sexism, does not address sufficiently "political economic issues" that structure the lives of women in the South and North (2002: 310). This is the result of a politics of recognition overshadowing a politics of redistribution. The latter requires a more thoroughgoing solidarity of more-privileged women (and men) who choose to be against imperialism, settler colonialism, racism, global capitalism, sexism, and heterosexism with less-privileged women (and men) who are critiquing and resisting these forces that ultimately threaten the planet and thus all on it.

Combining a politics of recognition with a politics of redistribution will also require coalitional solidarities among women's movements and mixed movements. In order to build more intersectional coalitions, Mohanty (2003) recommends a "feminist solidarity" model for thought and action. This model sees the local and global as mutually constituted and, through comparative analysis, focuses "not just on the intersections of race, class, nation, and sexuality in different communities of women but on mutuality and co- implication, which suggests attentiveness to the interweaving of the histories of these communities" (Mohanty 2003: 242). This enables an alternative mapping of what connects and divides women (and men) based on redirecting attention to "global capitalism, and the uncovering of the naturalization of its masculinist and racist values," which compromise peoples and the planet (Mohanty 2003: 250). As this text has argued, it is the power of gender that breeds the dichotomous thinking that operates to prevent or mitigate this remapping and the more fully developed solidarities that can arise from it. As Bernice Johnson Reagon (2000) has famously argued, coalitions are a matter of survival and can be built only through the praxis of acting together on particular projects at particular times (Gilmore 2008). They are not entered into because participants are similar to each other, are friendly with each other, or are safe from each other, but because "that's the only way you can figure you can stay alive" in the face of the widespread crises of representation, insecurity, and sustainability that affect all but the most privileged and that need to be resisted collectively in both small and large ways (Reagon 2000: 344).[7] And although, as Audre Lorde (2008) famously argued, it is problematic to "dismantle the Master's house" with the "Master's tools," even the tools that are implicated in neoliberal governmentality can be used for dismantling and rebuilding projects because many such tools arose, albeit in a more de-radicalized and distanced form than was intended, from social movement analysis and agitation.

One such tool is the Internet, especially in the form of social media, which has created a lively world of virtual politics that is having major material effects on offline worlds and is more accessible to more and more women. Although cyberpolitics, including "cyberfeminism," is not new, the use of Facebook, Twitter, YouTube, and blogs that circulate through smart phones and other handheld devices to mobilize ordinary people to take to the streets has made a range of powerful political actions possible, from the successful toppling of authoritarian governments, such as the Mubarek regime in Egypt, during the Arab Spring in 2011, and the widespread Occupy movement against neoliberal economic austerity touched off in the same year, to the 2017 worldwide Women's March.

However, it is important to refrain from imagining that social media are sufficient for building inclusive and sustainable social movements. Indeed, the digital divide between nations and genders is still wide and deep (see Chart 6.1), and online media, like offline media, are still dominated by men as producers and subjects. According to Mary Hawkesworth, although the majority of males and females in the global North were Internet users and constituted the majority of Internet users in the world by 2006, relatively few people in the global South had access to the Internet, with, for example, only 15 percent of Brazilians, 8.6 percent of Chinese, 6.8 percent of Egyptians, and 3.6 percent of all Africans online and with women

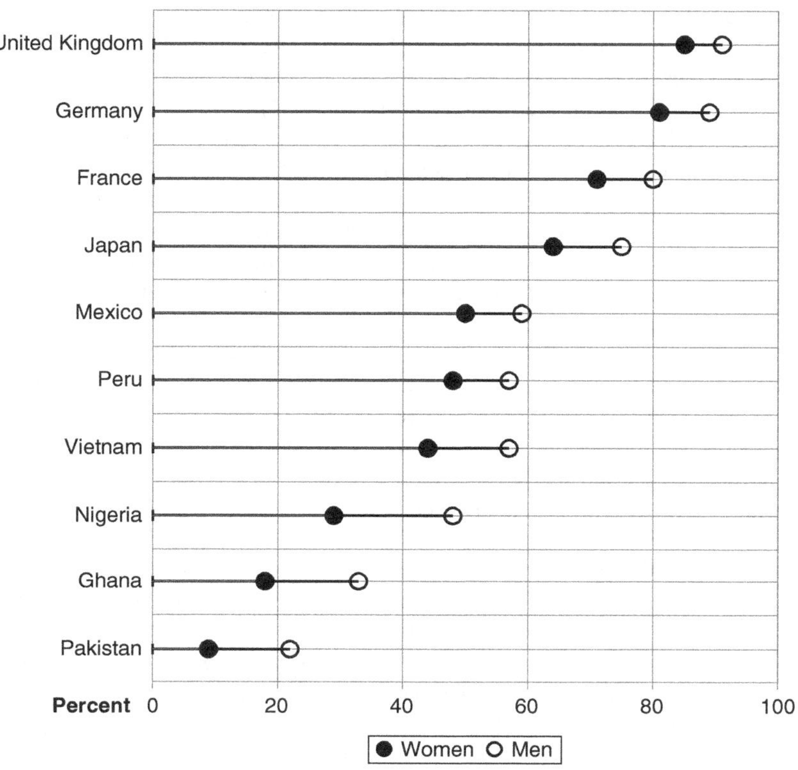

Chart 6.1 Gendered Digital Divides between North/South and Men/Women*

Source: Drawn from Poushter, Jacob. 2016. "Internet access growing worldwide but remains higher in advanced economies." *Pew Research Center*. Available at: www.pewglobal.org/2016/02/22/internet-access-growing-worldwide-but-remains-higher-in-advanced-economies/.

*Based on adult respondents who use the Internet or report owning a smartphone.

constituting only 20–24 percent of Internet users in Africa (2012: 307). Moreover, Hawkesworth points to a 2010 study of offline and online news media in 108 countries that found that women were the subjects of only 23 percent of offline news stories and only 11 percent of online news stories and rarely appeared in business and government news, were only 20 percent of experts quoted in all news stories,[8] and were underrepresented as news reporters both offline (40 percent) and online (36 percent) (2012: 303). Even worse, she documents that in the wider world of the Internet, racist, sexist, and homophobic Web sites, social networking sites, and gaming sites proliferate, as do cyberharassment and cyberstalking, particularly of women (Hawkesworth 2012: 304–306; see also Nagle 2017). English, as the hegemonic language of global commerce and governance, dominates the Web, which is also the space most heavily surveilled by security states, most used for targeted marketing (both licit and illicit) to further ever-greater consumption of disposable goods and people, and least available to grassroots women's groups in the South (Hawkesworth 2012: 311).

The rise of Twitter hashtag campaigns focused on the plight of women and girls in the global South have also been highly problematized by feminists. These include such hashtags as #BringBackOurGirls (referring to the schoolgirls kidnapped in Nigeria by the Islamist terrorist group Boko Haram in 2014) and #IAmMalala (referring to the Pakistani girl, Malala Yousafzai, who survived an attempted murder of her for attending school in 2012 and was awarded the Nobel Peace Prize for supporting girls' education—just one of a number of women who have received that prize in the last few decades[9]). Among the feminist critiques of these campaigns is that they create the illusion that global North (re)tweeters really understand the suffering of such girls and the wider forces, in which distant and more privileged supporters are implicated, that produced their suffering (Berentz 2016). Such hashtags can serve as a reenactment of "neocolonial global hierarchies while seemingly making a depoliticized appeal to solidarity" (Barentz 2016: 524). And, of course, we are now witness to the constant circulation of deception and hate via Twitter by new (and older) authoritarian leaders—most significantly, Trump and Putin.

Thus, despite claims about the Internet's accessibility, inclusion, and even democratizing nature, and the promise of the World Summits on the Information Society (WSIS) held since 2003 to empower women and other marginalized groups, it is more often a space of depoliticization than politicization, embodying and replicating gendered divisions of power, violence, labor, and resources and furthering the power of gender. Nevertheless, like all other "Master's" tools, it can be and has been used selectively, creatively, and subversively by feminist and other GJMs.

It is also the case that the gendered dichotomies of universalist–particularist, global–local, online–offline, global feminism–transnational feminism, NGOs–grassroots organizations, experts–activists, theory–practice, and individual–collective (see Table 6.1), the former of which in each pairing gains more attention in global politics-as-usual, are increasingly less operant on the ground. As Maiguashca (2016) has more recently argued, transnational feminism is now far more descriptive of social movements that simultaneously consist of grassroots, NGO, and TFN organizing. As she puts it, a transnational "feminist activist may find herself lobbying a government one day, protesting against it on another and running a neighborhood educational workshop on a third" (Maiguashca 2016: 116). Thus, we see much more mixing of strategies and actors engaged in ongoing coalitional struggles to build solidarity across internal and external borders through demanding much greater accountability from state, market, and civil society actors.

In terms of power differentials between grassroots and transnational women's organizations in the context of development, Millie Thayer's (2010) study reveals not only destructive, but also productive tensions between a Western feminist development organization and a rural women workers movement in Brazil. In their interactions, although structured by neocolonial

Table 6.1 Gendered Divisions in the Global Justice Movement

Masculinized	*Feminized*
Universalist	Particularist
Global	Local
NGOs	Grassroots organizations
Online	Offline
Global feminism	Transnational feminism
Theory	Practice
Experts	Activists
Individual	Collective

and neoliberal relations, the women workers were able to openly assert their autonomy, demand a more radical aid agenda, and insist on projects that furthered their needs and politics in relation to their local conditions and struggles. As neoliberal pressures intensified on the development organization to increase "efficiencies" and employ quick fixes in its work, the grassroots organization allied with the development organization to push back on these donor demands, taking the most militant and uncompromising stands that enabled the development organization more negotiating space to resist new donor imperatives. Key to what Amanda Lock Swarr and Richa Nagar (2010) call "critical transnational feminist praxis" is a refusal to enact the hierarchical dichotomies between experts and activists, theory and practice, and individual and collective knowledge and an ongoing commitment to be critical of one's own social and intellectual positions and accountable to others with whom one is collaborating through sustained dialogic encounters.

Latin America more generally has become a site of experiments to resist neoliberal governance. Although some of these experiments are in disarray (in Venezuela and Brazil most recently), Leftist governments elected in Ecuador and Bolivia continue down the path of enabling much greater involvement of civil society, including the poor, indigenous peoples, feminists, and LGBT activists, in governing and redistributing wealth and resources, particularly to the poor and indigenous. As feminist and other critical scholars (Macdonald and Ruckert 2009; Friedman 2017; Keating and Lind 2017) note, there are reasons to be skeptical about how "post-neoliberal" and inclusive these states are as they are still embedded in the larger global economy, depend on resource exploitation, and are unevenly "democratic" and "progressive." Nevertheless, they do point to how national and regional contexts can begin to shift to other, non-market priorities.

As further evidenced by the World Social Forums and calls for "Earth Democracy" arising from them and the many social movements that make up the GJM,[10] resistance to the larger architectures and priorities of neoliberalism has not ended under neoliberal governmentality: its assumptions and rules continue to be contested both offline and online. Although digital divides continue between men and women, rich and poor, ethnic majorities and ethnic minorities, and North and South, the explosion of transnational, national, and even local organizing would not have been possible without ICTs. Cyberfeminism has enabled UN gender architectures, transnational and national feminist NGOs, and even grassroots women's organizations to monitor policies, exchange information, and build solidarity networks on an unprecedented scale. As Wendy Harcourt (1999) points out, the Web has opened up new political spaces for diverse women who can, at times, bypass discriminatory spatial structures and represent themselves and their struggles in less mediated ways, while also contesting exclusivist constructions of cultural and national identity. This is not to dismiss or underestimate the commercial control, violence promotion, and disembodiment in which the Web is deeply implicated, but it does tell a "tale" of another Internet that is being subversively appropriated to "confront political and social issues of the day" and to negotiate "intercultural and intracultural exchange" both online and offline (Franklin 2004: 2–3). However, as Gillian Youngs (2005) points out, "cybercitizenship" remains quite unequal, requiring a politics of redistribution in relation to ICTs as well.

Popular culture, despite the extreme commodification of it that promotes gratuitous violence, can also be a site and a stimulant of political resistance. Consider the case of Pussy Riot (Box 6.1), the three-woman punk rock band in Russia that was sentenced to up to three years in prison for staging an iconoclastic performance against Russian authoritarian leader Vladimir Putin in a Russian Orthodox church in 2012 (Gessen 2014). Scantily and provocatively dressed and rocking and railing against the state and the church for its complicity with the state, the band, which includes two mothers, courageously transgressed normative

Box 6.1 Performing Resistance

There is a long history of feminists and other social justice activists using performative art, music, theater, and popular culture as forms of protest. The Russian Pussy Riot punk band, arrested and jailed by the Russian authorities for their 2011 anti-Putin performance at a Moscow cathedral, have since their release become globally known for their feminist and human rights-inspired performances and music videos (increasingly in English and widely available on YouTube) against authoritarianism in Russia, the US, and other parts of the world. You can learn more about how they became feminist performance activists and about their music, trials, and convictions in *Words Can Break Cement* (2014), a biography by Martha Gessen. CodePink, a US-based feminist anti-militarist movement, protests theatrically in pink against US-supported invasions and occupations in several parts of the world. As they say they have learned in their YouTube video, "Hot Pink Ladies in Action: 10 Year Anniversary of Codepink Creativity," it is important "to have fun" while resisting deadly global politics-as-usual.

Hot Pink Ladies in Action: 10 Year Anniversary of CodePink Creativity www.youtube.com/watch?v=_k-XJDB-asQ

gender, political, and religious boundaries. Two members were jailed and staged a hunger strike (a method most associated with feminist resistance to imprisonment stretching back to the Western suffragettes) after being denied parole, while the third was released on appeal and testified at a European Commission hearing about increasing human rights abuses in Putin's Russia. Trans and cultural studies theorist J. Jack Halberstam (2012) finds in pop star Lady Gaga's gender transgressive and bombastic performances (not her reformist politics) inspiration for what he calls "gaga feminism," which is about refusing the logic of domination in whatever form it takes and which continually seeks new forms of thinking, communicating, cooperating, provisioning, and organizing.[11] This feminism, he argues, infuses the GJM, whose transnational, imaginative, and disruptive protests take multiple and evolving forms in and appropriate to each local context.

Feminist resistance directed at challenging the crises of representation, insecurity, and sustainability also takes other symbolic forms that do not require large-scale mobilizations, technological access, or pop culture fame. Women have used the few resources available to them to pioneer many forms of protest that have gained global recognition: these include donning the veil to protest Western imperialism, as women did in the Iranian Revolution; engaging in guerrilla theater, as the US feminist peace protest group CODEPINK does; setting up women's peace camps outside nuclear weapons installations, as the women of Greenham Common in Britain pioneered; holding silent vigils to protest those "disappeared" by military dictatorships, for which the Argentinean Mothers of the Plaza de Mayo are famous; staging silent street protests against the Israeli occupation of Palestine, which was started by Women in Black (and which now has chapters in at least 28 countries protesting war and violence); or hugging trees to save them, for which the local Chipko women's movement in India is internationally known. And as part of "peoples' renewal movements" and movements engaging in "postcapitalist" practices (Gibson-Graham 2006) such as barter and other reciprocal-provisioning activities, women, often in concert with many other "others," are working toward more feminist futures.

Feminist scholars, too, have been a part of the deconstruction and reconstruction of global politics, engaging in a range of theoretical, material, and discursive interventions. In the following conclusion, key reconceptualizations of global politics from feminist, queer, and trans perspectives offered in this text are reviewed and amplified toward further engendering global justice. Such insights that rearrange how we think about world politics derived from feminist IR and related scholarship illuminate, without resolving, how the power of gender in global politics might be challenged. The stakes are high and the road is long, but the more ways to travel it, the better.

Conclusion: Toward Engendering Global Justice

The world faces old and new challenges, particularly in terms of global security and political economy. The post-9/11 climate of fear and uncertainty—exacerbated by the US-led "war on terror"—generates hypermasculine thinking and acting. The more recent breakdown of financial arrangements in the US, with devastating effects worldwide, generates economic perplexity and a frantic search for fixes. In these contexts, realities and representations of uncertainty, chaotic conditions, and looming crises operate, not surprisingly, to amplify desires for clarity, predictability, and social order. These have manifested in the rise of the far-right and new (as well as the maintenance of older) authoritarian governments in the global North as well as South. As argued throughout this text, there are indeed multiple crises, and collective longing for easy answers and quick fixes is understandable. But given the ominous developments associated with desires for simplistic answers built on sacrificing civil liberties, human rights, human security, and the health of the planet, a more fundamental transformation in ways of identifying, thinking, and acting is required. This text has argued that the power of gender as a meta-lens and hegemonic worldview itself is key to producing crises of global proportion. The problem, then, is that paths of least resistance—conventional ways of responding—are not only inadequate but also part of, indeed productive of, the problem. Hence, deconstructing the power of gender is a necessary component of addressing these crises and transforming global politics as-usual. This is obviously no simple or short-term project but one that is delayed or sidelined at great risk. It is urgent that we all get on with asking not only "How do we fix this problem?" but also "How do we transform the systems that produce and reproduce these problems?"

In considering what might illuminate and potentially guide the development of alternative lenses and transformational politics, it is important to recognize that we are never "outside" of the system we critique, meaning that no perspective can avoid complicity or claim innocence. The choice is not about whether we participate in the institutional practices constituting our life worlds but only how, in what ways, and with what effects. Do we take paths of least resistance that inexorably reproduce global politics-as-usual, or do we attempt to be critically aware of structural violence and wary of too-easy analyses and quick fixes? What have we learned in this text that might help us construct, however provisionally, forms of intersectional feminism that avoid exclusions, appropriations, and impositions and move us to greater global justice?

As argued in Chapter 1, intersectional feminist lenses and practices are required to avoid essentialist, universalist, and dichotomous notions of gender as well as reducing gender to "women" and reducing feminism to being concerned only with gender. Intersectional feminism encompasses critiques of all power relations—including those based on gender, race, class, sexuality, nation, and so on—and their interrelations. These structure gender and gendered divisions of power, violence, and labor and resources the world over, which are productive of the contemporary crises of representation, insecurity, and sustainability. Although there has been increasing interest and action on the part of international leaders and policymakers to instrumentally empower women to solve such crises, we are also seeing a backlash in the form of the rise of the far-right to international agendas, especially those that advocate gender equality. However, intersectional feminism directs us beyond "adding women" or just repositioning women and men to a wider critique of relations of equality at all levels and attempts to transform them. But in order to better see intersections among inequalities, the concept of the power of gender was introduced and defined as a meta-lens that naturalizes and reproduces essentializing, dichotomizing, stratifying, and depoliticizing thought and action—a process present in the making of all hierarchical divisions and oppositions. Intersectional feminism works to destabilize the power of gender through complicating any homogenous notion of women and men, while trans and queer experiences and perspectives disrupt sex, gender, and sexuality binaries themselves. As Laura Sjoberg (2012) argues, trans lives and perspectives highlight the complexity of living in between genders and, therefore, worlds. Living such a life requires "disidentification" with assigned sex and/or gender roles to enable the creation of hybrid sex and/or gender identities and relations that rest on reworking constructs of sex and gender in non-oppositional ways. The process of disidentification has implications not only for breaking down the psychosocial dynamics of oppositional sex and gender identity formations from which the power of gender stems at its deepest level, but also for rethinking all oppositional relations. It also has implications for "queering," or making strange, normativities that set up hierarchies and the normalization of those hierarchies.

In Chapter 2, feminist and other critical IR were distinguished from mainstream IR, focusing particularly on how the power of gender operates in positivist mainstream approaches to naturalize hierarchical dichotomies and produce a focus on and desires for top-down order and control, most often sought through state-led militaristic means but also via neoliberal capitalist arrangements, both of which keep structural inequalities in place. By contrast, intersectional feminist IR is "grounded in the human experience," "attentive to gender and other social constructions to identify emancipatory potential (and not practice forms of oppression in research)," "self-reflective," and "cognizant of the ongoing nature of the processes under study and the research process" (Ackerly and True 2006: 255–256). As such, intersectional feminist IR sees itself as collective inquiry that seeks to be supportive of and accountable to the struggles of subjugated people in global politics; this process entails not only privileging examinations of material oppressions and resistances, but also deconstructing oppressive discursive practices and reconstructing alternative conceptual frameworks for rethinking global politics.

A number of these reconceptualization strategies were engaged in Chapters 3 through 5. Chapter 3 argued that mainstream IR greatly underestimates the amount and kinds of power operant in global politics and how the power of gender is at work in naturalizing power-over systems. When we recognize how much typically unseen coercive power it takes to run this inequitable system, we begin to see why feminists argue that the deployment of coercive power is ultimately destructive of those who rule as well as those who are ruled. Disabling people—especially women—by depriving them of even the most basic needs so that the few can accumulate wealth and weaponry destroys genuinely popular support for states, international organizations, and their leaders. In the absence of genuine popular support and consent as the sources of legitimacy for those in power, coercion is the only mechanism available to insecure rulers, who must rely on dividing, impoverishing, and degrading people and the planet to maintain their power as we are seeing in sharp relief today within several so-called democracies. Therefore, "we" (referring here and throughout this conclusion to congeries of individuals, collectivities, and coalitions that make the political choice to progressively challenge global politics-as-usual in favor of global justice) must question not only the validity but also the efficacy of "power-over" as the mechanism for organizing global politics or solving global problems.

One alternative to coercive power that was introduced in Chapter 3 is the more feminist concept of enabling power, which draws upon feminist theorizing about the high degree of reciprocity, interconnectedness, and hybridity typifying most social relations and encounters. Christine Sylvester (1992) uses the term "relational autonomy" to describe a form of enabling power and contrasts it with the masculinist and imperialist ideal of "reactive autonomy" (valuing independence over interdependence and order over justice), which permeates the practice of international relations. The reactive autonomy model discounts most social reality and renders apolitical the emotional and relational webbing that gives life meaning as well as the practices of social reproduction that ensure everyday life and generational survival. Reactive autonomy assumes that cooperative relations are virtually impossible without some forms of hierarchical rule and coercion. In contrast, relational autonomy assumes that cooperation typifies human relations when they are relatively equal and is destroyed in the presence of inequality, "othering," and coercion.

Developing a more relational autonomy orientation would move us toward engendering global justice more deeply than simply "adding women" (and other subjugated groups) to existing power structures as a simplistic approach to addressing gender and gendered divisions of power. Although as Chapter 3 revealed, women in all their diversity remain sorely underrepresented in most and the highest power structures, without deeper institutional changes, simply "adding women" through quotas and the like can generate unrepresentative tokens whose presence may fuel complacency, as we have seen in exercise of neoliberal governmentality, rather than sustained efforts at transforming representational politics. And simply "adding women" to public power without adding men to domestic labor and caretaking, and without holding elite men (and women) responsible for undermining webs of care through neoliberal and militaristic policies, effectively exacerbates the crisis of social reproduction. On the other hand, "adding women" cannot take the form of a simple reversal that merely privileges feminine "care" over masculine "coercion." In such a reversal, not only gender dichotomies but also features of the feminine concept of care that oppress women would remain in place. Specifically, because caring has historically been a demand imposed upon subordinated groups and is, in this sense, inextricable from relations of inequality, a care model may offer insights on, but not solutions to, oppressive social relations. Caring that exclusively takes the form of sacrificing self or group interests is just another framing of inequality.

Emphasizing relational autonomy as a model of international relations would assist women and other subjugated people in terms of a redistribution of resources to ease their lives and enable their political participation, but we also need to facilitate autonomy for women and other groups denied this (sometimes of the reactive sort) through the realization of a gender and other forms of equality that entail a politics of recognition. Full equality, not only *between* men and women but also *among* women and *among* men, cannot be achieved unless all men have an equal responsibility for (social) reproductive or relational work (from the household through to the international arena) and diverse (in terms of race, class, sexuality, and nation) women have an equal say in how the world is organized. Through such a process, practices of leadership could be altered by redefining authority (Jones 1993). When the relationship between leaders and followers shifts from a command–obedience structure based on fear of loss of protection and the maintenance of (an unjust) order toward a more consensual egalitarian model, possibilities are opened up for transforming who can lead, what the basis of leadership could be, how it can be shared equally, and what shifts in direction it could take. Thus, to significantly counter the crisis of representation requires a politics of recognition that acknowledges and empowers subjugated voices and marginalized alternatives, and a politics of redistribution that enables more democratic (equal and consensual) participation by the many and not just the elite few.

Chapter 4 challenged the assumption that violence is largely the result of anarchic international relations in contrast to supposedly "peaceful" domestic communities. This obscures the question of the amount of and the way in which violence is deployed from the personal and local to the national and global levels. We know that domestic violence—a euphemism for the wide range of physical and emotional abuse suffered mostly by wives and children in families, but also a reference to the everyday violence inflicted on a range of peoples subjugated by gender, race, sexuality, and national origin—is widespread throughout the world. Hence, it makes little sense to argue that the level and frequency of violent conflict are what separates international relations from domestic relations. Feminist IR scholars have provided quantitative evidence that domestic and international violence are intimately connected, with the amount of the former predicting the amount of the latter. They have also found that although interstate warfare may have declined, other forms of armed conflict, and most especially gender violence in peace and wartime, have not. Through this lens, international violence and the crisis of insecurity identified in this text are bound up with historically institutionalized and deeply internalized constructions of gender and heteronormativity (which are always raced and classed). The power of gender establishes expectations that women are peaceful and men are violent, thereby sustaining protection rackets that keep all enthralled to the dictates of militarized security. Such security is productive of all manner of human insecurities, and its imperial form rests on deep patterns of colonization and racialization through which war and conquest is justified, often in the name of the "security myth" of saving (deserving) women ("ours" or "theirs") from racialized men.

The model of masculinity that is currently hegemonic encourages males to assume assertive, arrogant, aggressive, and power-over ways of thinking and acting that effectively produce conditions of conflict, "othering," competition, and structural violence. In addition, military security policies and practices can be seen, in part, as the pursuit of masculinist reactive autonomy, which can tolerate no interdependent relations. This model and its demands do less to empower men than subject them to crippling emotional and physical harm and unrelenting pressure to prove their manhood, when, in reality, any claims to such status are fragile and precarious. Insofar as this model is valorized, women aspire to it as well—in part to enjoy the status and unreconstructed authority it affords and in part to realize its material benefits, such as higher pay. Indeed, the gender division of violence obscures the long history of women who have engaged in political and other forms of violence, which belies the notion that they are naturally peaceful or in need of protection. Nevertheless, as Chapter 4 showed, these assumptions are so strong and so vital to keeping the war system in place that there remains remarkable resistance to women serving in, particularly state, militaries.

But "adding women" to militaries where violence is constitutive raises different issues from adding them to positions of formal political authority. The aggressive and hypermasculinized climate of militaries is particularly hostile to feminized identities and bodies, which means that women and feminized men are not and arguably cannot be treated as equal, no matter how well intentioned individual agents and policies might be. Merely increasing women's presence in militaries without also analyzing the power of gender will simply "resex" militaries to a certain degree without challenging the masculinism and imperialism of the war system and the ways of thinking and acting it engenders. Indeed, as Sylvester (2013) has more recently argued, war is not just something that is made, but more importantly makes us through the embodied and emotional experiences of it to which we must critically attend if we are to de-normalize it within ourselves and the wider world on the path to global justice.

Similarly, merely defining peace as the absence of the direct violence of war simply obscures the deep structural inequalities that both give rise to and are the result of violence. As we saw in Chapter 4, simply "adding women" to institutionalized structures of peacemaking, peacekeeping, and peacebuilding may provide some voice, a few more resources, and (weak and problematic) prohibitions on some forms of gender violence, but does little to challenge the masculinist, colonial, and neoliberal nature of these projects that are not designed to significantly address the prerogatives and costs of war nor the inequalities that produce and are produced by war. As Cynthia Enloe (2017a) recently noted, women peace activists connecting around the world insist that letting armed men write peace agreements and post-conflict constitutions and form post-conflict political parties while under-resourcing women's movements and civil society will never result in peace. Sustaining sexism, racism, classism, heterosexism, and gendered nationalism has heretofore been vital to sustaining militarism and the "us" and "them" mentality that goes along with it. Thus, any serious attempt to end war must involve significant alterations in local, national, and global hierarchies that construct the gendered division of violence.

With reference to the crisis of insecurity, the power of gender as a meta-lens naturalizes us–them as a necessarily hierarchical and oppositional dichotomy, which then fuels arrogance, distrust, fear, and often violence. Ultimately, it divides the human community into unequal and opposed beings who must resort to violence to settle disputes. This violent process may alter who the winners and losers are, but it rarely reduces systemic inequalities and keeps reproducing violence. By adopting the lens of reactive autonomy, IR practitioners—even without intending to—reproduce expectations of hostile and competitive behavior, which, in turn, generate uncooperative and defensive responses. This is how we find ourselves caught in self-perpetuating, vicious cycles, such as arms races and wars on terror, that produce more expressions of "terror" by hypermasculinist "othering" and outlawing all dissent. In contrast, the model of relational autonomy encourages mutual respect and cooperation. For this model to flourish in IR would require that we not only alter our lenses but also make profound changes in our individual and collective practices. Agathangelou and Ling (2009) have coined the term "worldism" to describe a global politics that recognizes already existing multiple worlds that are inextricably embedded within each other, are capable of reframing each other's worldviews, and are mutually accountable to each other. In their view, shifting from the lens that the father, the general, and the wealthy know best exposes how non-sensical it is to perpetuate the hegemonic self–other (non)relation in the face of the inescapable intertwinement and mutual constitution of worlds.

There is nothing simple or easy about identifying and institutionalizing alternatives to violence-as-usual to produce greater global justice. Generating alternatives presumes as a starting point both a politics of recognition that cultivates respect rather than "othering" and a politics of redistribution that minimizes inequalities and the grievances that so often fuel conflicts. Such strategies entail an emphasis on a restructuring in thought and action of valorized and devalorized identities of states, nations, and people, coupled with analyses of class, race, gender, nation, and sexuality stratifications and violences that produce and are produced by virulent us–them and self–other dichotomies.

Chapter 5 provided an analysis of the gender and gendered dimensions of neoliberal globalization, a process that has exacerbated gender(ed) divisions of labor and resources set in motion since colonial times and accelerating with the rise of first industrial and then global capitalism. The present crisis of sustainability, referring to the dual crises of social reproduction and environmental sustainability, derives significantly from the power of gender to devalorize not only women, but also the poor and working class, indigenous peoples, and nature. Chapter 5 also addressed the problematics of neoliberal inclusions of women into the existing global political economy to buffer financial crises, lessen poverty, and adapt to climate change.

Whereas the desirability of "adding women" to institutions designed for direct violence (and especially imperialist means and ends) is hotly debated, "adding women" (and other less economically privileged people) to the public realm of political power-wielders and the business world of economic income earners would seem a less contestable feminist goal. And, of course, feminists have worked long and hard to promote these projects. However, as we have seen, neoliberalism so marketizes and circumscribes political institutions and human relations and subjectivities that gaining such footholds does not necessarily translate into feminist gains more broadly defined as the development of global justice. Indeed, this is underscored when we consider how women were (briefly) held out as saviors of an unjust financial system. Neoliberalism has leavened gendered economic inequalities downward, with some women increasingly enjoying some of the benefits of access to higher political and economic positions, but many men "falling down" economically. This "race to the bottom" for many men and this "staying at the bottom" for many women are not the kind of equality that feminists envision. Indeed, as Saskia Sassen (2014) has found in her statistical study, economic inequalities among, but particularly within, states have reached "savage" proportions, resulting in a global pattern of simply expelling economically displaced people and cordoning off environments laid to waste rather than engaging in inclusion and remediation. Far more people (women and subordinated men) should be "moving up" as envisioned by the SDGs, but this cannot occur without wider (not just women's) responsibilities for taking care of social reproduction and the environment upon which all else depends.

With reference to the crisis of sustainability, the power of gender operates to valorize productive over reproductive, formal over informal, and paid over unpaid labor. This has left women primarily responsible for serving others and ever willing to put family survival ahead of their own (despite small and problematic efforts to get men to shoulder more of this work), but it has also ensured that social reproduction more generally is devalorized and underresourced by those at the top. Even if increasing more diverse women's presence at the top of corporate and IFI hierarchies might translate into more humane and gender-sensitive labor and social reproduction policies, the fact remains that few women and few men can actually be at the top of pyramidal hierarchies. Increasing the number of women in higher-paying, male-dominated occupations may increase some women's wages and status. But that would not necessarily lead to challenging the global gendered dichotomy between productive and reproductive labor, which renders the latter "non-work." Also, drawing poor rural women into circuits of capital through microcredit might enable some entrepreneurial women to prosper, and it might "feel good" to Western consumers to funnel a little of their shopping dollars to campaigns that assist such women to be entrepreneurs. But none of these moves disrupt the logic of capital accumulation or the growth imperative it establishes. They do not lead to questioning what is produced, why, and under what circumstance, or whose bodies are exploited in the process, whose backyards are surrendered to the waste produced, or how actual resources are distributed. Yet these are the underlying problems generating the crisis of sustainability, and to address them, we need transformative strategies.

In addition to others just cited, it is necessary to undermine the gendered dichotomy of "modern" and "traditional" that pervades the thinking and practices of development agencies.

The power of gender creates an association between "women's work" and "primitive" economic and technological practices found in indigenous societies in the global South and North societies. This association tends to discredit the knowledge and agency of women in development processes and devalues the quite complex, self-sufficient, and ecologically sustainable economic activities and technologies in which many women (and some men) engage in traditional indigenous societies. Undermining this association and the devaluation of women, indigenous cultures, and the land on which they depend requires questioning the kind of progress that masculinism and modernity have brought to us. Indigenous peoples, often led by women, as in the case of the Idle No More[12] movement of First Nations in Canada, are resisting their destruction in the name of progress, and their rights to self-determination and protection of their lands and ecosystems have been recognized in the 2008 UN Declaration of the Rights of Indigenous Peoples (UNDRIP),[13] but neocolonial development continues apace as long as masculinist modernity remains valorized.

Moving beyond the power of gender also involves questioning the premises of neoliberal capitalism: the imperative of growth, commodification of the life world, and pursuit of profits for some at the expense of well-being for all. By making visible the costs of current economic priorities, as well as who (most women and all marginalized peoples) and what (the environment) bear the brunt of these costs, states and corporations would find it harder to justify a great deal of what they claim is wealth-generating activity. Such costs include the realities that few are benefiting from the wealth that many workers are producing and that the formal sector of so-called productive work is dependent on the reproductive and informal sectors, rather than the reverse. Keeping the reproductive and informal sectors undervalued is "functional" only for those few at the top who reap greater profits as a result of this under- or devaluation.

Instead of having an equal say in what and how resources are to be used, women, the poor and working class, the indigenous, and people of the global South more generally are treated as resources themselves. In fact, all states (and corporations) appropriate women's (and many men's) bodies and labor to extend their resource base and thus their power within and outside state borders. Yet this fact is concealed by the gendered division of resources. However, when an intersectional feminist lens is used to view global politics, the positions of women and other marginalized people in a state's and a corporation's resource base are revealed, permitting those used as resources to specify strategies of resistance against this appropriation of their bodies and labor.

More privileged women and men have a responsibility to change and curb their consumption in resistance to the endless promotion of a consumer culture by neoliberal forces. The more privileged benefit—in the form of cheap consumer goods—from the cheap labor of primarily poor and racialized women (and feminized men) of the global South and North. Moreover, although men, especially in the global North, have far greater ecological footprints, all those with economic privilege are sentencing the most vulnerable to the vagaries of climate change. Being unmindful of consumption practices is at the expense of creating international solidarity among women (and men) to struggle against the global gendered division of labor and the exploitative practices of neoliberal capitalism. Ultimately, moving toward greater global justice will involve increasing not only the presence of women in male-dominated occupations and institutions at all levels but also recognizing the power of gender to perpetuate differential valorization of skills, bodies, identities, jobs, and resources in ways that reproduce and cumulatively deepen inequalities.

Respect for nature as a partner in, not a slave to, the world community must be accompanied by respect for the needs of the vast majority of women, racial, sexual, and gender minorities in the global North, and peoples of the global South more generally to enjoy a much greater share of the world's resources. At the same time, it is incumbent on those who struggle for equity in parenting, work, consuming, soldiering, officeholding, decision-making, and property owning to concern themselves with transforming these activities in ways that are not ecologically harmful. We must engage a politics of redistribution to ensure more equitable access to and control over resources, and a politics of recognition to address shifting identities borne of global migrations and the citizenship claims they raise to move toward global justice. Both entail rejecting the symbolic and material valorization of hegemonic masculinity at the expense of all that is feminized. If we do not seek to transform the gendered divisions of labor and resources simultaneously, we individually and collectively face an ever-deepening and widening crisis of sustainability. On the one hand, feminizing employment without enlarging responsibility for care undermines social reproduction, and exploitative production processes—especially the dangerous, debilitating, and demeaning work that is the survival option for too many—create disposable people and even countries. On the other hand, excessive and irresponsible growth disposes of natural resources, creates disposable waste that further degrades the environment, and depletes the resources upon which we all depend.

This final chapter has focused on the many movements comprising the GJM and the ways in which transnational and intersectional feminist activists have enabled this movement of movements of which they are a part to become more representative as well as more aware of cross-cutting inequalities and injustices and the complexities of challenging them. As the preceding, and, in fact, this entire text, suggests, moving toward the goals of the GJM is ever more urgent in this time of the ascendancy of regressive responses to global crises. Such goals may seem utopian, but without envisioning them, we cannot work toward them. The good news is that no matter where we are, we can engage in global justice activism, for, as we have seen, such activism goes on in local, national, and global contexts, offline and online, and through grassroots and NGO organizing and even with and within governmental and intergovernmental institutions. It is important, however, to remain conscious of any aspects of activism that reproduce gendered power relations and to work in solidarity with others toward just relations for all. The resource lists provided by this text offer many avenues to get involved in the GJM. In one sense, we have no choice but to become involved. Contemporary global processes force us to develop new understandings of who "we," as humans, are and how "we," as global citizens and planetary stewards, must act. In another sense, we willingly seek systemic transformations because we desire more than coercive and divisive politics, diffusely imposed discipline, globalized fear, and commodified life worlds. We demand lives of meaning and value and the actualization of justice. And whatever our commitments to justice, we cannot pursue them if we retain the power of gender as a meta-lens that produces and at the same time normalizes inequalities and, hence, injustice. There is no single or simple strategy to follow, but crucially important is a commitment to repoliticizing thought and action to resist what continually divides the world, yet binds it to deadening and destructive patterns.

Notes

1 See Women's March at www.womensmarch.com.

2 For personal stories of violence against women in Syria, see the Human Rights Watch July 2, 2014 report, "'We are Still Here': Women on the Front Lines of Syria's Conflict" at www.hrw.org/report/2014/07/02/we-are-still-here/women-front-lines-syrias-conflict. Also see Enloe (2017b) for an account of an alternative peace negotiation to end the war in Syria organized by transnational feminists in 2014.

3 See Cities for CEDAW at www.citiesforcedaw.org.

4 See World Social Forum (2016) at www.fsm2016.org/en/sinformer/.
5 See listings of examples in the Web and Video Resources list under Gender and Gender-Related NGOs at the end of this text (p. 000) and in the e-resource accompanying this text (www.routledge.com/9780813350851).
6 For a series of trenchant critiques of the co-optation and deradicalization of feminism by global capital, see Fraser (2009), McRobbie (2009), and Eisenstein (2009).
7 Staudt's (2008) extensive study of and participation in women's cross-border organizing against femicide at the US–Mexico border shows the extreme obstacles presented by "the border" to that organizing despite such proximity, but she argues that borderlands—as hybrid spaces where the intersection of local, national, and global is so visible—are particularly important sites for the development of coalition politics "on the ground."
8 As a way to correct the paucity of women experts consulted by the news media and policymakers, a constantly updated directory of female experts on domestic and international politics from around the world has been created under the banner of #WomenAlsoKnowStuff (see https://womenalsoknowstuff.com/).
9 See Nobel Prize.Org: The Official Web Site of the Nobel Prize at www.nobelprize.org/nobel_prizes/peace/laureates/.
10 For numerous examples of explicitly and implicitly feminist struggles against neoliberal globalization, see Naples and Desai (2002), Waller and Marcos (2005), Moghadam (2005), Hawkesworth (2006), and Marchand and Runyan (2011).
11 Zalewski (2013) urges a discontinuity project of breaking up the self-imposed boundaries of what constitutes feminism, particularly IR feminism, opening it up to new, unfamiliar, and even jarring formulations, such as "gaga feminism."
12 See Idle No More at www.idlenomore.ca/.
13 See UNDRIP at www.un.org/esa/socdev/unpfii/documents/DRIPS_en.pdf.

Chapter 6

Questions for Discussion

1 What is the global justice movement, what are some movements and organizations that are involved in it, and what are its visions?
2 How have feminists struggled for voice and leadership in the global justice movement and struggled among themselves to develop more inclusive and intersectional feminist movements?
3 How have feminist and other social justice groups engaged in more coalition-building across global–local, universalist–particularist, NGO–grassroots, policymaking focus–civil society change focus, and digital divides?
4 How might you become involved in the global justice movement to counter the crises of representation, insecurity, and sustainability? How would you employ an intersectional feminist lens in doing so?

Activities for Further Research

1 Watch the video, "Can We Shop to End Poverty" with Ananya Roy at www.youtube.com/watch?v=mpuf-N66CGI. What is the difference between engaging in collective and face-to-face dialogic activities and just buying a T-shirt or making a donation or only being online? How might actions with (not over or under or distant from) others be more productive for and more accountable with respect to crossing gendered divides and reversing the crises of representation, violence, and sustainability that ultimately hurt us all?
2 Review the websites of such global South-based and global North-based NGOs as Development Alternatives with Women for a New Era (at www.dawnnet.org/feminist-resources/),

Madre (www.madre.org/), Women Living Under Muslim Laws (at www.wluml.org/), and Women in Black (at www.womeninblack.org/about-women-in-black/). How are they informed by perspectives of women across the global South and North? How do they interconnect their issues, struggles, and even in some cases organizations? What does this tell us about coalition-building and feminist global justice organizing in practice?

3 Actively participating in global justice movements, actions, and projects, broadly defined, can be particularly empowering. Consider the testimonies of women who participated in the Arab Spring protests in Tahrir Square in Cairo, Egypt, in "Four Women, One Revolution" (at www.youtube.com/watch?v=kVMVc_8fzO0&t=201s), "Women Climate Defenders" from different parts of the world (at www.youtube.com/watch?v=TdzsFdhMMDI), and women, men, and children at the Washington, DC, Women's March in "Why I March" (at www.youtube.com/watch?v=oc2GepjlWLQ). How is this kind of empowerment different from market-based or power-over empowerment? How can it inform and bring about alternative relations at the local, national, and global level? Why is it just as important to study global justice movements as the actions of states and IGOs to understand and to change global politics?

Web and Video Resources

Select Web Resources

Gender, Gender-Related, and Other Relevant IGO Policies/Documents

Beijing Platform for Action (BPA)—Fourth World Conference on Women (September 1995)
www.un.org/womenwatch/daw/beijing/platform

Convention on the Elimination of All Forms of Discrimination Against Women (CEDAW 1979)
www.un.org/womenwatch/daw/cedaw

International Convention on the Elimination of All Forms of Racial Discrimination (ICERD 1965)
www.ohchr.org/EN/ProfessionalInterest/Pages/CERD.aspx

International Convention on the Protection of the Rights of All Migrant Workers and Members of Their Families (1990)
www.humanrights.se/wp-content/uploads/2012/01/Convention-on-the-Protection-of-all-Migrant-Workers.pdf

International Labour Organization Convention on Domestic Workers (2011)
www.ilo.org/dyn/normlex/en/f?p=NORMLEXPUB:12100:0::NO::P12100_ILO_CODE:C189

Paris Climate Agreement
www.unfccc.int/files/essential_background/convention/application/pdf/english_paris_agreement.pdf

Rome Statute of the International Criminal Court (ICC) (1998)
www.legal.un.org/icc/statute/romefra.htm

United Nations Convention on the Rights of the Child (1989)
www.ohchr.org/EN/ProfessionalInterest/Pages/CRC.aspx

United Nations Convention Relating to the Status of Refugees (1951)
www.unhcr.org/en-us/1951-refugee-convention.html

United Nations Convention Relating to the Status of Stateless Persons (1954)
www.unhcr.org/ibelong/wp-content/uploads/1954-Convention-relating-to-the-Status-of-Stateless-Persons_ENG.pdf

United Nations Declaration on the Rights of Indigenous Peoples (UNDRIP 2008)
www.un.org/esa/socdev/unpfii/documents/DRIPS_en.pdf

United Nations Development Programme Gender Inequality Index (2010)
www.hdr.undp.org/en/statistics/gii/

United Nations Economic and Social Council Resolution 1997/2 (Gender Mainstreaming 1997)
www.un.org/womenwatch/osagi/pdf/ECOSOCAC1997.2.PDF

United Nations Framework Convention on Climate Change (UNFCCC)/Kyoto Protocol (1997)
www.unfccc.int/kyoto_protocol/items/2830.php

United Nations Human Rights Council Resolution on Protecting Against Violence and Discrimination based on Sexual Orientation and Gender Identity (2016)
www.ohchr.org/EN/Issues/Discrimination/Pages/LGBTUNResolutions.aspx

United Nations Protocol to Prevent, Suppress, and Punish Trafficking in Persons (2000)
www.ohchr.org/Documents/ProfessionalInterest/ProtocolonTrafficking.pdf

United Nations Security Council Resolution 1325 (2000)
https://undocs.org/S/RES/1325(2000)

United Nations Security Council Resolution 1820 (2008)
www.undocs.org/en/S/RES/1820%282008%29

United Nations Security Council Resolution 1888 (2009)
www.undocs.org/en/S/RES/1888%282009%29

United Nations Security Council Resolution 1889 (2009)
www.undocs.org/en/S/RES/1889%282009%29

United Nations Security Council Resolution 1960 (2010)
www.undocs.org/en/S/RES/1960%282010%29

United Nations Security Council Resolution 2106 (2013)
www.undocs.org/en/S/RES/2106%282013%29

United Nations Security Council Resolution 2122 (2013)
www.undocs.org/en/S/RES/2122%282013%29

United Nations Security Council Resolution 2242 (2015)
www.undocs.org/en/S/RES/2242(2015)

United Nations Sustainable Development Goals (SDGs)
www.un.org/sustainabledevelopment/sustainable-development-goals/

Universal Declaration of Human Rights (1948)
www.un.org/Overview/rights.html

Gender and Gender-Related IGOs

United Nations Entity for Gender Equality and the Empowerment of Women (UN WOMEN)
www.unwomen.org/en
@UN_Women
#HeForShe

United Nations Fund for Population Activities (UNFPA)
www.unfpa.org/

Other IGOs

Food and Agriculture Organization of the United Nations (FAO)
www.fao.org

International Monetary Fund (IMF)
www.imf.org

International Organization for Migration (IOM)
www.iom.int

Inter-Parliamentary Union (IPU)
www.ipu.org

Joint United Nations Program on HIV/AIDS (UNAIDS)
www.unaids.org

Office of the United Nations High Commissioner for Refugees (UNHCR)
www.unhcr.org

Organization for Economic Cooperation and Development (OECD)
www.oecd.org

United Nations (UN)
www.un.org

United Nations Development Programme (UNDP)
www.undp.org

United Nations Economic and Social Council (ECOSOC)
www.un.org/ecosoc

United Nations Educational, Scientific, and Cultural Organization (UNESCO)
www.en.unesco.org

United Nations Environment Program (UNEP)
www.unenvironment.org

World Bank
www.worldbank.org

World Health Organization (WHO)
www.who.int

World Trade Organization (WTO)
www.wto.org

Gender and Gender-Related NGOs and Information

African Feminist Forum
www.africanfeministforum.com

African Women's Development Fund
www.awdf.org

AI My Body, My Rights Campaign
www.amnesty.org/en/get-involved/my-body-my-rights/

All Women's Action Society
www.awam.org.my

Amnesty International (AI)
www.amnesty.org

Association for Women's Rights in Development (AWID)
www.awid.org

Blackgirl International
www.blackgirl.org

Black Lives Matter
www.blacklivesmatter.com

Boston Consortium on Gender, Security, and Human Rights
www.genderandsecurity.org

Center for Reproductive Rights
www.reproductiverights.org

Center for Women's Global Leadership
www.cwgl.rutgers.edu

CLADEM
www.cladem.org/eng/

CODEPINK
www.codepink.org

Development Alternatives with Women for a New Era (DAWN)
www.dawnnet.org

Egyptian Feminist Union
www.efuegypt.org/en/

European Women's Lobby
www.womenlobby.org

Equality Now
www.equalitynow.org

FEMEN
www.femen.org

Feminist Majority Foundation (FMF)
www.feminist.org

Femmes Africa Solidarité (FAS)
www.fasngo.org

50/50: Gender, Sexuality and Social Justice
www.opendemocracy.net/5050

Gender cc–Women for Climate Justice
www.gendercc.net

GenderIT.org
www.genderit.org

Gender Quotas Database
www.idea.int/data-tools/data/gender-quotas

Global Alliance Against Trafficking in Women (GAATW)
www.gaatw.org

Global Fund for Women
www.globalfundforwomen.org

Green Belt Movement
www.greenbeltmovement.org

Guerilla Girls
www.guerrillagirls.com

Human Rights Watch
www.hrw.org

Human Rights Watch—Women's Rights
www.hrw.org/topic/womens-rights

Idle No More
www.idlenomore.ca/

Incite!: Women of Color Against Violence
www.incite-national.org

Institute for Women's Policy Research (IWPR)
www.iwpr.org

International Alert
www.international-alert.org/gender

International Alliance of Women
www.womenalliance.org

International Center for Research on Women (ICRW; Re:Gender merged with)
www.icrw.org

International Community of Women Living with HIV/AIDS (ICW)
www.icwglobal.org

International Feminist Journal of Politics (IFJP)
www.ifjpjournal.org

International Lesbian, Gay, Bisexual, Trans, and Intersex Association (ILGA)
www.ilga.org

International Studies Association (ISA)
www.isanet.org

Isis Women's International Cross-Cultural Exchange (Isis-WICCE)
www.isis.or.ug

Korean Women's Association United
www.women21.or.kr/kwau

Leap Manifesto
www.leapmanifesto.org/en/the-leap-manifesto/

MADRE
www.madre.org
#Madre

Make Every Woman Count
www.makeeverywomancount.org/index.php

Me Too Movement
www.metoomvmt.org
#MeToo

Navdanya—Research Foundation for Science, Technology, and Ecology (RFSTE)
www.navdanya.org

Nobel Peace Laureates
www.nobelprize.org/nobel_prizes/peace/laureates/

OutRight Action International
www.outrightinternational.org

Pan Pacific and Southeast Asia Women's Association (PPSEAWA)
www.ppseawa.org

PeaceWomen: A Project of the Women's International League for Peace and Freedom
www.peacewomen.org
@Peace_Women

Pro Mujer
www.promujer.org

Radical Women
www.radicalwomen.org

Revolutionary Association of the Women of Afghanistan (RAWA)
www.rawa.org

Scotland's Feminist Organization: Engender
www.engender.org.uk

Sisters in Islam
www.sistersinislam.org.my

The Alliance for International Women's Rights
www.aiwr.org

The BRIDGE Project
www.bridge.ids.ac.uk

The Center for Global Development
www.cgdev.org

The Sisterhood Is Global Institute (SIGI)
www.sigi.org

WIDE+
www.wideplus.org

Women for Human Rights
www.whr.org.np

Women for Women's Human Rights-New Ways
www.wwhr.org

Women in Black
www.womeninblack.org

Women in International Security (WIIS)
www.wiis-brussels.org

Women in Informal Employment: Globalizing and Organizing (WIEGO)
www.wiego.org

Women Learning Partnership for Rights, Development, and Peace
www.learningpartnership.org

Women Living Under Muslim Laws (WLUML)
www.wluml.org

Women's Action for New Directions (WAND)
www.wand.org/

#WomenAlsoKnowStuff
https://womenalsoknowstuff.com/

Women's Environment and Development Organization (WEDO)
www.wedo.org
#WomenClimateJustice

Women's Global Empowerment Fund
www.wgefund.org

Women's International League for Peace and Freedom (WILPF International)
http://wilpf.org

Women's March
www.womensmarch.com
#globalwomensmarch

Women's Refugee Commission
www.womensrefugeecommission.org

Women's Research and Education Institute (WREI)
www.wrei.org

WomenStats Project
www.womanstats.org

World Social Forum
www.fsm2016.org/en/

Select Video Resources

Women Make Movies
www.wmm.com

Bamako (dir. Abderrahmane Sissako, 2006)

Beyond Gay: The Politics of Pride (dir. Bob Christie, 2009)

Can You Hear Me? Israeli and Palestinian Women Fight for Peace (dir. Lily Rivlin and Margaret Murphy, 2006)

Cowboys in Paradise (dir. Amit Virmani, 2009)

El Contrato (dir. Min Sook Lee, 2003)

G.I. Jane (dir. Ridley Scott, 1997)

Life + Debt (dir. Stephanie Black, 2001)

Maquilapolis (dir. Vicky Funari and Sergio de la Torre, 2006)

Rape Is . . . (dir. Margaret Lazarus and Renner Wunderlich, 2002)

Seek My Face, Hear My Voice: Foreign Domestic Workers in Hong Kong (dir. Seyoung Lee, 2010)

Seniorita Extraviada (dir. Lourdes Portillo, 2001)

The Invisible War (dir. Kirby Dick, 2012)

The Women Outside: Korean Women and the U.S. Military (dir. J. T. Takagi and Hye Jung Park, 1995)

Women on the Frontlines (dir. Lisa Hepner and Patricia Smith Melton, 2003)

Women, Peace, and War (PBS TV) series (dir. Gini Reticker, 2011):
- *Peace Unveiled*
- *War Redefined*
- *The War We Are Living*
- *I Came to Testify*
- *Pray the Devil Back to Hell*

Which Way Home (dir. Rebecca Cammisa, 2009)

Zero Dark Thirty (dir. Kathryn Bigelow, 2012)

And countless YouTube and Vimeo resources on women, gender, and global issues, such as the following:

"A Punk Prayer" trailer (on Pussy Riot, 2013)
www.youtube.com/watch?v=E8K8WRRzbQs

"Can We Shop to End Poverty?" with Ananya Roy (Global POV Production, 2013)
www.youtube.com/watch?v=mpuf-N66CGI

"Feminism in the Age of Trump?" (interview with Cynthia Enloe, 2017)
www.counteractionmag.com/current-issue/2017/7/12/feminism-in-the-age-of-trump-interview-with-cynthia-enloe

"Four Women, One Revolution" (by Granta Magazine, 2011)
www.youtube.com/watch?v=kVMVc_8fzO0&t=201s

"If Lehman brothers were Lehman sisters" (Irene van Staveren TEDx talk, 2016)
www.youtube.com/watch?v=pcl0kEeN4mk

"International Relations: Feminism and International Relations" (Open University Talk by Kimberly Hutchings, 2014)
www.youtube.com/watch?v=ajAWGztPUiU

"Make America Great Again" (by Pussy Riot, 2016)
www.youtube.com/watch?v=s-bKFo30o2o

"Men, Peace, and Security: Agents of Change" (by United States Institute of Peace, 2014)
www.youtube.com/watch?v=LEAYxr8Xo7I

"The Hidden Face of Globalization" (four-part series produced by the National Labor Committee, 2008)
www.youtube.com/watch?v=8Bhodyt4fmU

"Queer International Relations-Cynthia Weber" (talk at University of Ottawa, 2016)
www.youtube.com/watch?v=H8MgE0fc9Ws

"Side by Side—Women, Peace, and Security" (produced by UN Women, 2012)
www.youtube.com/watch?v=a2Br8DCRxME

"Solutions to the Food and Ecological Crisis Facing Us Today"
(Vandana Shiva TEDx talk, 2012)
www.youtube.com/watch?v=ER5ZZk5atlE

"This Changes Everything" trailer (based on the book by Naomi Klein, 2015)
www.youtube.com/watch?v=YQhflH4alO0

"Who Sees Poverty?" with Ananya Roy (Global POV Production, 2012)
www.youtube.com/watch?v=hrW8ier__4Q

"Who's Counting? Marilyn Waring on Sex, Lies and Global Economics" (produced by National Film Board of Canada, 2016)
www.youtube.com/watch?v=WS2nkr9q0VU

"Why I March" (by RachelRose, 2017)
www.youtube.com/watch?v=oc2Gepj1WLQ

"Women and Climate Change" (produced by Gender cc–Women for Climate Justice, 2011)
www.youtube.com/watch?v=j1JdAmCJF5o

"Women Climate Defenders" (produce by MADREspeaks, 2017)
www.youtube.com/watch?v=TdzsFdhMMDI

References

Ackerly, Brooke A. 2008. *Universal Human Rights in a World of Difference*. Cambridge: Cambridge University Press.

Ackerly, Brooke A., Maria Stern, and Jacqui True, eds. 2006. *Feminist Methodologies for International Relations*. Cambridge: Cambridge University Press.

Ackerly, Brooke A., and Jacqui True. 2006. "Studying the Struggles and Wishes of the Age: Feminist Theoretical Methodology and Feminist Theoretical Methods." In Brooke A. Ackerly, Maria Stern, and Jacqui True, eds., *Feminist Methodologies for International Relations*, 241–260. Cambridge: Cambridge University Press.

Agathangelou, Anna, and L. H. M. Ling. 2004. "The House of IR: From Family Power Politics to the Poisies of Worldism." *International Studies Review* 6(4): 21–49.

Agathangelou, Anna, and L. H. M. Ling. 2009. *Transforming World Politics: From Empire to Multiple Worlds*. London: Routledge.

Agathangelou, Anna M. 2013. "Neoliberal Geopolitical Order and Value: Queerness as a Speculative Economy and Anti-blackness as Terror." *International Feminist Journal of Politics* 15(4): 453–476.

Agathangelou, Anna M., and Heather M. Turcotte. 2016. "Reworking Postcolonial Feminisms in the Sites of IR." In Jill Steans and Daniela Tepe-Belfrage, eds., *Handbook on Gender in World Politics*, 41–50. Cheltenham: Edward Elgar.

Agustín, Laura Maria. 2007. *Sex at the Margins: Migration, Labour Markets, and the Rescue Industry*. London: Zed Books.

Al-Ali, Nadje, and Nicola Pratt. 2009. *What Kind of Liberation? Women and the Occupation of Iraq*. Berkeley, CA: University of California Press.

Alexander, M. Jacqui. 2005. *Pedagogies of Crossing: Meditations on Feminism, Sexual Politics, Memory, and the Sacred*. Durham, NC: Duke University Press.

Alvarez, Lizette, and Erik Eckholm. 2009. "Purple Heart Is Ruled Out for Traumatic Stress." *New York Times*, January 8. www.nytimes.com/2009/01/08/us/08purple.html (accessed February 9, 2009).

Alvarez, Sonia. 1999. "Advocating Feminism: The Latin American Feminist NGO 'Boom.'" *International Feminist Journal of Politics* 1(2): 181–209.

Anderson, Bridget. 2000. *Doing the Dirty Work? The Global Politics of Domestic Labour*. London: Zed Books.

Antrobus, Peggy. 2006. "Gender Equality in the New Millennium: Goal or Gimmick?" *Caribbean Quarterly* 52(2/3): 39–50.

Anzaldúa, Gloria. 1999. *Borderlands/La Frontera: The New Mestiza*. 2nd ed. San Francisco, CA: Aunt Lute Books.

Ashley, Richard. 1989. "Living on Borderlines: Man, Poststructuralism, and War." In James Der Derian and Michael J. Shapiro, eds., *International/Intertextual Relations: Postmodern Readings of World Politics*, 259–322. Lexington, MA: Lexington Books.

Aslanbeigui, Nahid, and Gale Summerfield. 2000. "The Asian Crisis, Gender, and the International Financial Architecture." *Feminist Economics* 6(3): 81–104.

Aslanbeigui, Nahid, and Gale Summerfield. 2001. "Risk, Gender, and Development in the 21st Century." *International Journal of Politics, Culture, and Society* 15(1): 7–26.

Baaz, Maria Eriksson, and Maria Stern. 2013. *Sexual Violence as a Weapon of War? Perceptions, Prescriptions, Problems in the Congo and Beyond*. London: Zed Books.

Bach, Jonathan. 2011. "Remittances, Gender, and Development." In Marianne H. Marchand and Anne Sisson Runyan, eds., *Gender and Global Restructuring: Sightings, Sites, and Resistances*, 129–142. 2nd ed. London: Routledge.

Baker, Peter. 2016. "Raise of Donald Trump Tracks Growing Debate Over Global Fascism." *New York Times*, May 28. www.nytimes.com/2016/05/29/world/europe/rise-of-donald-trump-tracks-growing-debate-over-global-fascism.html (accessed December 18, 2017).

Bakker, Isabella, ed. 1994. *The Strategic Silence: Gender and Economic Policy*. London: Zed Books.

Bakker, Isabella, and Stephen Gill, eds. 2003. *Power, Production, and Social Reproduction: Human In/Security in the Global Political Economy*. Basingstoke: Palgrave Macmillan.

Barber, Pauline Gardiner. 2011. "Women's Work Unbound: Philippine Development and Global Restructuring." In Marianne H. Marchand and Anne Sisson Runyan, eds.,*Gender and Global Restructuring: Sightings, Sites, and Resistances*, 143–162. 2nd ed. London: Routledge.

Basu, Amrita, ed. 2017. *Women's Movements in the Global Era: The Power of Local Feminisms*. Boulder, CO: Westview Press.

Barthwal-Datta, Monika, and Soumita Basu. 2015. "Land, Water and Food." In Laura J. Shepherd, ed., *Gender Matters in Global Politics: A Feminist Introduction to International Relations*, 197–209. 2nd ed. London: Routledge.

Bedford, Kate. 2009. *Gender, Sexuality, and the Reformed World Bank*. Minneapolis, MN: University of Minnesota Press.

Bedont, Barbara. 2005. "The Renewed Popularity of the Rule of Law: Implications for Women, Impunity, and Peacekeeping." In Dyan Mazurana, Angela Raven-Roberts, and Jane Parpart, eds., *Gender, Conflict, and Peacekeeping*, 83–108. Lanham, MD: Rowman and Littlefield.

Belkin, Aaron. 2012. *Bring Me Men: Military Masculinity and the Benign Façade of American Empire, 1898–2001*. New York: Columbia University Press.

Benería, Lourdes. 1995. "Toward a Greater Integration of Gender in Economics." *World Development* 23(11): 1839–1850.

Benería, Lourdes. 2003. *Gender, Development, and Globalization: Economics as if All People Mattered*. New York: Routledge.

Benhabib, Seyla, and Drucilla Cornell, eds. 1987. *Feminism as Critique: On the Politics of Gender in Late-Capitalist Societies*. Cambridge: Polity Press.

Berentz, Helen. 2016. "Hashtagging Girlhood: #IAmMalala, #BringBackOurGirls and Gendering Representation of Global Politics." *International Feminist Journal of Politics* 18(4): 513–527.

Bergeron, Suzanne L. 2003. "Challenging the World Bank's Narrative of Inclusion." In Amitava Kumar, ed., *World Bank Literature*, 157–171. Minneapolis, MN: University of Minnesota Press.

Blee, Kathleen M., and Sandra McGee Deutsch. 2012. *Women of the Right: Comparisons and Interplay Across Borders*. University Park, PA: University of Pennsylvania Press.

Bordo, Susan. 2017. *The Destruction of Hillary Clinton*. New York: Melville House.

Brenner, Johanna. 2009. "Transnational Feminism and the Struggle for Global Justice." In Jai Sen and Peter Waterman, eds., *World Social Forum: Challenging Empires*, 26–37. 2nd ed. Montreal: Black Rose Books.

Brittan, Arthur. 1989. *Masculinity and Power*. Oxford: Basil Blackwell.

Brown, Katherine E. 2011. "Blinded by the Explosion? Security and Resistance in Muslim Women's Suicide Terrorism." In Laura Sjoberg and Caron E. Gentry, eds., *Women, Gender, and Terrorism*, 194–226. Athens, GA: University of Georgia Press.

Brown, Sarah. 1988. "Feminism, International Theory, and International Relations of Gender Inequality." *Millennium Journal of International Studies* 17(3): 461–475.

Brown, Wendy. 2015. *Undoing the Demos: Neoliberalism's Stealth Revolution*. New York: Zone Books.

Bunch, Charlotte, and Niamh Reilly. 1994. *Demanding Accountability: The Global Campaign and Vienna Tribunal for Women's Human Rights*. New York: United Nations Development Fund for Women (UNIFEM) and Center for Women's Global Leadership (CWGL).

Buss, Doris, and Didi Herman. 2004. *Globalizing Family Values: The Christian Right in International Politics*. Minneapolis, MN: University of Minnesota Press.

Butler, Judith. 1990. *Gender Trouble: Feminism and the Subversion of Identity*. London: Routledge.

Caglar, Gülay. 2013. "Gender Mainstreaming." *Politics & Gender* 9(3): 336–344.

Caglar, Gülay, Elisabeth Prügl, and Susanne Zwingel, eds. 2012. *Feminist Strategies in International Governance*. London: Routledge.

Cameron, Darla, and Bonnie Berkowitz. 2016. "The State of Gay Rights Around the World." *The Washington Post*. www.washingtonpost.com/graphics/world/gay-rights/ (accessed July 11, 2017).

Campbell, David. 1992. *Writing Security: United States Foreign Policy and the Politics of Identity*. Minneapolis, MN: University of Minnesota Press.

Cape Chameleon. 2016. "Women in the South African Army: Fighting for Gender Transformation." www.capechameleon.co.za/2016/09/women-south-african-army/ (accessed May 15, 2017).

Carreon, Michelle E., and Valentine M. Moghadam. 2015. " 'Resistance is Fertile: Revisiting Maternalist Frames Across Cases of Women's Mobilization." *Women's Studies International Forum* 51: 19–30.

Carver, Terrell. 1996. *Gender Is Not a Synonym for Women*. Boulder, CO: Lynne Rienner.

Catalyst. 2017. *Pyramid: Women in S&P 500 Companies*. New York: Catalyst. www.catalyst.org/knowledge/women-sp-500-companies (accessed July 14, 2017).

Chan-Tiberghien, Jennifer. 2004. "Gender Skepticism or Gender-Boom? Poststructural Feminisms, Transnational Feminisms, and the World Conference Against Racism." *International Feminist Journal of Politics* 6(3): 454–484.

Chappell, Louise, and Lisa Hill. 2006. *The Politics of Women's Interests: New Comparative Perspectives*. London: Routledge.

Chowdhury, Geeta, and Sheila Nair, eds. 2002. *Power, Postcolonialism, and International Relations: Reading Race, Gender, and Class*. London: Routledge.

Chowdhury, Najma, and Barbara J. Nelson et al. 1994. "Redefining Politics: Patterns of Women's Political Engagement from a Global Perspective." In Barbara J. Nelson and Najma Chowdhury, eds., *Women and Politics Worldwide*, 3–24. New Haven, CT: Yale University Press.

Clausewitz, Carl von. 2004. *On War*. Whitefish, MT: Kessinger.

Cockburn, Cynthia. 2012. *Antimilitarism: Political and Gender Dynamics of Peace Movements*. London: Palgrave Macmillan.

Cohen, Benjamin J. 2008. *International Political Economy: An Intellectual History*. Princeton, NJ: Princeton University Press.

Cohn, Carol. 2008. "Mainstreaming Gender in UN Security Policy: A Path to Political Transformation?" In Shirin Rai and Georgina Waylen, eds., *Global Governance: Feminist Perspectives*, 185–206. Basingstoke: Palgrave Macmillan.

Cohn, Carol, ed. 2013. *Women & Wars: Contested Histories, Uncertain Futures*. Cambridge: Polity Press.

Cohn, Carol, and Ruth Jacobson. 2013. "Women and Political Activism in the Face of War and Militarization." In Carol Cohn, ed., *Women & Wars: Contested Histories, Uncertain Futures*, 102–123. Cambridge: Polity Press.

Collins, Patricia Hill. 1991. *Black Feminist Thought: Knowledge, Consciousness, and the Politics of Empowerment*. New York: Routledge.

Connell, R. W. 1987. *Gender and Power*. Cambridge: Polity Press.

Connell, R. W. 1995. *Masculinities*. Berkeley, CA: University of California Press.

Cook, Rebecca, ed. 1994. *Human Rights of Women: National and International Perspectives*. Philadelphia, PA: University of Pennsylvania Press.

Council of Europe Regional Study. 2016. Women's Political Representation in the Eastern Partnership Countries. www.rm.coe.int/CoERMPublicCommonSearchServices/DisplayDCTMContent?documentId=09000016806c3fa5 (accessed April 27, 2017).

Cox, Robert W. 1987. *Production, Power, and World Order: Social Forces in the Making of History*. New York: Columbia University Press.

Crenshaw, Kimberlé. 1991. "Mapping the Margins: Intersectionality, Identity Politics, and Violence Against Women of Color." *Stanford Law Review* 43: 1241–1299.

Dahl, Robert A. 1961. *Who Governs? Democracy and Power in an American City*. New Haven, CT: Yale University Press.

Dahlerup, Drude. 2006a. "Conclusion." In Drude Dahlerup, ed., *Women, Quotas, and Politics*, 293–307. London: Routledge.

Dahlerup, Drude. 2006b. "Introduction." In Drude Dahlerup, ed., *Women, Quotas, and Politics*, 3–31. London: Routledge.

Dahlerup, Drude, Zeina Hilal, Nana Kalandadze, and Rumbidzai Kandawasvika-Nhundu. 2014. "Atlas of Electoral Gender Quotas." International IDEA: Institute for Democracy and Electoral Assistance. Co-Published with Inter-Parliamentary Union, Stockholm University. www.idea.int/publications/catalogue/atlas-electoral-gender-quotas (accessed April 25, 2017).

D'Amico, Francine. 2015. "LGBT and (Dis)United Nations: Sexual and Gender Minorities, International Law, and UN Politics." In Manuela Lavinas Picq and Marcus Thiel, eds., *Sexualities in World Politics: How LBGTQ Claims Shape International Relations*, 54–74. London: Routledge.

Darrow, Barb. 2016. "There Are Hardly Any Women Leading Fortune 1000 Companies." *Fortune.com*. www.fortune.com/2016/09/06/fortune-1000-still-led-by-men/ (accessed July 11, 2017).

Dauvergne, Peter, and Genevieve LeBaron. 2014. *Protest Inc.: The Corporatization of Activism*. Cambridge: Polity Press.

Davis, Lisa. 2013. *The Seeking Accountability and Effective Response for Gender-Based Violence Against Syrian Women: Women's Inclusion in Peace Processes*. www.law.cuny.edu/academics/clinics/iwhr/publications/Seeking-Accountability-and-Effective-Response-for-Sexual-and-Gender-Based-Violence-Against-Syrian-Women-Womens-Inclusion-in-Peace-Processes.pdf (accessed December 19, 2017).

Defence People Group, Department of Defence, Australia. 2015. *Women in the ADF Report 2014-15: Supplement to the Defence Annual Report 2014–15*. www.defence.gov.au/annualreports/14-15/downloads/Women_in_the_ADF_Report.pdf (accessed May 8, 2017).

De Goede, Marieke. 2005. *Virtue, Fortune, and Faith: A Genealogy of Finance*. Minneapolis, MN: University of Minnesota Press.

DeLargy, Pamela. 2013. "Sexual Violence and Women's Health in War." In Carol Cohn, ed., *Women & Wars: Contested Histories, Uncertain Futures*, 54–79. Cambridge: Polity Press.

della Porta, Donatella. 2007. *The Global Justice Movement: Cross-National and Transnational Perspectives*. London: Routledge.

Den Boer, Andrea. 2016. "Gender as a Variable in International Relations Research." In Jill Steans and Daniela Tep-Belfrage, eds., *Handbook on Gender and World Politics*, 15–23. Cheltenham: Edward Elgar.

Department of Defense (DOD). 2013. *Department of Defense Annual Report on Sexual Assault in the Military*. www.sapr.mil/public/docs/reports/FY13_DoD_SAPRO_Annual_Report_on_Sexual_Assault.pdf (accessed May 10, 2017).

Department of Defense (DOD). 2017. *Department of Defense Annual Report on Sexual Assault in the Military*. www.sapr.mil/public/docs/reports/FY16_Annual/FY16_SAPRO_Annual_Report.pdf (accessed May 10, 2017).

Der Derian, James, and Michael J. Shapiro. 1989. *International/Intertextual Relations: Postmodern Readings of World Politics*. Lexington, KY: Lexington Books.

Detraz, Nicole, 2012. *International Security and Gender*. Cambridge: Polity.

Detraz, Nicole. 2015. *Environmental Security and Gender*. London: Routledge.

Diamond, Larry, Marc F. Plattner, and Christopher Walker. 2016. *Authoritarianism Goes Global: The Challenge to Democracy*. Baltimore, MD: Johns Hopkins University Press.

Dionne, Jr., E. J., Norman J. Ornstein, and Thomas E. Mann. 2017. *One Nation Under Trump: A Guide for the Perplexed, the Disillusioned, the Desperate, and the Not-Yet Deported*. New York: St. Martin's Press.

Disabled American Veterans (DAV). 2015. "Women Veterans: The Long Journey Home." www.dav.org/wp-content/uploads/women-veterans-study.pdf (accessed May 15, 2017).

Eager, Paige Whaley. 2014. *Waging Gendered Wars: U.S. Military Women in Afghanistan and Iraq*. Farnham: Ashgate.

Ehrenreich, Barbara, and Arlie R. Hochschild, eds. 2002a. *Global Woman: Nannies, Maids, and Sex Workers in the New Economy*. New York: Metropolitan Books.

Ehrenreich, Barbara, and Arlie R. Hochschild, eds. 2002b. "Introduction." In Barbara Ehrenreich and Arlie R. Hochschild, eds., *Global Woman: Nannies, Maids, and Sex Workers in the New Economy*, 1–14. New York: Metropolitan Books.

Eichler, Maya. 2015. *Gender and Private Security in Global Politics*. Oxford: Oxford University Press.

Einhorn, Barbara, and Eileen Janes Yeo, eds. 1995. *Women and Market Societies: Crisis and Opportunity*. Aldershot: Edward Elgar.

Eisenstein, Hester. 2009. *Feminism Seduced: How Global Elites Use Women's Labor and Ideas to Exploit the World*. Boulder, CO: Paradigm Publishers.

Eisenstein, Zillah R. 2004. *Against Empire: Feminisms, Racisms, and the West*. London: Zed Books.

Eisenstein, Zillah R. 2007. *Sexual Decoys: Gender, Race, and War in Imperial Democracy*. London: Zed Press.

Elias, Juanita, and Adrienne Roberts, eds. 2018. *Handbook on the International Political Economy of Gender*. Cheltenham: Edward Elgar.

Ellerby, Kara. 2017. *No Shortcut to Change: An Unlikely Path to a More Gender-Equitable World*. New York: New York University Press.

Elshtain, Jean Bethke. 1987. *Women and War*. New York: Basic Books.

Elshtain, Jean Bethke. 1992. "Sovereignty, Identity, Sacrifice." In V. Spike Peterson, ed., *Gendered States: Feminist (Re)Visions of International Relations Theory*, 141–154. Boulder, CO: Lynne Rienner.

Enloe, Cynthia. 1983. *Does Khaki Become You? The Militarization of Women's Lives*. Boston, MA: South End Press.

Enloe, Cynthia. 1989. *Bananas, Beaches, and Bases: Making Feminist Sense of International Politics*. Berkeley, CA: University of California Press.

Enloe, Cynthia. 1990. "Women and children: Making Feminist Sense of the Persian Gulf Crisis." *Village Voice*, September 25: 29ff.

Enloe, Cynthia. 1993. *The Morning After: Sexual Politics at the End of the Cold War*. Berkeley, CA: University of California Press.

Enloe, Cynthia. 2000. *Maneuvers: The International Politics of Militarizing Women's Lives*. Berkeley, CA: University of California Press.

Enloe, Cynthia. 2007. *Globalization and Militarism: Feminists Make the Link*. Lanham, MD: Rowman and Littlefield.

Enloe, Cynthia. 2013. *Seriously! Investigating Crashes and Crises as if Women Mattered*. Berkeley, CA: University of California Press.

Enloe, Cynthia. 2014. *Bananas, Beaches, and Bases: Making Feminist Sense of International Politics*. 2nd ed. Berkeley, CA: University of California Press.

Enloe, Cynthia. 2017a. "Peace Has to be Built: What Feminist Activists Have Taught Me about Peace." *International Studies Review* 19(1): 135–136.

Enloe, Cynthia. 2017b. *The Big Push: Exposing and Challenging the Persistence of Patriarchy*. Oakland, CA: University of California Press.

Eschle, Catherine. 2001. *Global Democracy, Social Movements, and Feminism*. Boulder, CO: Westview Press.

Eschle, Catherine. 2005. "Constructing 'the Anti-Globalisation Movement.'" In Catherine Eschle and Bice Maiguashca, eds., *Critical Theories, International Relations, and the "Anti-Globalization Movement"*, 17–35. London: Routledge.

Eschle, Catherine, and Bice Maiguashca, eds. 2005. *Critical Theories, International Relations, and the "Anti-Globalization Movement"*. London: Routledge.

Eschle, Catherine, and Bice Maiguashca, eds. 2010. *Making Feminist Sense of the Global Justice Movement*. Lanham, MD: Rowman & Littlefield.

European Commission. 2015. Gender Balance on Corporate Boards: Europe is Cracking the Glass Ceiling. www.ec.europa.eu/justice/gender-equality/files/womenonboards/factsheet_women_on_boards_web_2015-10_en.pdf (accessed April 12, 2017).

European Country of Origin Information Network. 2015. "Russia: Military Service, Including Amendments to Military Service; Whether Women Are Treated Differently Than Men; Whether Holders of Military Books Are Treated Differently Than Conscripted Persons; Consequences of Draft Evasion and Availability of an Appeal Process (2006-April 2015) [RUS105142.E]." www.ecoi.net/local_link/318559/443774_en.html (accessed May 15, 2017).

European Institute for Gender Equality (EIGE). 2017. "Largest Listed Companies: Presidents, Board Members and Employee Representatives. Gender Statistics Database for the European Institute for Gender Equality." www.eige.europa.eu/gender-statistics/dgs/indicator/wmidm_bus_bus__wmid_comp_compbm (accessed April 12, 2017).

Fall, Yassine. 2001. "Gender and Social Implications of Globalization: An African Perspective." In Rita Mae Kelly et al., eds., *Gender, Globalization, and Democratization*, 49–74. Lanham, MD: Rowman and Littlefield.

Faludi, Susan. 2007. *The Terror Dream: Fear and Fantasy in Post-9/11 America*. New York: Metropolitan Books/Henry Holt.

Fausto-Sterling, Anne. 1992. *Myths of Gender: Biological Theories About Women and Men*. 2nd ed. New York: Basic Books.

Fausto-Sterling, Anne. 2000. "The Five Sexes, Revisited." *The Sciences* 40(4): 19–23.

Federici, Sylvia. 2004. *Caliban and the Witch: Women, the Body, and Primitive Accumulation*. New York: Autonomedia.

Fernandez-Kelly, Maria Patricia. 1983. *For We Are Sold, I and My People: Women in Industry in Mexico's Frontier*. Albany, NY: State University of New York Press.

Floro, Maria, and Gary Dymski. 2000. "Financial Crisis, Gender, and Power: An Analytical Framework." *World Development* 28(7): 1269–1283.

Foucault, Michel. 1991. "Governmentality." In Graham Burchell, Colin Gordon, and Peter Miller, eds., *The Foucault Effect: Studies in Governmentality*, 87–104. Chicago, IL: University of Chicago Press.

Franklin, M. I. 2004. *Postcolonial Politics, the Internet, and Everyday Life: Pacific Traversals Online*. London: Routledge.

Fraser, Nancy. 1997. *Justice Interruptus: Critical Reflections on the "Postsocialist" Condition*. New York: Routledge.

Fraser, Nancy. 2009. "Feminism, Capitalism, and the Cunning of History." *New Left Review* 56: 97–117.

Friedenwall, Lenita, Drude Dahlerup, and Hege Skjeie. 2006. "The Nordic Countries: An Incremental Model." In Drude Dahlerup, ed., *Women, Quotas, and Politics*, 55–82. London: Routledge.

Friedman, Elisabeth Jay. 2017. "Seeking Rights from the Left: Gender and Sexuality in Latin America." In Amrita Basu, ed., *Women's Movements in the Global Era: The Power Local Feminisms Second Edition*, 265–298. Boulder, CO: Westview Press.

Fuentes, Annette, and Barbara Ehrenreich. 1983. *Women in the Global Factory*. Boston, MA: South End Press.

Gender Quotas Database. 2017. "About Quotas." www.idea.int/data-tools/data/gender-quotas (accessed April 13, 2017).

Gentry, Caron E., and Laura Sjoberg. 2015. *Beyond Mothers, Monsters, Whores: Thinking about Women's Violence in Global Politics*. London: Zed Books.

Gentry, Caron E., Laura J. Shepherd, and Laura Sjoberg, eds. Forthcoming 2019. *The Routledge Handbook of Gender and Security*. London: Routledge.

Gessen, Martha. 2014. *Words Will Break Cement*. New York: Riverhead Books.

Ghosh, Nandita. 2007. "Women and the Politics of Water: An Introduction." *International Feminist Journal of Politics* 9(4): 443–454.

Gibbons-Neff, Thomas. 2017. "'It's Marine Corps Wide': Female Marines Detail Harassment in Wake of Nude Photos Scandal." *Washington Post*, March 7. www.washingtonpost.com/news/checkpoint/wp/2017/03/07/its-marine-corps-wide-female-marines-detail-harassment-in-wake-of-nude-photos-scandal/?utm_term=.436989271f1c (accessed December 19, 2017).

Gibson-Graham, J. K. 2006. *A Postcapitalist Politics*. Minneapolis, MN: University of Minnesota Press.

Giddings, Paula. 1984. *When and Where I Enter: The Impact of Black Women on Race and Sex in America*. New York: Bantam Books.

Giles, Wenona, and Jennifer Hyndman. 2004. "Introduction: Gender and Conflict in a Global Context." In Wenona Giles and Jennifer Hyndman, eds., *Sites of Violence: Gender and Conflict Zones*, 3–23. Berkeley, CA: University of California Press.

Gillies, Shannon. 2015. "Number of Women in Defence 'Inadequate.'" RNZ. www.radionz.co.nz/news/national/270496/number-of-women-in-defence-%27inadequate%27 (accessed May 8, 2017).

Gilmore, Stephanie, ed. 2008. *Feminist Coalitions: Historical Perspectives on Second-Wave Feminism in the United States*. Urbana, IL: University of Illinois Press.

Goetz, Anne Marie, and Rina Sen Gupta. 1996. "Who Takes the Credit? Gender, Power, and Control over Loan Use in Rural Credit Programs in Bangladesh." *World Development* 24(1): 45–64.

Goldstein, Joshua S. 2001. *War and Gender: How Gender Shapes the War System and Vice Versa*. Cambridge: Cambridge University Press.

Goldstein, Joshua S. 2011. *Winning the War on War: The Decline of Armed Conflict Worldwide*. New York: Dutton.

Goodyear, Michael, and Ronald Weitzer. 2011. "International Trends in the Control of Sexual Services." In Susan Dewey and Patty Kelly, eds., *Policing Pleasure: Sex Work, Policy, and the State in Global Perspective*, 16–30. New York: New York University Press.

Government of Canada. 2014. "Women in the Canadian Armed Forces." www.forces.gc.ca/en/news/article.page?doc=women-in-the-canadian-armed-forces/hie8w7rm (accessed May 8, 2017).

Grant, Rebecca. 1994. "The Cold War and the Feminine Mystique." In Peter R. Beckman and Francine D'Amico, eds., *Women, Gender, and World Politics: Perspectives, Policies, and Prospects*, 119–130. Westport, CT: Bergin and Garvey.

Grewal, Inderpal. 2005. *Transnational America: Feminisms, Diasporas, Neoliberalisms*. Durham, NC: Duke University Press.

Grewal, Inderpal, and Caren Kaplan, eds. 1994. *Scattered Hegemonies: Postmodernity and Transnational Feminist Practices*. Minneapolis, MN: University of Minnesota Press.

Grewal, Inderpal, and Caren Kaplan. 2001. "Global Identities: Theorizing Transnational Studies of Sexuality." *GLQ* 7(4): 663–679.

Griffin, Penny. 2016. "Feminist Political Economy." In Jill Steans and Daniela Tepe-Belfrage, eds., *Handbook on Gender in World Politics*, 345–353. Cheltenham: Edward Elgar.

Guerrero, MA Jaimes. 1997. "Exemplars of Indigenism: Native North American Women for Decolonization and Liberation." In Cathy J. Cohen, Kathleen B. Jones, and Joan C. Tronto, eds., *Women Transforming Politics: An Alternative Reader*, 205–222. New York: New York University Press.

Hague, Euan. 1997. "Rape, Power, and Masculinity: The Construction of Gender and National Identities in the War in Bosnia-Herzegovina." In Ronit Lentin, ed., *Gender and Catastrophe*, 50–63. London: Zed Books.

Halberstam, J. Jack. 2012. *Gaga Feminism: Sex, Gender, and the End of Normal*. Boston, MA: Beacon Press.

Harcourt, Wendy, ed. 1999. *Women@Internet: Creating New Cultures in Cyberspace*. London: Zed Books.

Harding, Sandra. 1986. *The Science Question in Feminism*. Ithaca, NY: Cornell University Press.

Harding, Sandra. 1991. *Whose Science? Whose Knowledge? Thinking from Women's Lives*. Ithaca, NY: Cornell University Press.

Hardt, Michael, and Antonio Negri. 2000. *Empire*. Cambridge, MA: Harvard University Press.

Harvey, David. 2003. *The New Imperialism*. Oxford: Oxford University Press.

Hawkesworth, Mary E. 2006. *Globalization and Feminist Activism*. Lanham, MD: Rowman and Littlefield.

Hawkesworth, Mary E. 2012. *Political Worlds of Women: Activism, Advocacy, and Governance in the Twenty-First Century*. Boulder, CO: Westview Press.

Henderson, Sarah L., and Alana S. Jeydel. 2010. *Women and Politics in a Global World*. 2nd ed. Oxford: Oxford University Press.

Henry, Nicola. 2011. *War and Rape: Law, Memory, and Justice*. London: Routledge.

Hesford, Wendy S., and Wendy Kozol, eds. 2005. *Just Advocacy? Women's Human Rights, Transnational Feminisms, and the Politics of Representation*. New Brunswick, NJ: Rutgers University Press.

Hoogensen, Gunhild, and Bruce O. Solheim. 2006. *Women in Power: World Leaders Since 1960*. Westport, CT: Praeger.

Hooper, Charlotte. 1998. "Masculinist Practices and Gender Politics: The Operation of Multiple Masculinities in International Relations." In Marysia Zalewski and Jane Parpart, eds., *The "Man" Question in International Relations*, 28–53. Boulder, CO: Westview Press.

Hooper, Charlotte. 2001. *Manly States: Masculinities, International Relations, and Gender Politics*. New York: Columbia University Press.

Hossein, Caroline Shenaz. 2016. *Politicized Microfinance: Money, Power, and Violence in the Black Americas*. Toronto: University of Toronto Press.

Hozić, Aida A. and Jacqui True, eds. 2016. *Scandalous Economics: Gender and the Politics of Financial Crisis*. Oxford: Oxford University Press.

Hua, Julietta. 2011. *Trafficking Women's Human Rights*. Minneapolis, MN: University of Minnesota Press.

Hudson, Heidi. 2005. "Peacekeeping Trends and Their Gender Implications for Regional Peacekeeping Forces in Africa: Progress and Challenges." In Dyan Mazurana, Angela Raven-Roberts, and Jane Parpart, eds., *Gender, Conflict, and Peacekeeping*, 111–133. Lanham, MD: Rowman and Littlefield.

Hudson, Heidi. 2018. "Close(d) Encounters: Feminist Security Studies Engages Feminist (International) Political Economy and the Return to the Basics." In Juanita Elias and Adrienne Roberts, eds., *Handbook on the International Political Economy of Gender*, 137–141. Cheltenham: Edward Elgar.

Hudson, Valerie, and Patricia Leidl. 2015. *The Hilary Doctrine: Sex & American Foreign Policy*. New York: Columbia University Press.

Hudson, Valerie, Mary Caprioli, Bonnie Ballif-Spavill, Rose McDermott, and Chad F. Emmett. 2008/9. "The Heart of the Matter: The Security of Women and the Security of States." *International Security* 33(3): 7–45.

Human Resources (HR) Council. 2017. "Labour Force Statistics." www.hrcouncil.ca/labour/statistics.cfm (accessed April 12, 2017).

International Lesbian, Gay, Bisexual, Trans and Intersex Association (ILGA). 2016. "State-Sponsored Homophobia: A World Survey of Sexual Orientation Laws: Criminalisation, Protection and Recognition." www.ilga.org/downloads/02_ILGA_State_Sponsored_Homophobia_2016_ENG_WEB_150516.pdf (accessed December 18, 2017).

International Monetary Fund (IMF). 2017a. "IMF Executive Directors and Voting Power." www.imf.org/external/np/sec/memdir/eds.aspx (accessed April 12, 2017).

International Monetary Fund (IMF). 2017b. "Senior Officials of the International Monetary Fund." www.imf.org/external/np/sec/memdir/officers.htm (accessed April 12, 2017).

International Trade Centre (ITC). 2017. "Management." www.intracen.org/itc/about/how-itc-works/management/ (accessed April 12, 2017).

International Criminal Court (ICC). 2017. "Who's Who." www.icc-cpi.int/about/judicial-divisions/biographies/Pages/default.aspx# (accessed April 12, 2017).

International Court of Justice (ICJ). 2017. "The Court: Current Members." http://www.icj-cij.org/court/index.php?p1=1&p2=2&p3=1 (accessed April 12, 2017).

INCITE! Women of Color Against Violence. 2007. *The Revolution Will Not Be Funded: Beyond the Non-Profit Industrial Complex*. Cambridge, MA: South End Press.

Inter-Parliamentary Union (IPU). 2015. "Women in Parliament: 20 Years in Review." www.ipu.org/pdf/publications/WIP20Y-en.pdf (accessed April 5, 2017).

Inter-Parliamentary Union (IPU). 2017a. "Women in Politics: 2017 Map." www.beta.ipu.org/resources/publications/infographics/2017-03/women-in-politics-2017?utm_source=Inter-Parliamentary+Union+%28IPU%29&utm_campaign=550dedbec7-EMAIL_CAMPAIGN_2017_02_23&utm_medium=email&utm_term=0_d1ccee59b3-550dedbec7-258891957 (accessed April 5, 2017).

Inter-Parliamentary Union (IPU). 2017b. "Women in National Parliaments: World Classification." www.ipu.org/wmn-e/classif.htm (accessed April 27, 2017).

Irvine, Jill A. 2013. "Leveraging Change: Women's Organizations and the Implementation of UNSCR 1325 in the Balkans." *International Feminist Journal of Politics* 15(1): 20–38.

Jagger, Alison M. 1983. *Feminist Politics and Human Nature*. Totowa, NJ: Rowman and Allenheld.

Jansson, Maria. 2017. "The Logic of Protection: Narratives of HIV/AIDS in the UN Security Council." *International Feminist Journal of Politics* 19(1): 71–85.

Jeffords, Susan. 1989. *The Remasculinization of America: Gender and the Vietnam War*. Bloomington, IN: Indiana University Press.

Joachim, Jutta M. 2007. *Agenda Setting, the UN, and NGOs: Gender Violence and Reproductive Rights*. Washington, DC: Georgetown University Press.

Joekes, Susan, and Ann Weston. 1995. *Women and the New Trade Agenda*. New York: UNIFEM.

Jones, Branwen Gryffydd. 2006. *Decolonizing International Relations*. Lanham, MD: Rowman & Littlefield.

Jones, David E. 1997. *Women Warriors: A History*. London: Brassey's.

Jones, Kathleen B. 1993. *Compassionate Authority: Democracy and the Representation of Women*. New York: Routledge.

Kampwirth, Karen. 2002. *Women and Guerilla Movements: Nicaragua, El Salvador, Chiapas, Cuba*. University Park, PA: Penn State University Press.

Kamrani, Marjan E., and Federica Gentile. 2013. "Securing the State: The Relationship Between Anti–Sex Trafficking Legislation and Organizing and the Fortressing of North America." In Anne Sisson Runyan, Amy Lind, Patricia McDermott, and Marianne Marchand, eds., *Feminist (Im)Mobilities in Fortress(ing) North America: Rights, Citizenships, and Identities in Transnational Perspective*, 115–132. Farnham: Ashgate.

Kaufman, Joyce P., and Kristen P. Williams. 2007. *Women, the State, and War: A Comparative Perspective on Citizenship and Nationalism*. Lanham, MD: Lexington Books.

Keating, Christine, and Amy Lind. 2017. "Plural Sovereignty and la Familia Diversa in Ecuador's 2008 Constitution." *Feminist Studies* 43(2): 291–313.

Keck, Margaret, and Karen Sikkink. 1998. *Activists Beyond Borders: Transnational Advocacy Networks in International Politics*. Ithaca, NY: Cornell University Press.

Kempadoo, Kamala, ed. 2005. *Trafficking and Prostitution Reconsidered: New Perspectives on Migration, Sex Work, and Human Rights*. Boulder, CO: Paradigm Publishers.

Keohane, Robert O. 2005. *After Hegemony: Cooperation and Discord in the World Political Economy*. Princeton, NJ: Princeton University Press.

Kimmel, Michael. 2008. *Guyland*. New York: HarperCollins.

King, Samantha. 2013. "Philanthrocapitalism and the Healthification of Everything." *International Political Sociology* 7(1): 96–98.

Klein, Naomi. 2007. *The Shock Doctrine: The Rise of Disaster Capitalism*. New York: Metropolitan Books/Henry Holt.

Klein, Naomi. 2014. *This Changes Everything: Capitalism vs. The Climate*. New York: Simon & Schuster.

Klein, Naomi. 2017. *No is Not Enough: Resisting Trump's Shock Politics and Winning the World We Need*. Chicago, IL: Haymarket Books.

Koeszegi, Sabine T., Eva Zedlacher, and Rene Hudribusch. 2014. "The War against the Female Soldier? The Effects of Masculine Culture on Workplace Aggression." *Armed Forces & Society* 40(2): 226–251.

Kristof, Nicholas D., and Sheryl WuDunn. 2009. *Half the Sky: Turning Oppression into Opportunity for Women Worldwide*. New York: Vintage Books.

Laclau, Ernesto, and Chantal Mouffe. 1985. *Hegemony and the Socialist Strategy: Toward a Radical Democratic Politics*. London: Verso Books.

Leatherman, Janie L. 2011. *Sexual Violence and Armed Conflict*. Cambridge: Polity Press.

Lind, Amy, ed. 2010. *Development, Sexual Rights, and Global Governance*. New York: Routledge.

Lips, Hilary. 1991. *Women, Men, and Power*. Mountain View, CA: Mayfield.

Lomsky-Feder, Edna, and Orna Sasson-Levy. 2015. "Serving the Army as Secretaries: Intersectionality, Multi-level Contract and Subjective Experience of Citizenship." *The British Journal of Sociology* 66(1): 173–192.

Lorde, Audre. 2008. "The Master's Tools Will Never Dismantle the Master's House." Reprinted in Alison Bailey and Chris Cuomo, eds., *The Feminist Philosophy Reader*, 49–50. New York: McGraw-Hill.

Lovenduski, Joni. 2015. *Gendering Politics, Feminising Political Science*. Colchester: ECPR Press.

Luibhéid, Eithne, and Lionel Cantú Jr., eds. 2005. *Queer Migrations: Sexuality, U.S. Citizenship, and Border Crossings*. Minneapolis, MN: University of Minnesota Press.

Macdonald, Cameron Lynne, and Carmen Sirianni, eds. 1996. *Working in the Service Society*. Philadelphia, PA: Temple University Press.

Macdonald, Laura. 1994. "Globalizing Civil Society: Interpreting International NGOs in Central America." *Millennium* 23: 227–285.

Macdonald, Laura, and Arne Ruckert, eds. 2009. *Post-Neoliberalism in the Americas*. New York: Palgrave Macmillan.

Mackie, Vera. 2001. "The Language of Globalization, Transnationality, and Feminism." *International Feminist Journal of Politics* 3(2): 180–206.

Maiguashca, Bice. 2016. "Transnational Feminist Politics: A Concept that has Outlived its Usefulness?" Steans, Jill and Daniela Tepe-Belfrage, eds., *Handbook on Gender in World Politics*, 110–117. Cheltenham: Edward Elgar.

Marchand, Marianne H., and Anne Sisson Runyan, eds. 2011. *Gender and Global Restructuring: Sightings, Sites, and Resistances*. 2nd ed. London: Routledge.

Martin, Janet M., and MaryAnne Borelli. 2016. *The Gendered Executive: A Comparative Analysis of Presidents, Prime Ministers, and Chief Executives*. Philadelphia, PA: Temple University Press.

Masters, Cristina. 2008. "Bodies of Technology and the Politics of the Flesh." In Jane L. Parpart and Marysia Zalewski, eds., *Rethinking the Man Question: Sex, Gender, and Violence in International Relations*, 87–108. London: Zed Books.

Mathers, Jennifer G. 2013. "Women and State Military Forces." In Carol Cohn, ed., *Women & Wars: Contested Histories, Uncertain Futures*, 124–145. Cambridge: Polity Press.

Matland, Richard E. 2006. "Electoral Quotas: Frequency and Effectiveness." In Drude Dahlerup, ed., *Women, Quotas, and Politics*, 275–292. London: Routledge.

McDermott, Roger. 2013. "The Role of Women in Russia's Army." Eurasia Daily Monitor Volume: 10 Issue: 213. The Jamestown Foundation. www.jamestown.org/program/the-role-of-women-in-russias-armed-forces/ (accessed May 15, 2017).

McClintock, Anne. 1995. *Imperial Leather: Race, Gender, and Sexuality in the Colonial Contest*. New York: Routledge.

McCracken, Angela. 2014. *The Beauty Trade: Youth, Gender, and Fashion Globalization*. Oxford: Oxford University Press.

McGinley, Laurie, and Amy Goldstein. 2017. "Trump Reverses Abortion-related U.S. Policy, Bans Funding to International Health Groups." *Washington Post*. www.washingtonpost.com/news/to-your-health/wp/2017/01/23/trump-reverses-abortion-related-policy-to-ban-funding-to-international-health-groups/?utm_term=.4471780767f7 (accessed April 11, 2017).

McRobbie, Angela. 2009. *The Aftermath of Feminism: Gender, Culture, and Social Change*. London: Sage.

Mearsheimer, John J. 2001. *The Tragedy of Great Power Politics*. New York: Norton.

Mendoza, Breny. 2002. "Transnational Feminisms in Question." *Feminist Theory* 3(3): 295–314.

Merchant, Carolyn. 1980. *The Death of Nature: Women, Ecology, and the Scientific Revolution*. San Francisco, CA: Harper and Row.

Merry, Sally Engle. 2016. *The Seduction of Quantification: Measuring Human Rights, Gender Violence, and Sex Trafficking*. Chicago, IL: University of Chicago Press.

Mies, Maria. 1986. *Patriarchy and Accumulation on a World Scale: Women in the International Division of Labour*. London: Zed Books.

Mies, Maria, Veronika Bennholdt-Thomsen, and Claudia von Werlhof. 1988. *Women: The Last Colony*. London: Zed Books.

Military.com. 2015. "Women in Combat: Silver Stars, Combat Action Badges and Casualties." www.military.com/daily-news/2015/08/31/women-in-combat-silver-stars-combat-action-badges-casualties.html (accessed May 15, 2017).

Moghadam, Valentine M., ed. 1994. *Democratic Reform and the Position of Women in Transitional Economies*. Oxford: Oxford University Press.

Moghadam, Valentine M. 2005. *Globalizing Women: Transnational Feminist Networks*. Baltimore, MD: Johns Hopkins University Press.

Mohanty, Chandra Talpade. 2003. *Feminism Without Borders: Decolonizing Theory, Practicing Solidarity*. Durham, NC: Duke University Press.

Montagu, Ashley. 1974. *The Natural Superiority of Women*. New York: Collier Books.

Moon, Katharine H. S. 1997. *Sex Among Allies: Military Prostitution in U.S.-Korea Relations*. New York: Columbia University Press.

Morgenthau, Hans Joachim. 1948. *Politics Among Nations: The Struggle for Power and Peace*. New York: A.A. Knopf.

Nagel, Joane. 2016. *Gender and Climate Change: Impacts, Science, Policy*. New York: Routledge.

Nagle, Angela. 2017. *Kill All the Normies: The Online Culture Wars from Tumblr and 4Chan to the Alt-Right and Trump*. Winchester: Zero Books.

Naples, Nancy, and Manisha Desai, eds. 2002. *Women's Activism and Globalization: Linking Local Struggles and Transnational Politics*. New York: Routledge.

National Council for Research on Women (NCRW). 2006. *Gains and Gaps: A Look at the World's Women*. New York: NCRW.

Nayak, Meghana, and Eric Selbin. 2010. *Decentering International Relations*. London: Zed Books.

Nikolic-Ristanovic, Verna. 1996. "War and Violence Against Women." In Jennifer Turpin and Lois Ann Lorentzen, eds., *The Gendered New World Order: Militarism, Development, and the Environment*, 195–210. New York: Routledge.

North Atlantic Treaty Organization (NATO). 2017. "Latvian Army Female Officer." YouTube Channel. www.youtube.com/watch?v=XHtM9sgB828 (accessed May 15, 2017).

Office of Global Women's Issues. 2017. "Office of Global Women's Issues." US Department of State. www.state.gov/s/gwi/ (accessed April 11, 2017).

Okin, Susan Moller. 1979. *Women in Western Political Thought*. Princeton, NJ: Princeton University Press.

Okojo, Kamene. 1994. "Women and the Evolution of a Ghanaian Political Synthesis." In Barbara J. Nelson and Najma Chowdhury, eds., *Women and Politics Worldwide*, 285–297. New Haven, CT: Yale University Press.

Oliver, Kelly. 2007. *Women as Weapons of War: Iraq, Sex, and the Media*. New York: Columbia University Press.

Ong, Aihwa. 2006. *Neoliberalism as Exception: Mutations of Citizenship and Sovereignty*. Durham, NC: Duke University Press.

Onuf, Nicholas G. 1989. *World of Our Making: Rules and Rule in Social Theory and International Relations*. Columbia, SC: University of South Carolina Press.

Oosterveld, Valerie. 2005. "Prosecution of Gender-Based Crimes in International Law." In Dyan Mazurana, Angela Raven-Roberts, and Jane Parpart, eds., *Gender, Conflict, and Peacekeeping*, 94–117. Lanham, MD: Rowman and Littlefield.

Out. 2016. "Same-Sex Marriages Begin in Greenland." www.out.com/news-opinion/2016/4/01/same-sex-marriages-begin-greenland (accessed May 1, 2017).

Parashar, Swati, J. Ann Tickner, and Jacqui True, eds. 2018. *Revisiting Gendered States: Feminist Imaginings of the State in International Relations*. Oxford: Oxford University Press.

Parker, Kim, Anthony Cilluffo, and Renee Stepler. 2017. "6 Facts about the U.S. Military and Its Changing Demographics." Pew Research Center. www.pewresearch.org/fact-tank/2017/04/13/6-facts-about-the-u-s-military-and-its-changing-demographics/ (accessed May 8, 2017).

Parpart, Jane L., and Marysia Zalewski, eds. 2008. *Rethinking the Man Question: Sex, Gender, and Violence in International Relations*. London: Zed Books.

Parr, Adrian. 2009. *Hijacking Sustainability*. Cambridge, MA: MIT Press.

Pateman, Carole. 1988. *The Sexual Contract*. Cambridge: Polity Press.

Patten, Eileen, and Kim Parker. 2011. "Women in the U.S. Military: Growing Share, Distinctive Profile." Pew Research Center. www.pewsocialtrends.org/2011/12/22/women-in-the-u-s-military-growing-share-distinctive-profile/2/#a-snapshot-of-active-duty-women?src=prc-number (accessed May 8, 2017).

Peters, Julia, and Andrea Wolper, eds. 1995. *Women's Rights, Human Rights: International Feminist Perspectives*. New York: Routledge.

Peterson, V. Spike. 2003. *A Critical Rewriting of Global Political Economy: Integrating Reproductive, Productive, and Virtual Economies*. London: Routledge.

Peterson, V. Spike. 2007. "Thinking Through Intersectionality and War." Special Issue on "Race, Gender, Class, Sexuality, and War." *Race, Gender, and Class* 14(3/4): 10–27.

Peterson, V. Spike. 2014. "Sex Matters: A Queer History of Hierarchies." *International Feminist Journal of Politics* 16(3): 389–409.

Peterson, V. Spike, and Laura Parisi. 1998. "Are Women Human? It's Not an Academic Question." In Tony Evans, ed., *Human Rights Fifty Years On: A Radical Reappraisal*, 132–160. Manchester: University of Manchester Press.

Pettman, Jan Jindy. 1996. *Worlding Women: A Feminist International Politics*. London: Routledge.

Phillips, Anne. 1991. *Engendering Democracy*. University Park, PA: Penn State University Press.

Pierson, Ruth Roach, ed. 1987. *Women and Peace: Theoretical, Historical, and Practical Perspectives*. London: Croom Helm.

Picq, Manuela Lavinas, and Marcus Thiel, eds. 2015. *Sexualities in World Politics: How LBGTQ Claims Shape International Relations*. London: Routledge.

Poster, Winifred, and Zakia Salime. 2002. "The Limits of Microcredit: Transnational Feminism and USAID Activities in the United States and Morocco." In Nancy A. Naples and Manisha Desai, eds., *Women's Activism and Globalization*, 189–219. New York: Routledge.

Prügl, Elisabeth. 2016. "'Lehman Brothers and Sisters': Revisiting Gender and Myth after the Financial Crisis." In Aida A. Hozić and Jacqui True, eds., *Scandalous Economics: Gender and the Politics of Financial Crisis*, 21–40. Oxford: Oxford University Press.

Prügl, Elisabeth, and Markus Thiel, eds. 2009. *Diversity in the European Union*. New York: Palgrave Macmillan.

Puar, Jasbir. 2007. *Terrorist Assemblages: Homonationalism in Queer Times*. Durham, NC: Duke University Press.

Rai, Shirin M. 2002. *Gender and the Political Economy of Development*. Cambridge: Polity Press.

Rai, Shirin M. 2008. "Analyzing Global Governance." In Shirin Rai and Georgina Waylen, eds., *Global Governance: Feminist Perspectives*, 19–42. Basingstoke: Palgrave Macmillan.

Randall, Vicky. 1987. *Women and Politics: An International Perspective*. 2nd ed. Chicago, IL: University of Chicago Press.

Reagon, Bernice Johnson. 2000. "Coalition Politics: Turning the Century." In Barbara Smith, ed., *Home Girls: A Black Feminist Anthology*, 343–355. New Brunswick, NJ: Rutgers University Press.

Richey, Lisa Ann, and Stefano Ponte. 2011. *Brand Aid: Shopping Well to Save the World*. Minneapolis, MN: Quadrant/University of Minnesota Press.

Richter-Montpetit, Malenie. 2014. "Beyond the Erotics of Orientalism: Lawfare, Torture and Racial-Sexual Grammars of Legitimate Sufferings." *Security Dialogue* 45(1): 43–62.

Rincker, Meg. 2017. *Empower by Design: Decentralization and the Gender Policy Trifecta*. Philadelphia, PA: Temple University Press.

Roberts, Adrienne. 2016. "Finance, Financialization, and the Production of Gender." In Aida A. Hozić and Jacqui True, eds., *Scandalous Economics: Gender and the Politics of Financial Crisis*, 57–75. Oxford: Oxford University Press.

Rodda, Annabel. 1991. *Women and the Environment*. London: Zed Books.

Rowley, Michelle. 2011. "'Where the Streets Have No Name': Getting Development Out of the (RED)?" In Marianne H. Marchand and Anne Sisson Runyan, eds. *Gender and Global Restructuring: Sightings, Sites, and Resistances*, 78–98. 2nd ed. London: Routledge.

Roy, Ananya. 2010. *Poverty Capitalism*. New York: Routledge.

Ruddick, Sara. 1984. "Preservative Love and Military Destruction." In Joyce Trebilcot, ed., *Mothering: Essays in Feminist Theory*, 231–262. Totowa, NJ: Rowman and Allanheld.

Runyan, Anne Sisson. 2018. "Disposable Waste, Lands, and Bodies under Canada's Gendered Nuclear Colonialism." *International Feminist Journal of Politics* 20(1): 24–38.

Runyan, Anne Sisson, Amy Lind, Patricia McDermott, and Marianne H. Marchand, eds. 2013. *Feminist (Im)Mobilities in Fortress(ing) North America: Rights, Citizenships, and Identities in Transnational Perspective*. Farnham: Ashgate.

Russo, Ann. 2006. "The Feminist Majority Foundation's Campaign to Stop Gender Apartheid: The Intersections of Feminism and Imperialism in the United States." *International Feminist Journal of Politics* 8(6): 557–580.

Said, Edward. 1979. *Orientalism*. New York: Vintage Books.

Said, Edward. 1993. *Culture and Imperialism*. New York: Knopf.

Sang-Hun, Choe. 2009. "Ex-Prostitutes Say South Korea and the U.S. Enabled Sex Trade Near Bases." *New York Times*, January 8.

Sanjay, Seth, ed. 2016. *Postcolonial Theory and International Relations*. London: Routledge.

Sassen, Saskia. 2014. *Expulsions: Brutality and Complexity in the Global Economy*. Cambridge, MA: The Belknap Press of Harvard University Press.

Seager, Joni. 1997. *The State of Women in the World Atlas*. 2nd ed. New York: Penguin Books.

Seager, Joni. 2009. *The Penguin Atlas of Women in the World*. 4th ed. New York: Penguin Books.

Sen, Gita, and Caren Grown for Development Alternatives with Women for a New Era (DAWN). 1987. *Development, Crises, and Alternative Visions: Third World Women's Perspectives*. New York: Monthly Review Press.

Sen, Jai, and Peter Waterman, eds. 2009. *World Social Forum: Challenging Empires*. Montreal: Black Rose Books.

Sharoni, Simona. 1995. *Gender and the Israeli-Palestinian Conflict: The Politics of Women's Resistance*. Syracuse, NY: Syracuse University Press.

Sharoni, Simona. 1998. "Gendering Conflict and Peace in Israel/Palestine and the North of Ireland." *Millennium: Journal of International Studies* 27: 1061–1089.

Shepherd, Laura J. 2008. *Gender, Violence, and Security*. London: Zed Books.

Shepherd, Laura J. ed. 2015. *Gender Matters in Global Politics: A Feminist Introduction to International Relations*. 2nd ed. London: Routledge.

Shiva, Vandana. 2005. *Earth Democracy*. Cambridge, MA: South End Press.

Simmons, Beth A. 2009. *Mobilizing for Human Rights: International Law and Domestic Politics*. Cambridge: Cambridge University Press.

Sjoberg, Laura. 2012. "Toward Trans-Gendering International Relations." *International Political Sociology* 6(4): 337–354.

Sjoberg, Laura. 2016. *Women as Wartime Rapists; Beyond Sensationalism and Stereotyping*. New York: New York University Press.

Sjoberg, Laura, Grace D. Cooke, and Stacy Reiter Neal. 2011. "Introduction: Women, Gender, and Terrorism." In Laura Sjoberg and Caron E. Gentry, eds., *Women, Gender, and Terrorism*, 1–25. Athens, GA: University of Georgia Press.

Sjoberg, Laura, and Caron E. Gentry. 2007. *Mothers, Monsters, Whores: Women's Violence in Global Politics*. London: Zed Books.

Sjoberg, Laura, and Caron E. Gentry, eds. 2011. *Women, Gender, and Terrorism*. Athens, GA: University of Georgia Press.

Sjoberg, Laura and Jessica L. Peet. 2011. "Targeting Civilians in War: Feminist Contributions." In J. Ann Tickner and Laura Sjoberg, eds., *Feminism and International Relations: Conversations about the Past, Present and Future*, 167–187. London: Routledge.

Sjoberg, Laura, Heidi Hudson, and Cynthia Weber. 2015. "Gender and Crisis in Global Politics: Introduction." *International Feminist Journal of Politics* 17(4): 529–535.

Skard, Torlid. 2015. *Women of Power: Half a Century of Female Presidents and Prime Ministers Worldwide*. Bristol: Policy Press.

Smiley, Tavis, and Cornel West. 2012. *The Rich and the Rest of Us: A Poverty Manifesto*. New York: SmileyBooks.

Smith, Dan. 1997. *The State of War and Peace Atlas*. London: Penguin Books.

Smith, Hilda L., and Berenice A. Carroll. 2000. *Women's Political and Social Thought: An Anthology*. Bloomington, IN: Indiana University Press.

Smith, Nicola. 2016. "The Global Political Economy of Sex Work." In Jill Steans and Daniela Tepe-Belfrage, eds. *Handbook on Gender in World Politics*, 370–377. Cheltenham: Edward Elgar.

Spade, Dean. 2015. *Normal Life: Administrative Violence, Critical Trans Politics and the Limits of Law*. Durham, NC: Duke University Press.

Spivak, Gayatri Chakravorty. 1987. *In Other Worlds: Essays in Cultural Politics*. London: Methuen.

Spivak, Gayatri Chakravorty. 1988. "Can the Subaltern Speak?" In Cary Nelson and Lawrence Grossberg, eds., *Marxism and the Interpretation of Culture*, 271–313. Urbana, IL: University of Illinois Press.

Spivak, Gayatri Chakravorty. 1999. *A Critique of Postcolonial Reason: Toward a History of the Vanishing Present*. Cambridge, MA: Harvard University Press.

Squires, Judith. 2007. *The New Politics of Gender Equality*. Basingstoke: Palgrave Macmillan.

Staudt, Kathleen. 2008. "Gender, Governance, and Globalization at Borders: Femicide at the US-Mexico Border." In Shirin Rai and Georgina Waylen, eds., *Global Governance: Feminist Perspectives*, 234–253. Basingstoke: Palgrave Macmillan.

Steans, Jill. 2006. *Gender and International Relations*. 2nd ed. New Brunswick, NJ: Rutgers University Press.

Steans, Jill, and Daniela Tepe-Belfrage, eds. 2016. *Handbook on Gender in World Politics*. Cheltenham: Edward Elgar.

Stern, Maria. 2016. "Poststructuralist Feminism in World Politics." In Jill Steans and Daniela Tepe-Belfrage, eds. *Handbook on Gender in World Politics*, 33–40. Cheltenham: Edward Elgar.

Stiehm, Judith Hicks. 1989. *Arms and the Enlisted Woman*. Philadelphia, PA: Temple University Press.

Stienstra, Deborah. 1999. "Of Roots, Leaves, and Trees: Gender, Social Movements, and Global Governance." In Mary K. Meyer and Elisabeth Prügl, eds., *Gender Politics in Global Governance*, 260–272. Lanham, MD: Rowman and Littlefield.

Stryker, Susan, and Stephen Whittle. 2006. *The Transgender Reader*. New York: Routledge.

Sudbury, Julia, ed. 2005. *Global Lockdown: Race, Gender, and the Prison-Industrial Complex*. New York: Routledge.

Sutton, Barbara, Sandra Morgen, and Julie Novkov, eds. 2008. *Security Disarmed: Critical Perspectives on Gender, Race, and Militarization*. New Brunswick, NJ: Rutgers University Press.

Swarr, Amanda Lock, and Richa Nagar. 2010. *Critical Transnational Feminist Praxis*. Albany, NY: State University of New York Press.

Sylvester, Christine. 1992. "Feminists and Realists View Autonomy and Obligation in International Relations." In V. Spike Peterson, ed., *Gendered States: Feminist (Re)Visions of International Relations Theory*, 155–178. Boulder, CO: Lynne Rienner.

Sylvester, Christine. 2013. *War as Experience: Contributions from International Relations and Feminist Analysis*. London: Routledge.

Thames, Frank C., and Margaret S. Williams. 2013. *Contagious Representation: Women's Political Representation in Democracies Around the World*. New York: New York University Press.

Thayer, Millie. 2010. *Making Transnational Feminism: Rural Women, NGO Activists, and Northern Donors in Brazil*. New York: Routledge.

The Institute for National Security Studies (INSS). 2017. "INSS Insight No. 887, January 5, 2017. Suicide Bombings in 2016: The Highest Number of Fatalities. Ilana Kricheli, Yotam Rosner, Aviad Mendelboim, and Yoram Schweitzer." www.inss.org.il/uploadImages/systemFiles/No.%20887%20-%20Terrorism%202016%20report_website.pdf (accessed May 10, 2017).

Tickner, J. Ann. 1993. *Gender in International Relations*. New York: Columbia University Press.

Tickner, J. Ann. 2001. *Gendering World Politics: Issues and Approaches in the Post–Cold War Era*. New York: Columbia University Press.

Tickner, J. Ann. 2006. "Feminism Meets International Relations: Some Methodological Issues." In Brooke Ackerly, Maria Stern, and Jacqui True, eds., *Feminist Methodologies for International Relations*, 19–41. Cambridge: Cambridge University Press.

Tickner, J. Ann. 2014. *A Feminist Voyage Through International Relations*. Oxford: Oxford University Press.

Tickner, J. Ann, and Laura Sjoberg, eds. 2011. *Feminism and International Relations: Conversation about the Past, Present and Future*. London: Routledge.

Tilghman, Andrew. 2016. MilitaryTimes. "Military Sex Assault: Just 4 Percent of Complaints Result in Convictions." www.militarytimes.com/story/veterans/2016/05/05/military-sexual-assault-complaints-result-few-convictions/83980218/ (accessed May 15, 2017).

Towns, Ann, and Birgitta Niklasson. 2016. "Gender, International Status, and Ambassador Appointments." *Foreign Policy Analysis* 13(3): 521–540.

Tripp, Aili Marie, Myra Marx Ferree, and Cristina Ewig, eds. 2013. *Gender, Violence, and Human Security: Critical Feminist Perspectives*. New York: New York University Press.

True, Jacqui. 2012. *The Political Economy of Violence Against Women*. Oxford: Oxford University Press.

Truong, Thanh-Dam. 2000. "A Feminist Perspective on the Asia Miracle and Crisis." *Journal of Human Development* 1(1): 159–164.

2020 Women on Boards. 2016. "Gender Diversity Index: 2011-2016 Progress of Women Corporate Directors by Company Size, State and Sector." www.2020wob.com/sites/default/files/2016_GDI_Report_Final.pdf (accessed December 18, 2017).

United Nations (UN). 2000. *The World's Women 2000: Trends and Statistics*. New York: United Nations.

United Nations (UN). 2016. "Report of the UN Secretary-General: Mainstreaming a Gender Perspective into all Policies and Programmes in the United Nations System." www.undocs.org/en/E/2016/57 (accessed April 11, 2017).

United Nations (UN). 2017. "Sustainable Development Knowledge Platform." www.sustainabledevelopment.un.org/hlpf (accessed April 5, 2017).

United Nations Development Fund for Women (UNIFEM). 2008. *Progress of the World's Women 2008/2009: Who Answers to Women?* New York: UNIFEM. www.unifem.org/progress/2008/media/POWW08_Report_Full_Text.pdf (accessed February 6, 2009).

United Nations Development Programme (UNDP). 1997. *Human Development Report 1997*. New York: Oxford University Press.

United Nations Entity for Gender Equality and the Empowerment of Women (UN Women). 2011. *Progress of the World's Women 2011–2012: In Pursuit of Justice*. New York: UN Women. www.progress.unwomen.org/pdfs/EN-Report-Progress.pdf (accessed May 1, 2013).

United Nations Entity for Gender Equality and the Empowerment of Women (UN Women). 2015. "Progress of the World's Women 2015-2016: Transforming Economies, Realizing Rights." progress.unwomen.org/en/2015/pdf/UNW_progressreport.pdf (accessed May 23, 2017).

United Nations Entity for Gender Equality and the Empowerment of Women (UN Women). 2016a. "Status of Women in the United Nations System." www.unwomen.org/en/digital-library/publications/2016/12/status-of-women-in-the-united-nations-system. (accessed April 5, 2017).

United Nations Entity for Gender Equality and the Empowerment of Women (UN Women). 2016b. "UN Women Annual Report 2015–2016." www2.unwomen.org/-/media/annual%20report/attachments/sections/library/un-women-annual-report-2015-2016-en.pdf?vs=3016 (accessed April 13, 2017).

United Nations High Commissioner for Refugees (UNHCR). 2016. "Global Trends: Forced Displacement in 2016." www.unhcr.org/en-us/statistics/unhcrstats/5943e8a34/global-trends-forced-displacement-2016.html (accessed December 18, 2017).

United Nations Secretariat Department of Economic and Social Affairs (UN DESA). 2010. *The World's Women 2010: Trends and Statistics*. New York: UN Secretariat Department of Economic and Social Affairs. www.unstats.un.org/unsd/demographic/products/Worldswomen/WW_full%20report_color.pdf (accessed May 1, 2013).

United Nations Secretariat Department of Economic and Social Affairs (UN DESA). 2013. *World Abortion Policies 2013: Trends and Statistics*. New York: UN Secretariat Department of Economic and Social Affairs. www.un.org/en/development/desa/population/publications/pdf/policy/WorldAbortion Policies2013/WorldAbortionPolicies2013_WallChart.pdf (accessed December 19, 2017).

Van Staveren, Irene. 2002. "Global Finance and Gender." In Jan Aart Scholte and Albrecht Schnabel, eds., *Civil Society and Global Finance*, 228–246. London: Routledge.

Vickers, Jean. 1991. *Women and the World Economic Crisis*. London: Zed Books.

Vickers, Jill. 2006. "The Problem with Interests: Making Political Claims for Women." In Louise Chappell and Lisa Hill, eds., *The Politics of Women's Interests*, 5–38. London: Routledge.

Waller, Marguerite, and Sylvia Marcos, eds. 2005. *Dialogue and Difference: Feminisms Challenge Globalization*. New York: Palgrave Macmillan.

Wallerstein, Immanuel. 1979. *The Capitalist World-Economy*. Cambridge: Cambridge University Press.

Waltz, Kenneth. 1959. *Man, the State and War: A Theoretical Analysis*. New York: Columbia University Press.

Weber, Cynthia. 2016. *Queer International Relations: Sovereignty, Sexuality and the Will to Knowledge*. Oxford: Oxford University Press.

Wendt, Alexander. 1999. *Social Theory of International Politics*. Cambridge: Cambridge University Press.

Whitworth, Sandra. 2004. *Men, Militarism, and UN Peacekeeping: A Gendered Analysis*. Boulder, CO: Lynne Rienner.

Whitworth, Sandra. 2008. "Militarized Masculinity and Post-Traumatic Stress Disorder." In Jane L. Parpart and Marysia Zalewski, eds., *Rethinking the Man Question: Sex, Gender, and Violence in International Relations*, 109–126. London: Zed Books.

Woehl, Stephanie. 2008. "Global Governance as Neoliberal Governmentality: Gender Mainstreaming in the European Employment Strategy." In Shrin Rai and Georgina Waylen, eds., *Gender and Global Governance: Feminist Perspectives*, 64–83. Basingstoke: Palgrave Macmillan.

Women's International League for Peace & Freedom. 2014. "You Get What You Pay For." www.wilpf.org/wp-content/uploads/2014/07/You-Get-What-You-Pay-For-Web.pdf (accessed December 19, 2017).

World Bank. 2017. "World Bank Group Leadership." www.worldbank.org/en/about/leadership/managers (accessed April 12, 2017).

World Economic Forum (WEF). 2016. "The Global Gender Gap Report." www3.weforum.org/docs/GGGR16/WEF_Global_Gender_Gap_Report_2016.pdf (accessed April 12, 2017).

World Social Forum. 2016. "Information." www.fsm2016.org/en/sinformer/ (accessed July 24, 2018).

World Trade Organization (WTO). 2017. "The Secretariat." www.wto.org/english/thewto_e/whatis_e/tif_e/org4_e.htm (accessed April 12, 2017).

Worldwide Guide to Women in Leadership. 2016. "Female Governors General." www.guide2womenleaders.com/Governor_Generals.htm (accessed April 12, 2017).

Youngs, Gillian. 2005. "Ethics of Access: Globalization and the Information Society." *Journal of Global Ethics* 1(1): 69–83.

Yuval-Davis, Nira. 1997. *Gender and Nation*. London: Sage.

Yuval-Davis, Nira. 2006. "Intersectionality and Feminist Politics." *European Journal of Women's Studies* 13(3): 193–209.

Zalewski, Marysia. 2013. *Feminist International Relations: Exquisite Corpse*. London: Routledge.

Zalewski, Marysia, and Jane Parpart, eds. 1998. *The "Man" Question in International Relations*. Boulder, CO: Westview Press.

Zieleńska, Marianna. 2012. "Gender Equality in Non-governmental Organisations." *Eurofound*. www.eurofound.europa.eu/observatories/eurwork/articles/labour-market/gender-equality-in-non-governmental-organisations (accessed April 12, 2017).

Zwingel, Susanne. 2005. "From Intergovernmental Negotiations to (Sub)National Change: A Transnational Perspective on the Impact of CEDAW." *International Feminist Journal of Politics* 7(3): 400–424.

Zwingel, Susanne. 2016. *Translating International Women's Right: The CEDAW Convention in Context*. New York: Palgrave Macmillan.

Index